BIOFEEDBACK
A Survey of the Literature

BIOFEEDBACK
A Survey of the Literature

FRANCINE BUTLER
University of Colorado Medical Center

IFI / PLENUM • NEW YORK · WASHINGTON · LONDON

Library of Congress Cataloging in Publication Data

Butler, Francine

  Biofeedback: A survey of the literature

  Includes index.
  1. Biofeedback training — Bibliography. I. Title.
  Z7204   B56B87   [BF319.5.B5]   016.1521'88   78-6159
  ISBN 0-306-65173-4

BF
319. 5
B 5
B87

© 1978 IFI/Plenum Data Company
A Division of Plenum Publishing Corporation
227 West 17th Street, New York, N.Y. 10011

Printed in the United States of America

This book is the result of a
symbiotic relationship between
the BSA and me.   It is
dedicated to the membership.

And to my mentor, Quixote, who
first taught me about science
and the mind.

Francine Butler
January, 1978

FOREWORD

In a rapidly growing area such as biofeedback, a need
for an extensive bibliography clearly exists. Both for
the practicing clinician as well as the researcher, a
convenient reference work is an important tool, for not
only has the field expanded quickly, but a similar growth
has occurred in related areas.

A glimpse at the contents will reveal the diversity
and richness of the sources contributing to the biofeedback area. Thus, we see questions pertaining to· mind-body
issues, the nature of the stress response and whether it
can be voluntarily modified, the rehabilitation of muscle
function after injury, the nature of learning in the
autonomic nervous system, cybernetics and control systems,
EEG and consciousness, the status of clinical applications,
and so forth. In addition, the reader will see many
references to related self-regulatory therapies--autogenic
training, behavioral self-control techniques, progressive
relaxation, among others. These related approaches are
valuable both as sources of clinical techniques which
complement biofeedback and as a source of hypotheses for
experimental work.

Eminently well-qualified to perform the task of
preparing the bibliography is the editor, Francine Butler.
Her day-to-day familiarity with the workings of the
Biofeedback Society of America, as well as its journal,
Biofeedback and Self-Regulation, have placed her in an
excellent position to assemble and select the important
references in the field. In addition to preparing the
reference list, the editor has prepared a detailed index
of topics. This will make the bibliography extremely
convenient for the user.

Finally, it is worth drawing attention to something which may remain hidden behind the seemingly matter-of-fact bibliographic entries. That is the sense of ferment and of grappling with genuine human issues which permeates the biofeedback area. We hope that the user of this bibliography will come to share our sense of excitement at participating in an area which has yet to assume its final shape.

Johann Stoyva

Department of Psychiatry

University of Colorado School of Medicine

Denver, Colorado

PREFACE

My own feelings toward science and research are
captured in the words of Albert Szent-Györgyi:

> The basic texture of research consists
> of dreams into which the threads of
> reasoning, measurement and calculation
> are woven.

In psychology there is a long history of thought or
dreams that the individual could exercise control over a
number of internal functions. Within biofeedback we have
come to see many of these dreams materialize.

In 1971 when Johann Stoyva was President of the
Biofeedback Research Society and I had just begun working
with the Society, the first project was to collect the
references in existence at that time. The result was the
1973 edition of <u>Biofeedback</u> <u>and</u> <u>Self-Control</u>: <u>A Bibliography</u>,
edited by F. Butler and J. Stoyva. This became a basic
reference.

I've since been in a very fortunate position as
Director of the Biofeedback Society. This has been a time
of development both for the field and for the Society. My
role has encompassed both active participation and passive
observation; perhaps the most important function has been
as archivist.

In the past five years publication in the area of
biofeedback and self-control has vastly expanded. Although
it is possible to retrieve necessary references from a
number of books currently on the market, it is difficult
to do. This collection was compiled and organized with
two specific goals in mind. The goals were based on the
inquiries addressed to our office, i.e., to provide information on the work of a specific individual or to

provide information on the status of biofeedback within a
given disorder or type of illness. Thus the first section
of the bibliography represents the published work in
biofeedback to date listed alphabetically by author. The
second section is a keyword index. Topics in the keyword
index were generated from titles of all the references
included in the bibliography. This system differs from
most others in that it does not rely on knowledge of a
particular muscle system or biofeedback modality.

The 1973 bibliography listed 850 references. Many of
these were basic psychophysiology papers. In addition
there was a large section on behavior therapy, because it
was helpful to have such material within a biofeedback
listing. Currently, if one wants to seek basic psychophysiology or behavior therapy works, one would go to the
literature in the primary discipline, not to the biofeedback bibliography. Thus, many of the references in these
areas from the 1973 edition have not been repeated. In
fact, in the order of 30-50% are not included in this
collection. Yet, the total number of references in this
collection is 2300, representing a five-fold increase.

This certainly can be considered a demonstration of
evidence that the field is progressing. We anticipate a
continued expansion with future developments in the area.

Acknowledgments

Thanks go to each of you kind enough to send me copies
of reprints so that they might be included in this collection, to Johann Stoyva for preparing the Foreword and to
David Paskewitz for his help in structuring the keyword
index.

With pleasure, I acknowledge the patience, under-
standing and endurance of Penny Hiernu for the preparation
of the manuscript.

CONTENTS

REFERENCES

The bibliographic listings are arranged alphabetically according to the first author's name.
Each letter of the alphabet begins on a new page.

1. Aarons, L.
    Subvocalization: Aural and EMG feedback in reading
    Perceptual and Motor Skills, 1971, 33:271-306-

2. Abboud, F.M.
    Relaxation, autonomic control and hypertension
      (Editorial)
    New England Journal of Medicine, 1976, 294:107-109

3. Abdullah, S.
    The use of biofeedback in meditation technique: An
      innovative combination in psychotherapy
    Journal of Contemporary Psychotherapy, 1973, 5:101-
      106

4. Abdullah, S.
    Biofeedback for asthmatic patients
    New England Journal of Medicine, 1974, 291:1037

5. Abdullah, S. & Schucman, H.
    Cerebral lateralization, bimodal consciousness and
      related developments in psychiatry
    Research Communications in Psychology, Psychiatry
      and Behavior, 1976, 1:671-679

6. Abramson, E.E.
    A review of behavioral approaches to weight control
    Behavior Research and Therapy, 1973, 11:547-556

7.   Ackner, B.
     The relationship between anxiety and the level of
        peripheral vasomotor activity
     Journal of Psychosomatic Research, 1956, 1:21-48

8.   Adams, J.A., Goetz, E.T. & Marshall, P.H.
     Response feedback and motor learning
     Journal of Experimental Psychology, 1972, 92:391-397

9.   Adams, J.A., Gopher, D. & Lintern, G.
     Effects of visual and proprioceptive feedback on
        motor learning
     Journal of Motor Behavior, 1977, 9:11-22

10. Adams, J.A., Marshall, P.H. & Goetz, E.T.
     Response feedback and short-term motor retention
     Journal of Experimental Psychology, 1972, 92:92-95

11. Ader, R. & Cohen, N.
     Behaviorally conditioned immunosuppression
     Psychosomatic Medicine, 1975, 37:333-340

12. Adler, C.S.
     Biofeedback, evolution, and the tools of mankind
     Proceedings of the Biofeedback Research Society
        Fifth Annual Meeting
     Colorado Springs, 1974, 2 (Abst.)

13. Adler, C.S. & Adler, S.M.
     The pragmatic application of biofeedback to head-
        aches -- a five-year clinical follow-up
     Biofeedback and Self-Regulation, 1976, 1:347-348
        (Abst.)

14. Adler, C.S. & Adler, S.M.
     Biofeedback psychotherapy for the treatment of
        headaches: A 5 year follow-up
     Headache, 1976, 16:189

15. Adler, S.M.
     The headache swamp: Pragmatic problems of biofeed-
        back treatment
     Proceedings of the Biofeedback Research Society
        Fifth Annual Meeting
     Colorado Springs, 1974, 3 (Abst.)

16. Adrian, E.D. & Matthews, B.H.C.
    The Berger rhythm: Potential changes from the
      occipital lobes in man
    Brain, 1934, 57:355-385

17. Agathon, M., et al.
    Attempted use of biological retroaction (biofeed-
      back) in the treatment of an anxiety neurosis
    Annals of Medicine and Psychology, (Paris), 1977,
      1:256-264

18. Agras, S.
    Relaxation therapy and high blood pressure
    Archives of General Psychiatry, 1977, 34:339-345

19. Agras, S. & Marshall, C.
    The application of negative practice to spasmodic
      torticollis
    American Journal of Psychiatry, 1965, 122:579-582

20. Ainslie, G.W. & Engel, B.T.
    Alteration of classically conditioned heart rate by
      operant reinforcement in monkeys
    Journal of Comparative and Physiological Psychology,
      1974, 87:373-382

21. Albanese, H. & Gaarder, K.
    Biofeedback treatment of tardive dyskinesia
    American Journal of Psychiatry, 1977, 134:1149-1150

22. Alberstein, B.
    Biofeedback and skin temperature control: A con-
      trolled study
    Psychophysiology, 1977, 14:115 (Abst.)

23. Albert, I.B., Simmons, J. & Walker, J.
    Massed and spaced practice in alpha enhancement
    Perceptual and Motor Skills, 1974, 39:1039-1042

24. Albino, R. & Burnand, G.
    Conditioning of the alpha rhythm in man
    Journal of Experimental Psychology, 1964, 67:539-544

25.   Alexander, A.B.
      Systematic relaxation and flow rates in asthmatic
         children: Relationship to emotional precipitants
         and anxiety
      Journal of Psychosomatic Research, 1972, 16:405-410

26.   Alexander, A.B.
      Generalization to other muscles during EMG bio-
         feedback training of the frontalis
      Psychophysiology, 1974, 11:232-233 (Abst.)

27.   Alexander, A.B.
      An experimental test of assumptions relating to the
         use of electromyographic biofeedback as a general
         relaxation training technique
      Psychophysiology, 1975, 12:656-662

28.   Alexander, A.B., French, C.A. & Goodman, N.J.
      A comparison of audio and visual feedback in bio-
         feedback assisted muscular relaxation training
      Psychophysiology, 1975, 12:119-123

29.   Alexander, A.B. & Hanson, D.G.
      An experimental test of assumptions relating to the
         use of EMG biofeedback as a general relaxation
         training technique
      Proceedings of the Biofeedback Research Society
         Fifth Annual Meeting
      Colorado Springs, 1974, 41 (Abst.)

30.   Alexander, A.B., Holland, P.W. & Wallace, H.M.
      Training and transfer of training effects in EMG
         biofeedback assisted muscular relaxation
      Psychophysiology, 1976, 13:181 (Abst.)

31.   Alexander, A.B., White, P.D. & Wallace, H.M.
      Training and transfer of training effects in EMG
         biofeedback assisted muscular relaxation
      Psychophysiology, 1977, 14:551-559

32.   Alexander, A.B., Miklich, D.R. & Hershkoff, H.
      The immediate effects of systematic relaxation
         training in peak expiratory flow rates in asth-
         matic children
      Psychosomatic Medicine, 1972, 34:388-394

33.   Allison, J.
       Respiratory changes during the practice of the
          technique of transcendental meditation
       Lancet, 1970, 7651:833-834

34.   Amato, A., Hermsmeyer, C. & Kleinman, K.
       Use of electromyographic feedback to increase in-
          hibitory control of spastic muscles
       Physical Therapy, 1973, 53:1063-1066

35.   Amenhauser, C.G. & Shipley, R.
       EMG and its effects on alcohol withdrawal
       Biofeedback and Self-Regulation, 1977, 2:311 (Abst.)

36.   Anand, B. & Chhina, G. S.
       Investigations on Yogis claiming to stop their heart
          beats
       Indian Journal of Medical Research, 1961, 49:90-94

37.   Anand, B.K., Chhina, G.S. & Singh, B.
       Some aspects of electroencephalographic studies in
          yogis
       Electroencephalography and Clinical Neurophysiology,
          1961, 13:451-456

38.   Ancoli, S.
       Authoritarianism, introspection, and alpha wave
          biofeedback conditioning
       Proceedings of the Biofeedback Research Society
          Sixth Annual Meeting
       Monterey, 1975, 35   (Abst.)

39.   Ancoli, S. & Green, K.F.
       Authoritarianism, introspection, and alpha wave
          biofeedback training
       Psychophysiology, 1977, 14:40-44

40.   Ancoli, S. & Kamiya, J.
       Methodological issues in alpha biofeedback training
       Biofeedback and Self-Regulation, 1977, 2:280 (Abst.)

41.   Andersen, P. & Anderson, S.A.
       Physiological Basis of the Alpha Rhythm
       New York: Appleton-Century Crofts, 1968

42.   Andrews, J.M.
      Neuromuscular re-education of hemiplegic with aid of
        electromyograph
      Archives of Physical Medicine and Rehabilitation,
        1964, 45:530-532

43.   Andreychuk, T. & Skriver, C.
      Hypnosis and biofeedback in the treatment of migraine
        headache
      Proceedings of the Biofeedback Research Society
        Fifth Annual Meeting
      Colorado Springs, 1974, 21 (Abst.)

44.   Andreychuk, T. & Skriver, C.
      Hypnosis and biofeedback in the treatment of
        migraine headache
      International Journal of Clinical and Experimental
        Hypnosis, 1975, 23:172-183

45.   Anliker, J.
      Biofeedback from the perspectives of cybernetics and
        systems science
      In J. Beatty & H. Legewie (Eds.), Biofeedback and
        Behavior, New York:Plenum Press, 1977

46.   Arengo, A.D. & Lewisdearengo, S.F.
      Biofeedback techniques and their importance for
        future of psychosomatic medicine
      Medicina-Buenes Aires, 1976, 36:267-270

47.   Astor, M.
      An introduction to biofeedback
      American Journal of Orthopsychiatry, 1977, 47:615-
        625

48.   Averill, J.
      Personal control over aversive stimuli and its
        relationship to stress
      Psychological Bulletin, 1973, 80:286-303

49.   Ax, A.F., Lootens, A.M. & Gorham, J.C., Jr., et al.
      Physiological arousal and learning with biofeedback
        as a measure of achievement motivation
      Biofeedback and Self-Regulation, 1977, 2:318 (Abst.)

50. Ayrapet'yants, E. Sh.
     The principle of temporary connections in the
       physiology of interoception
     Voprosy Fiziologii Interotseptsii, 1952, 1:5-23
     In: The Central Nervous System and Human Behavior,
       Translation from the Russian Medical Literature.
       Bethesda: Russian Scientific Translation Program,
       1959

51.   Bachrach, A.J., Erwin, W. & Mohr, J.P.
      The control of eating behavior in an anorexic by
         operant conditioning techniques
      In L. P. Ullman, L. Krasner (Eds.), Case Studies in
         Behavior Modification.
      New York: Holt, Rinehart & Winston, 1965, 153-163

52.   Badia, P. & Defran, R.H.
      Orienting responses and GSR conditioning: A
         dilemma
      Psychological Review, 1970, 77, 171-181

53.   Bagchi, B.K.
      Mental hygiene and the Hindu doctrine of relaxation
      Mental Hygiene, 1936, 20:424-440

54.   Bagchi, B.K.
      The adaptation and variability of response of the
         human brain rhythm
      Journal of Psychology, 1937, 3:463-485

55.   Bagchi, B.K.
      Mysticism and mist in India
      Journal of the American Society of Psychosomatic
         Dentistry and Medicine, 1969, 16:1-32

56.   Bagchi, B.K. & Wenger, M.A.
      Electro-physiological correlates of some yogi
         exercises
      In L. Van Bogaert & J. Radermecher (Eds.), Pro-
         ceedings of the First International Congress of
         Neurological Sciences, Brussels, 1957, Vol. III,
         EEG, Clinical Neurophysiology and Epilepsy.
      London: Pergamon Press, 1959, 132-149

57.   Baginsky, R.G.
      Voluntary control of motor unit activity by visual
         and aural feedback
      Electroencephalography and Clinical Neurophysiology,
         1969, 27:724-725 (Abst.)

58.   Bair, J.H.
      Development of voluntary control
      Psychological Reviews, 1901, 8:474-510

59. Bakal, D.A.
     Headache: A biopsychological perspective
     Psychological Bulletin, 1975, 8:369-382

60. Bakan, P. & Svorad, D.
     Resting EEG alpha and asymmetry of reflective
        lateral eye movements
     Nature, 1969, 223:975-976

61. Baker, B.L., Cohen, D.C. & Saunders, J.T.
     Self-directed desensitization for acrophobia
     Behavior Research and Therapy, 1973, 11, 79-89

62. Baker, B.L. & Kahn, M.
     A reply to "Critique of 'Treatment of insomnia by
        relaxation training': Relaxation training,
        Rogerian therapy or demand characteristics."
     Journal of Abnormal Psychology, 1972, 79:94-96

63. Baker, M., Regenas, E., Wolf, S.L. & Basmajian, J.V.
     Developing strategies for biofeedback -- application
        in neurologically handicapped patients
     Physical Therapy, 1977, 57:402-408

64. Ballard, P., Doerr, H. & Varni, J.
     Arrest of a disabling eye disorder using biofeedback
     Psychophysiology, 1972, 9:271 (Abst.)

65. Balshan, S.
     Muscle tension and personality in women
     Archives of General Psychiatry, 1962, 7:436-448

66. Banquet, J.P.
     EEG and meditation
     Electroencephalography and Clinical Neurophysiology,
        1972, 33:449-455

67. Banquet, J.P.
     Spectral analysis of the EEG in meditation
     Electroencephalography and Clinical Neurophysiology,
        1973, 35:143-151

68.   Banuazizi, A.
      Modification of an autonomic response by instru-
        mental conditioning
      Psychonomic Bulletin, 1967, 1:30

69.   Banuazizi, A.
      Discriminative shock avoidance learning of an auto-
        nomic response under curare
      Journal of Comparative and Physiological Psychology,
        1972, 81:336-346

70.   Barber, T.X.
      The necessary and sufficient conditions for hypnotic
        behavior
      American Journal of Clinical Behavior, 1960, 3:31-42

71.   Barber, T.X.
      Physiological effects of "hypnosis"
      Psychological Bulletin, 1961, 58:390-419

72.   Barber, T.X.
      Experimental controls and the phenomena of "hypnosis":
        A critique of hypnotic research methodology
      Journal of Nervous and Mental Disease, 1962, 134:
        493-505

73.   Barber, T.X.
      The effects of "hypnosis" on pain: A critical
        review of experimental and clinical findings
      Psychosomatic Medicine, 1963, 25, 303-333

74.   Barber, T.X.
      An empirically-based formulation of hypnotism
      The American Journal of Clinical Hypnosis, 1969,
        12:100-130

75.   Barber, T.X.
      Physiological effects of hypnosis and suggestion
      LSD, Marijuana, Yoga and Hypnosis
      Chicago: Aldine Publishing Co., 1970

76.   Barber, T.X.
      Implication for human capabilities and potentialities
      In T. X. Barber et al (Eds.), Hypnosis, Imagination
        and Human Potentialities
      New York: Pergamon Press, 1974

77.   Barber, T.X., DiCara, L.V., Kamiya, J., Miller,
      N.E., Shapiro, D. & Stoyva, J. (Eds.)
      Biofeedback and Self-Control, 1970
      Chicago: Aldine Publishing Co., 1971

78.   Barber, T.X., DiCara, L.V., Kamiya, J., Miller,
      N.E., Shapiro, D. & Stoyva, J. (Eds.)
      Biofeedback and Self-Control, 1975
      Chicago: Aldine Publishing Co., 1976

79.   Barefoot, J.C. & Straub, R.B.
      Opportunity for information search and the effect of
        false heart-rate feedback
      Journal of Personal and Social Psychology, 1971,
        17:154-157

80.   Barlow, D.H., Agras, W.S., Abel, G.G. et al.
      Case histories and shorter communications
      Biofeedback and reinforcement to increase hetero-
        sexual arousal in homosexuals
      Behavior Research and Therapy, 1975, 13:45-50

81.   Barlow, D.H., Blanchard, E.B., Hayes, S.C. &
      Epstein, L.H.
      Single case designs and clinical biofeedback ex-
        perimentation
      Biofeedback and Self-Regulation, 1977, 2:221-240

82.   Barlow, D.H. & Hersen, M.
      Single case experimental designs: Uses in applied
        clinical research
      Archives of General Psychiatry, 1973, 29:319-325

83.   Barr, R. & Abernethy, V.
      Single case study -- conversion reaction.
        Differential diagnosis in light of biofeedback
        research
      Journal of Nervous and Mental Disease, 1977, 164:
        287-292

84.   Barratt, P. & Herd, J.
      Subliminal conditioning of alpha rhythm
      Australian Journal of Psychology, 1964, 16:9-19

85. Barrett, B.
Reduction in rate of multiple tics by free operant
conditioning methods
Journal of Nervous and Mental Disease, 1962, 135:187-
195

86. Basmajian, J.V.
Control and training of individual motor units
Science, 1963, 141:440-441

87. Basmajian, J.V.
Conscious control of single nerve cells
New Scientist, 1963, 20:662-664

88. Basmajian, J.V.
Control of individual motor units
American Journal of Physical Medicine, 1967, 46:480-
486

89. Basmajian, J.V.
Microcosmic learning
In L. Smith (Ed.). Psychology of Motor Learning,
Proceedings of C.I.C. Symposium
Chicago: The Athletic Institute, 1970

90. Basmajian, J.V.
Neuromuscular facilitation techniques
Archives of Physical Medicine and Rehabilitation,
1971, 52:40-42

91. Basmajian, J.V.
Electromyography comes of age
Science, 1972, 176:603-609

92. Basmajian, J.V.
Control of individual motor units
American Journal of Physical Medicine, 1973, 52:257-
260

93. Basmajian, J.V.
Muscles alive: Their functions revealed by electro-
myography (3rd Edition)
Baltimore: Williams & Wilkins, 1974

94.   Basmajian, J.V.
      Facts vs. myths in EMG biofeedback
      Biofeedback and Self-Regulation, 1976, 1:369-371

95.   Basmajian, J.V.
      Motor learning and control: A working hypothesis
      Archives of Physical Medicine and Rehabilitation,
         1977, 58:38-41

96.   Basmajian, J.V.
      Learned control of single motor units
      In G. E. Schwartz and J. Beatty (Eds.), Biofeedback:
         Theory and Research
      New York: Academic Press, 1977

97.   Basmajian, J.V. (Ed.)
      Biofeedback: A Handbook for Clinicians
      Baltimore: Williams & Wilkins, in press

98.   Basmajian, J.V., Baeza, M. & Fabrigar, C.
      Conscious control and training of individual spinal
         motor neurons in normal human subjects
      Journal of New Drugs, 1965, 5:78-85

99.   Basmajian, J.V. & Cross, G.L.
      Duration of motor unit potentials from fine wire
         electrodes
      American Journal of Physical Medicine, 1971, 50:144-
         148

100. Basmajian, J.V., Forrest, W.J. & Shine, G.
      A simple connector for fine wire EMG electrodes
      Journal of Applied Physiology, 1966, 21:1680

101. Basmajian, J.V., Kukulka, C.G. & Narayan, M.G. et
         al.
      Biofeedback treatment of foot-drop after stroke
         compared with standard rehabilitation technique:
         Effects on voluntary control and strength
      Archives of Physical Medicine and Rehabilitation,
         1975, 56:231-236

102. Basmajian, J.V. & Newton, W.J.
      Feedback training of parts of buccinator muscle in
         man
      Psychophysiology, 1974, 11:92

103.   Basmajian, J.V., Regenos, E.M. & Baker, M.P.
        Rehabilitating stroke patients with biofeedback
        Geriatrics, 1977, 32:85-90

104.   Basmajian, J.V. & Samson, J.J.
        Standardization of methods in single motor unit
            training
        American Journal of Physical Medicine, 1973, 52:250-
            256

105.   Basmajian, J.V. & Simard, T.
        Effects of distracting movements in the control of
            trained motor units
        American Journal of Physical Medicine, 1967, 46:
            1427-1449

106.   Bauer, R.H.
        Short-term memory: EEG alpha correlates and the
            effect of increased alpha
        Behavioral Biology, 1976, 17:425-433

107.   Bauer, R.H. & Jones C.N.
        Feedback training of 36-44 Hz EEG activity in the
            visual cortex and hippocampus of cats: Evidence
            for sensory and motor involvement
        Physiology and Behavior, 1976, 17:885-890

108.   Baumgartner, P.
        Functional maintenance and retraining of the loco-
            motor system
        Gazette Medicale de France, 1964, 71:1763-1776 (Fr.)

109.   Baust, W. & Bohnert, B.
        The regulation of heart rate during sleep
        Experimental Brain Research, 1969, 7:169-180

110.   Bean, J.A., Kondo, C.Y., Travis, T.A., et al.
        Changes in heart rate associated with increases in
            occipital alpha
        Proceedings of the Biofeedback Research Society
            Sixth Annual Meeting
        Monterey, 1975, 65 (Abst.)

111. Bear
     Efficacy of alpha biofeedback training in elevating
        mood
     Journal of Consulting and Clinical Psychology, 1977,
        45:334

112. Beary, J.F. & Benson, H.
     A simple psychophysiologic technique which elicits
        the hypometabolic changes of the relaxation
        response
     Psychosomatic Medicine, 1974, 36:115-120

113. Beatty, J.
     Effects of initial alpha wave abundance and operant
        training procedures on occipital alpha and beta
        wave activity
     Psychonomic Science, 1971, 23:197-199

114. Beatty, J.
     Similar effects of feedback signals and instruction-
        al information on EEG activity
     Physiology and Behavior, 1972, 9:151-154

115. Beatty, J.
     Contributions of biofeedback methods to the under-
        standing of visceral and central nervous system
        functions
     In J. Beatty & H. Legewie (Eds.), Biofeedback and
        Behavior
     New York: Plenum Press, 1977

116. Beatty, J.
     Learned regulation of alpha and theta frequency
        activity in the human electroencephalogram
     In G. E. Schwartz & J. Beatty (Eds.), Biofeedback:
        Theory and Research
     New York: Academic Press, 1977

117. Beatty, J., Greenberg, A., Deibler, W.P., et al.
     Operant control of occipital theta rhythm affects
        performance in a radar monitoring task
     Science, 1974, 183:871-873

118. Beatty, J. & Kornfeld, C.
Relative independence of conditioned EEG changes
from cardiac and respiratory activity
Physiology and Behavior, 1972, 9:733-736

119. Beatty, J. & Legewie, H. (Eds.)
Biofeedback and Behavior
New York: Plenum Press, 1977

120. Beaty, E.T.
Feedback-assisted relaxation training as a treatment
for duodenal ulcers
Biofeedback and Self-Regulation, 1976, 1:323-324
(Abst.)

121. Beazel, H.A., Jr., Appel, M.A. & Murphy, W.D.
Effects of anxiety and extrinsic reinforcement on
operant conditioning of human heart rate decelerations
Psychophysiology, 1976, 13:176 (Abst.)

122. Becker-Carus, C.
Relationships between EEG, personality and vigilance
Electroencephalography and Clinical Neurophysiology,
1971, 30:519-526

123. Beckner, T.F., Shealy, C.N. & Gaumer, W.C.
Biofeedback training in the treatment of chronic
pain
Proceedings of the Biofeedback Research Society
Fifth Annual Meeting
Colorado Springs, 1974, 4 (Abst.)

124. Bell, I.R. & Schwartz, G.E.
Cognitive and somatic mechanisms in voluntary
control of heart rate
Proceedings of the Biofeedback Research Society
Fourth Annual Meeting
Boston, 1972, 23 (Abst.)

125. Bell, I. R. & Schwartz, G.E.
Voluntary control and reactivity of human heart rate
Psychophysiology, 1975, 12:339-348

126.   Belmaker, R., Proctor, E. & Feather, B.W.
        Muscle tension in human operant heart rate con-
            ditioning
        Conditional Reflex, 1972, 7:97-106

127.   Benjamins, J.
        The effectiveness of alpha feedback training and
            muscle relaxation procedures in systematic
            desensitization
        Biofeedback and Self-Regulation, 1976, 1, 352
            (Abst.)

128.   Benson, H.
        Conditional modifications of blood pressure
        In G. Onesti, K. E. Kim & J. H. Moyer (Eds.),
            Hypertension: Mechanisms and Management
        New York: Grune & Stratton, 1973

129.   Benson, H.
        Inate asset for combating stress
        Harvard Business Review, 1974, 52:49-60

130.   Benson, H.
        The Relaxation Response
        New York: William Morrow & Co., Inc., 1975

131.   Benson, H., Beary, J. F. & Carol, M.P.
        The Relaxation Response
        Psychiatry, 1974, 37:37-46

132.   Benson, H., Greenwood, M.M. & Klemchuk, H.
        Relaxation response: Psychophysiological aspects
            and clinical applications
        International Journal of Psychiatry in Medicine,
            1975, 6:87-98

133.   Benson, H., Herd, J.A., Morse, W.H. & Kelleher, R.T.
        Behavioral induction of arterial hypertension and
            its reversal
        American Journal of Physiology, 1969, 217:30-34

134.   Benson, H., Klemchuk, H.P. & Graham, J.R.
        The usefulness of the relaxation response in the
            therapy of headache
        Headache, 1974, 14:49-52

135.   Benson, H., Kotch, J.B.   & Crassweller, K.D.
       Relaxation response -- bridge between psychiatry and
          medicine
       Medical Clinics of North America, 1977, 61:929

136.   Benson, H., Kotch, J.B., Crassweller, K.D., et al.
       Historical and clinical considerations of the re-
          laxation response
       American Scientist, 1977, 65:441-445

137.   Benson, H., Marzetta, B.R. & Rosner, B.A.
       Decreased blood pressure associated with the regular
          elicitation of the relaxation response: A study
          of hypertension subjects
       In R. S. Eliot (Ed.), Contemporary Problems in
          Cardiology.   Vol I.   Stress and the Heart
       New York: Futura, 1974, 293-302

138.   Benson, H., Rosner, B.A. & Marzetta, B.R.
       Decreased systolic blood pressure in hypertension
          subjects who practiced meditation
       Journal of Clinical Investigation, 1973, 52:8a
          (Abst.)

139.   Benson, H., Rosner, B.A., Marzetta, B.R., et al.
       Decreased blood pressure in pharmacologically
          treated hypertensive patients who regularly
          elicited the relaxation response
       Lancet, 1974, 1:289-291

140.   Benson, H., Shapiro, D., Tursky, B. & Schwartz, G.E.
       Decreased systolic blood pressure through operant
          conditioning techniques in patients with essential
          hypertension
       Science, 1971, 173:740-742

141.   Benson, H. & Wallace, R.K.
       Decreased drug abuse with Transcendental Meditation:
          A study of 186 subjects
       In Zerafonetis, C. (Ed.):   Proceedings of the Inter-
          national Symposium on Drug Abuse
       Philadelphia: Lea & Febiger, 1972

142. Bergman, J.S. & Johnson, H.J.
      The effects of instructional set and autonomic
        perception on cardiac control
      Psychophysiology, 1971, 8:180-190

143. Bergman, J.S. & Johnson, H.J.
      Sources of information which affect training and
        raising of heart rate
      Psychophysiology, 1972, 9:30-39

144. Bernstein, D.A. & Borkovec, T.D.
      Progressive Relaxation Training: A Manual for the
        Helping Professionals
      Champaign, IL: Research Press, 1973

145. Bertelson, A. & Klein, M.
      The effects of autogenic and antiautogenic phrases
        on ability to increase and decrease hand temperature
      Proceedings of the Biofeedback Research Society
        Fifth Annual Meeting
      Colorado Springs, 1974, 57 (Abst.)

146. Bieker, M.A.
      A reliable technique for application of surface
        electrodes
      Biofeedback and Self-Regulation, 1977, 2:323 (Abst.)

147. Birbaumer, N.
      Biofeedback training: A critical review of its
        clinical applications and some possible future
        directions
      European Journal of Behavioral Analysis and Modi-
        fication, 1977, 1:235-251

148. Birbaumer, N.
      Operant enhancement of EEG-Theta activity
      In J. Beatty & H. Legewie (Eds.), Biofeedback and
        Behavior
      New York: Plenum Press, 1977

149. Birbaumer, N., Elbert, T. & Lutzenberger, W.
      Experiments on visceral perception
      Biofeedback and Self-Regulation, 1977, 2:322 (Abst.)

150. Birbaumer, N. & Lutzenberger, N.
An experiment on the feedback of the theta activity
of the human EEG (theta biofeedback)
Proceedings of the Biofeedback Research Society
Sixth Annual Meeting
Monterey, 1975, 34 (Abst.)

151. Birbaumer, N., Lutzenberger, W. & Sternmetz, P.
Simultaneous biofeedback of heart rate and frontalis
EMG as a pretraining for the biofeedback of EEG
theta activity
Biofeedback and Self-Regulation, 1976, 1:336 (Abst.)

152. Birbaumer, N. & Tunner, W.
EEG, evoked potentials, and desensitization
Archives of Psychology (Frankfurt), 1971, 123:225–
234

153. Birbaumer, N. & Wildgruber, C.
Experiment on the theta activity of the human EEG
European Journal of Behavioral Analysis and Modi-
fication, 1971, 1:133–136

154. Bird, B.L., Cataldo, M.F. & Cunningham, C.
Single-subject experimental analysis of EMG bio-
feedback effects in treating cerebral palsied
children
Biofeedback and Self-Regulation, 1977, 2:311–312
(Abst.)

155. Bird, B.L., Knapp, T.M., Newton, F.A., et al.
Operant conditioning of 40 Hz and alpha EEG rhythms
in visual cortex of cats: Relationship to other
EEG rhythms and behavior
Proceedings of the Biofeedback Research Society
Sixth Annual Meeting
Monterey, 1975, 17 (Abst.)

156. Birk, L.
Biofeedback -- furor therapeuticus
Seminars in Psychiatry, 1973, 5:361–364

157. Birk, L.
Biofeedback -- a clinician's overview
Seminars in Psychiatry, 1973, 5:563–565

158.   Birk, L. (Ed.).
        Biofeedback: Behavioral Medicine
        New York: Grune and Stratton, 1973

159.   Birk, L., Crider, A., Shapiro, D. et al.
        Operant conditioning of electrodermal activity
            under partial curarization
        Journal of Comparative and Physiological Psychology,
            1966, 62:965-966

160.   Black, A.H.
        The extinction of avoidance responses under curare
        Journal of Comparative and Physiological Psychology,
            1958, 51:519-524

161.   Black, A.H.
        Heart-rate changes during avoidance learning in
            dogs
        Canadian Journal of Psychology, 1959, 13:229-242

162.   Black, A.H.
        Cardiac conditioning in curarized dogs: The relation-
            ship between heart rate and skeletal behavior
        In W. F. Prokasy (Ed.), Classical Conditioning: A
            Symposium
        New York: Appleton-Century Crofts, 1965, 20-47

163.   Black, A. H.
        Transfer following operant conditioning in the
            curarized dog
        Science, 1967, 155:201-203

164.   Black, A.H.
        Operant conditioning in curarized dogs
        Conditional Reflex, 1967, 2:158 (Abst.)

165.   Black, A.H.
        Operant conditioning of autonomic responses
        Conditional Reflex, 1968, 3:130 (Abst.)

166.   Black, A.H.
        Mediating mechanisms of conditioning
        Conditional Reflex, 1970, 5:140-152

167.   Black, A.H.
       The direct control of neural processes by reward
          and punishment
       American Scientist, 1971, 59:236-245

168.   Black, A.H.
       Autonomic aversive conditioning in infrahuman
          subjects
       In R. F. Brush (Ed.), Aversive Conditioning and
          Learning
       New York: Academic Press, 1971, 3-104

169.   Black, A.H.
       The operant conditioning of central nervous system
          electrical activity
       In G. H. Bower (Ed.), The Psychology of Learning
          and Motivation. Vol 6
       New York: Academic Press, 1972, 47-95

170.   Black, A.H.
       The operant conditioning of the electrical activity
          of the brain as a method for controlling neural
          and mental processes
       In F. J. McGuigan & R. Schoonover (Eds.), Psycho-
          physiology of Thinking
       New York: Academic Press, 1973, 35-68

171.   Black, A.H.
       Operant autonomic conditioning: The analysis of
          response mechanisms
       In P. A. Obrist, et al (Eds.), Cardiovascular
          Psychophysiology
       Chicago: Aldine Publishing Co., 1974, 229-250

172.   Black, A.H.
       Operant conditioning of CNS electrical activity and
          the neural basis of learning
       In M. H. Chase & S. Fox (Eds.), Operant Control of
          the Electrical Activity of the Brain
       Los Angeles: UCLA Brain Research Institute, 1975,
          5-27

173.   Black, A.H. & Carlson, N.J.
       The conditioning of autonomic responses under
          curare-like drugs
       American Psychologist, 1957, 12:429

174. Black, A.H., Carlson, N.J. & Solomon, R.L.
      Exploratory studies of the conditioning of auto-
          nomic responses in curarized dogs
      Psychological Monographs, 1962, 76:1-31

175. Black, A.H. & Cott, A.
      A perspective on biofeedback
      In J. Beatty & H. Legewie (Eds.), Biofeedback and
          Behavior
      New York: Plenum Press, 1977

176. Black, A.H., Cott, A. & Pavloski, R.
      The operant learning theory approach to biofeedback
          training
      In G. E. Schwartz & J. Beatty (Eds.), Biofeedback:
          Theory and Research
      New York: Academic Press, 1977

177. Black, A.H. & Lang, W.H.
      Cardiac conditioning and skeletal responding in
          curarized dogs
      Psychology Review, 1964, 71:80-85

178. Black, A.H., Osborne, B. & Ristow, W.C.
      A note on the operant conditioning of autonomic
          responses
      In H. David & H.M.B. Hurwitz (Eds.), Operant-
          Pavlovian Interactions
      New York: Lawrence Ehrlbaum Assoc., (in press)

179. Black, A.H. & Young, G.A.
      The electrical activity of the hippocampus and
          cortex in dogs operantly trained to move and to
          hold still
      Journal of Comparative and Physiological Psychology,
          1972, 79:128-141

180. Black, A., Young, G.A. & Batenchuk, C.
      Avoidance training of hippocampal theta waves in
          flaxedilized dogs and its relation to skeletal
          movement
      Journal of Comparative and Physiological Psychology,
          1970, 70:15-24

181.   Blackwell, B., Bloomfield, S., Gartside, P., et al.
       Transcendental meditation in hypertension
       Lancet, 1976, 1:223-226

182.   Blanchard, E.B. & Abel, G.G.
       An experimental case study of the biofeedback
          treatment of a rape-induced psychophysiological
          disorder
       Behavior Therapy, 1976, 7:113-119

183.   Blanchard, E.B. & Epstein, L.H.
       The clinical usefulness of biofeedback
       In M. Hersen, R.M. Eisler & P. M. Miller (Eds.),
          Progress in Behavior Modification
       New York: Academic Press, 1977

184.   Blanchard, E.B. & Haynes, M.R.
       Biofeedback treatment in a case of Raynaud's Disease
       Journal of Behavior Therapy and Experimental
          Psychiatry, 1975, 6:230-234

185.   Blanchard, E.B., Haynes, M.R., Kallman, M.D., et
          al.
       A comparison of direct blood pressure feedback and
          electromyographic feedback on the blood pressure
          of normotensives
       Biofeedback and Self-Regulation, 1976, 1:445-451

186.   Blanchard, E.B., Haynes, M.R., Young, L.D., et al.
       The use of feedback training and a stimulus control
          procedure to obtain large magnitude increases in
          heart rate outside of the laboratory
       Biofeedback and Self-Regulation, 1977, 2:81-91

187.   Blanchard, E.B. & Scott, R.W.
       Behavioral tactics for clinical cardiac control
       In K. Calhoun, H. E. Adams, & K. M. Mitchell (Eds.),
          Innovative Treatment Methods in Psychopathology
       New York: Wiley, 1974

188.   Blanchard, E.B., Scott, R.W., Young, L.D., et al.
       The effects of feedback signal information content
          on the long-term self-control of heart rate
       Journal of General Psychology, 1974, 91:175-187

189. Blanchard, E. B., Scott, R.W., Young, L.D., et al.
     Effect of knowledge of response on the self-control
       of heart rate
     Psychophysiology, 1974, 11:251-264

190. Blanchard, E.B. & Young, L.D.
     Relative efficacy of visual and auditory feedback
       for self-control of heart rate
     Journal of General Psychology, 1972, 87:192-202

191. Blanchard, E.B. & Young, L.D.
     Self-control of cardiac functioning: A promise as
       yet unfulfilled
     Psychological Bulletin, 1973, 79:145-163

192. Blanchard, E.B. & Young, L.D.
     Of promises and evidence: A reply to Engel
     Psychological Bulletin, 1974, 81:44-46

193. Blanchard, E.B. & Young, L.D.
     Clinical application of biofeedback training:
       Review of evidence
     Archives of General Psychiatry, 1974, 30:573-589

194. Blanchard, E.B., Young, L.D. Haynes, M. R., et al.
     A simple feedback system for self-control of blood
       pressure
     Perceptual and Motor Skills, 1974, 39:891-898

195. Blanchard, E.B., Young, L.D. & Haynes, M.R.
     A simple feedback system for the treatment of
       elevated blood pressure
     Behavior Therapy, 1975, 6:241-245

196. Blanchard, E.B., Young, L.D., Haynes, M.R., et al.
     Long term instructional control of heart rate
       without exteroceptive feedback
     Journal of General Psychology, 1975, 92:291-292

197. Blanchard, E.B., Young, L.D. & Jackson, M.S.
     Clinical applications of biofeedback training
     Archives of General Psychiatry, 1974, 30:573-589

198. Blanchard, E.B., Young, L.D. & McLeod, P.
     Awareness of heart activity and self-control of
       heart rate
     Psychophysiology, 1972, 9:63-68

199.   Blanchard, E.B., Young, L.D., Scott, R.W., et al.
        Differential effects of feedback and reinforcement
          in voluntary acceleration of human heart rate
        Perceptual and Motor Skills, 1974, 38:683-691

200.   Blankstein, K.R.
        Test-retest consistency and stability of subject
          differences in bidirectional cardiac control: A
          one year follow-up of good versus poor controllers
        Proceedings of the Biofeedback Research Society
          Sixth Annual Meeting
        Monterey, 1975, 42 (Abst.)

201.   Blankstein, K.R.
        Note on relation of autonomic perception to volun-
          tary control of heart rate
        Perceptual and Motor Skills, 1975, 40:533-534

202.   Blankstein, K.R.
        Heart rate control, general anxiety, and subjective
          tenseness
        Behavior Therapy, 1975, 6:699-706

203.   Blankstein, K.R.
        Effect of cognitive mediation and instructions on
          self-regulation of heart rate
        Biofeedback and Self-Regulation, 1977, 2:300 (Abst.)

204.   Blankstein, K.R., Egner, K. & Tafts, J.
        Individual differences in the self-control of heart
          rate: Locus of control
        Proceedings of the Biofeedback Research Society
          Fifth Annual Meeting
        Colorado Springs, 1974, 87 (Abst.)

205.   Blankstein, K.R., Tafts, J. & D'Ambrosia, D.
        Psychopathy and the voluntary control of heart
          rate: Implications for lie detection
        Proceedings of the Biofeedback Research Society
          Fifth Annual Meeting
        Colorado Springs, 1974, 88 (Abst.)

206. Blankstein, K.R., Zimmerman, J. & Egner, K.
     Within-subject designs and the self-control of
       cardiac rate: Review of the literature and an
       experiment
     Proceedings of the Biofeedback Research Society
       Fifth Annual Meeting
     Colorado Springs, 1974, 89 (Abst.)

207. Blankstein, K.R., Zimmerman, J. & Egner, K.
     Within-subject control designs and voluntary bi-
       directional control of cardiac rate: Methodological
       comparison between pre-experimental and pre-trial
       baselines
     Journal of General Psychology, 1976, 95:161-175

208. Bleecker, E.R. & Engel, B.T.
     Learned control of cardiac rate and cardiac con-
       duction in the Wolff-Parkinson-White syndrome
     New England Journal of Medicine, 1973, 288:560-562

209. Bleecker, E.R. & Engel, B.T.
     Learned control of ventricular rate in patients
       with atrial fibrillation
     Psychosomatic Medicine, 1973, 35:161-170

210. Blizard, D.A., Cowings, P. & Miller, N.E.
     Visceral responses to opposite types of autogenic-
       training imagery
     Biological Psychology, 1975, 3:49-55

211. Block, J.D.
     Operant conditioned alleviation of pathological
       nystagmus
     Psychophysiology, 1969, 5:562 (Abst.)

212. Block, J.D., Lagerson, J., Zohman, L.R., et al.
     A feedback device for teaching diaphragmatic
       breathing
     American Review of Respiratory Diseases, 1969,
       100:577-578

213. Blovin, L., Pomerleau, A. & Malcuit, G.
     An attempt to place children's HR under the operant
       control of a Harlequin puppet
     Psychophysiology, 1977, 14:107 (Abst.)

214.   Bohm, M., Trlica, J. & Veljacikova, N.
        The EEG in different phases of essential vascular
           hypertension
        Electroencephalography and Clinical Neurophysiology,
           1967, 22:286-287

215.   Boller, J.D. & Flom, R.P.
        Developing a biofeedback facility: Inception to
           operation
        Biofeedback and Self-Regulation, 1977, 2:324-325
           (Abst.)

216.   Bonica, J.J. & Fordyce, W.F.
        Operant conditioning for chronic pain
        In J.J. Bonica, P. Procacci & C. A. Pagni (Eds.),
           Recent Advances on Pain, Pathophysiology and
           Clinical Aspects
        New York: Charles C. Thomas, 1974

217.   Booker, H., Rubow, R. & Coleman, P.
        Simplified feedback in neuromuscular retraining.
           An automated approach using electromyographic
           signals
        Archives of Physical Medicine and Rehabilitation,
           1969, 50:621-625

218.   Borkovec, T.D.
        The role of expectancy and physiological feedback
           in fear research: A review with special reference
           to subject characteristics
        Behavior Therapy, 1973, 4:491-505

219.   Borkovek, T.D.
        Physiological and cognitive processes in the re-
           gulation of anxiety
        In G. E. Schwartz & D. Shapiro (Eds.), Consciousness
           and Self-Regulation
        New York: Plenum Press, 1976, 261-312

220.   Borkovec, T.D. & Fowles, D.C.
        Controlled investigation of the effects of progressive
           and hypnotic relaxation on insomnia
        Journal of Abnormal Psychology, 1973, 82:153-158

221. Borkovec, T.D. & Glasgow, R.E.
      Boundary conditions of false heart-rate feedback
          effects on avoidance behavior: A resolution of
          discrepant results
      Behavior Research and Therapy, 1973, 11:171-177

222. Borkovec, T.D., Kaloupsek, D.G. & Slama, K.M.
      The facilitative effect of muscle tension release
          in the relaxation treatment of sleep disturbance
      Behavior Therapy, 1975, 6:301-309

223. Borkovek, T.D. & O'Brien, J.T.
      Relation of autonomic perception and its manipulation
          to the maintenance and reduction of fear
      Journal of Abnormal Psychology, 1977, 86:163-171

224. Borkovec, T.D., Steinmark, S.W. & Nau, S.D.
      Relaxation training and single-item desensitization
          in the group treatment of insomnia
      Journal of Behavior Therapy and Experimental
          Psychiatry, 1973, 4:401-403

225. Borkovec, T.D., Wall, R.L. & Stone, N.M.
      False physiological feedback and the maintenance of
          speech anxiety
      Journal of Abnormal Psychology, 1974, 83:164-168

226. Borkovec, T.D. & Weerts, T.C.
      Effects of progressive relaxation on sleep distur-
          bance: An electroencephalogic evaluation
      Psychosomatic Medicine, 1976, 38:173-180

227. Borrey, R., Grings, W.W. & Longstreet, B.J.
      A system for registering both true and false feed-
          back of the galvanic skin response
      Psychophysiology, 1969, 6:366-370

228. Botto, R.W., Galbraith, G.G. & Stein, R.M.
      Effects of false heart rate feedback and sex guilt
          upon attitudes toward sexual stimuli
      Psychological Reports, 1974, 35:267-274

229. Botto, R.W. & Stern, R.M.
      False heart rate feedback: The relationship of
          choice behavior and true EKG and GSR
      Psychophysiology, 1969, 5:582 (Abst.)

230.   Bouchard, C.
        Effects of success and failure signals on heart
            rate regulation
        Psychophysiology, 1976, 13:170 (Abst.)

231.   Bouchard, C. & Corson, J.A.
        Heart rate regulation with success and failure
            signals
        Psychophysiology, 1976, 13:69-74

232.   Bouchard, M. & Granger, L.
        The relative effects of instructions and monetary
            incentives in long-term voluntary control HR
            training
        Biofeedback and Self-Regulation, 1977, 2:300-301
            (Abst.)

233.   Bouchard, M. & Granger, L.
        The role of instructions versus instructions plus
            biofeedback in voluntary heart rate slowing
        Psychophysiology, 1977, 14:475-482

234.   Boudewyns, P.A.
        A comparison of the effects of stress vs relaxation
            instruction on the finger temperature response
        Behavior Therapy, 1976, 7:54-67

235.   Boudrot, R.
        An alpha detection and feedback control system
        Psychophysiology, 1972, 9:461-466

236.   Boudrot, R.
        A portable EEG alpha feedback module and cassette
            data recorder
        Proceedings of the Biofeedback Research Society
            Fifth Annual Meeting
        Colorado Springs, 1974, 106 (Abst.)

237.   Bowman, B.C. & Faust, D.S.
        EMG-autogenic training and cognitive-behavior
            modification: A multi-modal strategy for tension
            reduction for alcoholics
        Biofeedback and Self-Regulation, 1977, 2:312-313
            (Abst.)

238. Brady, J.P.
Metronome-conditioned relaxation: A new behavioral
procedure
British Journal of Psychiatry, 1973, 122:729-730

239. Brady, J.P., Luborsky, L. & Kron, R.E.
Blood pressure reduction in patients with essential
hypertension through metronome-conditioned relaxation: A preliminary report
Behavior Therapy, 1974, 5:203-209

240. Brady, J. V.
Ulcers in "executive" monkeys
Scientific American, 1958, 199:95-100

241. Brady, J.V., Porter, R.W., Conrad, D.G., et al.
Avoidance behavior and the development of gastro-
duodenal ulcers
Journal of the Experimental Analysis of Behavior,
1958, 1:69-72

242. Bram, P.
Biofeedback techniques in multi-modality treatment
Proceedings of the Biofeedback Research Society
Fifth Annual Meeting
Colorado Springs, 1974, 5 (Abst.)

243. Brandt, K.
The effects of relaxation training with analog HR
feedback on basal levels of arousal and response
to aversive tones in groups selected according
to Fear Survey scores
Psychophysiology, 1974, 11:242 (Abst.)

244. Braud, L.W., Lupin, M.N. & Braud, W.G.
The use of electromyographic biofeedback in the
control of hyperactivity
Journal of Learning Disabilities, 1975, 8:21-26

245. Breeden, S., Bean, J.A., Scandrett, S., et al.
EMG levels as indicators of "relaxation"
Proceedings of the Biofeedback Research Society
Sixth Annual Meeting
Monterey, 1975, 4 (Abst.)

246. Breeden, S.A. & Kondo, C.
     Using biofeedback to reduce tension
     American Journal of Nursing, 1975, 75:2010-2012

247. Bremner, F.J.
     Hippocampal activity during avoidance behavior in
       the rat
     Journal of Comparative and Physiological Psychology,
       1964, 58:16-22

248. Bremner, F.J., Moritz, F.& Benignus, V.
     EEG correlates of attention in humans
     Neuropsychologia, 1972, 10:307-312

249. Brener, J.
     Heart rate as an avoidance response
     The Psychological Record, 1966, 16:329-336

250. Brener, J.M.
     The measurement of heart rate
     In P. H. Venables & I. Martin (Eds.), Manual of
       Psychophysiological Methods
     Amsterdam: North Holland Publishing Co., 1967,
       103-132

251. Brener, J.
     Learned control of cardiovascular processes: Feed-
       back mechanisms and therapeutic applications
     In K. S. Calhoun, H.E. Adams, & K. M. Mitchell
       (Eds), Innovative Treatment Methods in Psycho-
       pathology
     New York: John Wiley & Sons, 1974, 245-272

252. Brener, J.
     A general model of voluntary control applied to the
       phenomena of learned cardiovascular change
     In P. Obrist et al (Eds.), Cardiovascular Psycho-
       physiology
     Chicago: Aldine Publishing Co., 1974

253. Brener, J.
     Factors influencing the specificity of voluntary
       cardiovascular control
     In L. DiCara (Ed.), Limbic and Autonomic Nervous
       Systems Research
     New York: Plenum Press, 1974, 335-368

254. Brener, J.
      Visceral perception
      In J. Beatty & H. Legewie (Eds.), Biofeedback and
         Behavior
      New York: Plenum Press, 1977

255. Brener, J.
      Sensory and perceptual determinants of voluntary
         visceral control
      In G. E. Schwartz & J. Beatty (Eds.), Biofeedback:
         Theory and Research
      New York: Academic Press, 1977

256. Brener, J. & Connally, S.R.
      Heart rate conditioning, somatomotor activity and
         oxygen consumption
      Psychophysiology, 1976, 13:180 (Abst.)

257. Brener, J. Eissenberg, E. & Middaugh, S.
      Respiratory and somatomotor factors associated with
         operant conditioning of cardiovascular responses
         in curarized rats
      In P. A. Obrist et al (Eds.), Cardiovascular
         Psychophysiology
      Chicago: Aldine Publishing Co., 1974, 51-275

258. Brener, J. & Goesling, W.
      Heart rate and conditioned activity
      Psychophysiology, 1969, 5:566-567 (Abst.)

259. Brener, J.M. & Hothersall, D.
      Heart rate control under conditions of augmented
         sensory feedback
      Psychophysiology, 1966, 3:23-28

260. Brener, J.M. & Hothersall, D.
      Paced respiration and heart rate control
      Psychophysiology, 1967, 4:1-6

261. Brener, J. & Jones, J.M.
      Interoceptive discrimination in intact humans:
         Detection of cardiac activity
      Physiology and Behavior, 1974, 13:763-767

262. Brener, J. & Kleinman, R.A.
Learned control of decreases in systolic blood
pressure
Nature, 1970, 226:1063-1064

263. Brener, J.M., Kleinman, R.A. & Goesling, W.J.
The effects of different exposures to augmented
sensory feedback on the control of heart rate
Psychophysiology, 1969, 5:510-516

264. Brener, J., Phillips, K. & Connally, S.R.
Oxygen consumption and ambulation during operant
conditioning of heart rate increases and decreases in rats
Psychophysiology, 1977, 14:483-491

265. Brener, J.M. & Shanks, E.M.
The interaction between instructions and augmented
sensory feedback in the training of cardiovascular
control
Proceedings of the Biofeedback Research Society
Fifth Annual Meeting
Colorado Springs, 1974, 95 (Abst.)

266. Bridgwater, G., Sherry, C.J. & Marczynski, T.J.
Alpha activity: The influence of unpatterned light
input and auditory feedback
Life Sciences, 1975, 16:729-739

267. Broadhurst, A. & Glass, A.
Relationship of personality measures to the alpha
rhythm of the electrencephalogram
British Journal of Psychiatry, 1969, 115:199-204

268. Brod, J., Fencl, V., Hejl, Z.,et al.
Circulatory changes underlying blood pressure
elevation during acute emotional stress (mental
arithmetic) in normotensives and hypertensive
subjects
Clinical Science, 1959, 18:269-279

269. Broff, D.L., Raskin, M. & Geisinger, D.
Management of interpersonal issues in systematic
desensitization
American Journal of Psychiatry, 1976, 133:791-794

270. Brogden, W.J.
     Conditioning and "voluntary" control
     Psychological Reports, 1961, 8:351-352

271. Brolund, J.W. & Schallow, J.R.
     The effects of reward on occipital alpha facilitation
        by biofeedback
     Psychophysiology, 1976, 13:236-241

272. Brooker, R.E.
     The effects of immediate feedback during relaxation
        training on the process of systematic desensiti-
        zation
     Dissertation Abstracts, 1972, 32B:4853

273. Brown, B.B.
     Specificity of EEG photic flicker responses to
        color as related to visual imagery ability
     Psychophysiology, 1966, 2:197-207

274. Brown, B.B.
     Recognition of aspects of consciousness through
        association with EEG alpha activity represented
        by a light signal
     Psychophysiology, 1970, 6:442-452

275. Brown, B.B.
     Awareness of EEG - subjective activity relationships
        detected within a closed feedback system
     Psychophysiology, 1971, 7:451-464

276. Brown, B.B.
     New Mind, New Body
     New York: Harper & Row, 1974

277. Brown, B.B.
     The Biofeedback Syllabus: A Handbook for the
        Psychophysiological Study of Biofeedback
     Springfield, Illinois: Charles C. Thomas, 1975

278. Brown, B.B.
     Biological awareness as a state of consciousness
     Journal of Altered States of Consciousness, 1975,
        2:1-14

279. Brown, B.B.
     Overview of biofeedback
     In J. I. Martin (Ed.), Proceedings of the San Diego
        Biomedical Symposium 1976 - Vol. 15
     New York: Academic Press, 1976

280. Brown, B.B.
     Stress and the Art of Biofeedback
     New York: Harper & Row, 1977

281. Brown, B., Fronek, A., Sargent, J., et al.
     Biofeedback Session: Excerpts from panel on
        instrumentation in biofeedback training
     In J. I. Martin (Ed.), Proceedings of the San Diego
        Biomedical Symposium 1976 - Vol. 15
     New York: Academic Press, 1976

282. Brown, B.B. & Klug, J.W.
     Exploration of EEG alpha bio-feedback as a tech-
        nique to enhance rapport
     Proceedings of the Biofeedback Research Society
        Fifth Annual Meeting
     Colorado Springs, 1974, 76 (Abst.)

283. Brown, B.B. & Klug, J.W. (Eds.)
     The Alpha Syllabus
     Springfield, Illinois: Charles C. Thomas, 1974

284. Brown, C.C. & Katz, R.A.
     Operant salivary conditioning in man
     Psychophysiology, 1967, 4:156-160

285. Brown, C.C. & Thorne, P.R.
     An instrument for signalling heart rate to un-
        restrained human subjects
     Psychophysiology, 1964, 1:192-194

286. Brown, C. & Wagman, A.
     Operant salivary conditioning in man
     Conditional Reflex, 1968, 3:128-129

287. Brown, T., Sambrooks, J.E. & Macculloch, M.J.
     Auditory thresholds and the effect of reduced
        auditory feedback of stuttering
     Acta Psychiatrica Scandinavia, 1975, 51:297

288. Brucker, B.S. & Ince, L.P.
Biofeedback as an experimental treatment for postural
hypotension in a patient with a spinal cord lesion
Archives of Physical Medicine and Rehabilitation,
1977, 58:49-53

289. Brucker, B.S., Pickering, T., Ince, L.P. et al.
Learned voluntary control of blood pressure as a
treatment for postural hypotension in spinal
cord injury patients
Biofeedback and Self-Regulation, 1977, 2:301 (Abst.)

290. Brudny, J., Grynbaum, B.B. & Korein, J.
Spasmodic torticollis: Treatment by feedback
display of EMG
Archives of Physical Medicine and Rehabilitation,
1974, 55:403-408

291. Brudny, J., Korein, J., Grynbaum, B.B., et al.
EMG feedback therapy: Review of treatment of 114
patients
Archives of Physical Medicine and Rehabilitation,
1976, 57:55-61

292. Brudny, J., Korein, J., Levidow, L., et al.
Sensory feedback therapy as a modality of treatment
in central nervous system disorders of voluntary
movement
Neurology, 1974, 24:925-932

293. Bry, B.M.
The operant conditioning of human EEGs
Dissertation Abstracts, 1970, 30:4805

294. Budzynski, T.H.
Feedback induced muscle relaxation and activation
level
Dissertation Abstracts International, 1970, 30:
4805-4806

295. Budzynski, T.H.
Some applications of biofeedback produced twilight
states
Fields Within Fields . . . Within Fields, 1972,
5:105-114

296. Budzynski, T.H.
     Biofeedback procedures in the clinic
     Seminars in Psychiatry, 1973, 5:537-547

297. Budzynski, T.H.
     A systems approach to some clinical applications of
        biofeedback
     Proceedings of the Biofeedback Research Society
        Fifth Annual Meeting
     Colorado Springs, 1974, 105 (Abst.)

298. Budzynski, T.H.
     Biofeedback and the twilight states of consciousness
     In G. E. Schwartz & D. Shapiro (Eds.), Conscious-
        ness and Self-Control
     New York: Plenum Press, 1976, 361-385

299. Budzynski, T.H.
     Clinical implications of electromyographic training
     In G. E. Schwartz & J. Beatty (Eds.), Biofeedback:
        Theory and Research
     New York: Academic Press, 1977

300. Budzynski, T.
     Tuning in on the twilight zone
     Psychology Today, 1977, August, 40-44

301. Budzynski, T.H. & Padnes, S., (Eds.)
     A Roche Scientific Series of Eight Monographs: How
        to make the involuntary voluntary
     Nutley, NJ: Hoffman LaRoche, 1976

302. Budzynski, T.H. & Peffer, K.E.
     Twilight state learning. The presentation of
        learning material during a biofeedback-produced
        altered state
     Proceedings of the Biofeedback Research Society
        Fifth Annual Meeting
     Colorado Springs, 1974, 97 (Abst.)

303. Budzynski, T.H. & Stoyva, J.M.
     An instrument for producing deep muscle relaxation
        by means of analog information feedback
     Journal of Applied Behavior Analysis, 1969, 2:231-
        237

304. Budzynski, T.H. & Stoyva, J.M.
An electromyographic technique for teaching volun-
tary relaxation of the masseter muscle
Journal of Dental Research, 1973, 52:116-119

305. Budzynski, T. & Stoyva, J.
Biofeedback techniques in behavior therapy
Originally published as: Biofeedback-techniken in
der verhaltenstherapie und im autogenen training
In N. Birbaumer (Ed.), Neuropsychologie der Angst.
Reieh Fortschritte der klinischen psychologie,
Bd. 3.
Munchen. Berlin, Wien: Verlag Urban & Schwarzenberg,
1973, 248-270

306. Budzynski, T.H. & Stoyva, J.M.
EMG-biofeedback bei unspezifischen und spezifischen
angstzustanden (EMG biofeedback in generalized
and specific anxiety disorders)
In H. Legewie & L. Nusselt (Eds.), Biofeedback-
Therapie: Lernmethoden in der Psychosomatik,
Neurologie und Rehabilitation (Fortschritte der
Klinischen Psychologie Vol 6) -
Munchen-Berlin-Wien: Urban & Schwarzenberg, 1975

307. Budzynski, T., Stoyva, J. & Adler, C.
Feedback-induced muscle relaxation: Application to
tension headache
Journal of Behavior Therapy and Experimental
Psychiatry, 1970, 1:205-211

308. Budzynski, T.H., Stoyva, J.M., Adler, C.S. &
Mullaney, D.
EMG biofeedback and tension headache: A controlled-
outcome study
Psychosomatic Medicine, 1973, 35:484-496

309. Budzynski, T.H., Stoyva, J.M. & Peffer, K.E.
Biofeedback techniques in psychosomatic disorders
In E. Foa & A. Goldstein (Eds.), Handbook of
Behavioral Interventions
New York: Wiley & Sons, in press

310. Budzynski, T.H., Stoyva, J.M., Thomas, D.L. et al.
     Performance under stress: A stress preventive
        biofeedback program
     Proceedings of the Biofeedback Research Society
        Fifth Annual Meeting
     Colorado Springs, 1974, 55 (Abst.)

311. Bundzen, P.V.
     Autoregulation of functional state of the brain:
        An investigation using photostimulation with
        feedback
     Federation Proceedings Transaction Supplement,
        1966, 25:551-554

312. Bundzen, P.V.
     Autoregulatory mechanisms of the central nervous
        system in the presence of photostimulation in the
        rhythm of the biopotentials
     Fiziologicheskii Zhurnal SSSR, 1968, 54:683-691

313. Bundzen, P.V. et al.
     Method of automatic photostimulation in the rhythm
        of cerebral bipotentials with a selectively
        controlled feedback system
     Fiziologicheskii Zhurnal SSSR, 1968, 54:1239-1243

314. Burgar, C.G. & Montgomery, P.S.
     A miniature device for measurement and feedback of
        average skin resistance
     Biofeedback and Self-Regulation, 1977, 2:324 (Abst.)

315. Burke, B.D.
     Susceptibility to delayed auditory feedback and
        dependence on auditory or oral sensory feedback
     Journal of Communication Disorders, 1975, 8:75-96

316. Burns, J.M. & Ascough, J.C.
     A physiological comparison of two approaches to
        relaxation and anxiety induction
     Behavior Therapy, 1971, 2:170-176

317. Bushman, J.A.
     Investigation of the behavior of the autonomic
        nervous system under stress
     Proceedings of the Royal Society of Medicine, 1973,
        66:477-478

318. Butler, J. & Stoyva, J.M.
      Biofeedback and Self-Regulation: A Bibliography
      Biofeedback Research Society, 1973

319. Butler, J.H., Abbott, B.M. & Bush, F.M.
      Biofeedback as a method of controlling bruxism
      Journal of Dental Research, 1976, 55:B310

320. Butollo, W.H.L.
      An experiment on the feedback of the theta activity
         of the human EEG. The struggle with falsifications
         and confirmations of hypotheses
      European Journal of Behavioral Analysis and Modi-
         fication, 1975, 1:275-132

321. Butterfield, W.H., Thomas, E.J. & Soberg, R.J.
      A device for simultaneous feedback of verbal and
         signal data
      Behavior Therapy, 1970, 1:395-401

322.   Cabral, R.J. & Scott, D.F.
       Effects of two desensitization techniques, biofeed-
       back and relaxation, on intractable epilepsy:
       Follow-up study.
       Journal of Neurological and Neurosurgical Psychiatry,
       1976, 39:504-507

323.   Caddy, G.R. & Lovibund, S.H.
       Self-regulation and discriminated aversive con-
       ditioning in the modification of alcoholics
       drinking behavior
       Behavior Therapy, 1976, 7:223-230

324.   Camacho, E.O.
       Comment on: Feedback of speech muscle activity
       during silent reading: Rapid extinction by C. D.
       Hardyck, L. F. Petrinovich, & D. W. Ellsworth
       (1966)
       Science, 1967, 157:581

325.   Campos, J.J. & Johnson, H.J.
       Affect, verbalization and directional fractionation
       of autonomic responses
       Psychophysiology, 1967, 3:285-290

326.   Canter, A., Kondo, C.Y. & Knott, J.R.
       A comparison of EMG feedback and progressive muscle
       relaxation training in anxiety neuroses
       British Journal of Psychiatry, 1975, 127:470-477

327.   Carlson, J.G.
       Locus of control and frontal electromyographic
       response training
       Biofeedback and Self-Regulation, 1977, 2:259-272

328.   Carlsoo, S. & Edfeldt, A.W.
       Attempts at muscle control with visual and auditory
       impulses as auxiliary stimuli
       Scandinavian Journal of Psychology, 1963, 4:231-235

329.   Carlsson, S.G. & Gale, E.N.
       Biofeedback in the treatment of long-term tempero-
       mandibular joint pain: An outcome study
       Biofeedback and Self-Regulation, 1977, 2: 161-172

330. Carlsson, S.G., Gale, E.N. & Ohman, A.
Treatment of temporomandibular joint syndrome
    biofeedback training
Journal of the American Dental Association, 1975,
    91:602-605

331. Carmona, A., Miller, N.E. & Dimierre, T.
Instrumental learning of gastric vascular tonicity
    responses
Psychosomatic Medicine, 1974, 36:156-163

332. Caronite, S.C.
The effects of biofeedback variables on the ac-
    quisition and retention of a differentiated
    electromyographic response
Dissertation Abstracts, 1972, 33B:1812

333. Carr, H.
Apparent control of the position of the visual
    field
Psychological Review, 1907, 14:357-382

334. Carr, H.
Voluntary control of the visual field
Psychological Review, 1908, 15:139-149

335. Carrera, F.& Adams, P. L.
An ethical perspective on operant conditioning
Journal of the American Academy of Child Psychiatry,
    1970, 9:607-623

336. Carroll, D.
Cardiac perception and cardiac control: A review
Biofeedback and Self-Regulation, 1977, 2::349-369

337. Cassel, R.N.
Fostering transcendental meditation using biofeed-
    back eliminates hoax and restores credibility to
    art
Psychology, 1976, 13:58-64

338. Cautela, J.R.
Behavior therapy and self-control: Techniques and
    implications
In C. M. Franks (Ed.), Behavior Therapy: Appraisal
    and Status
New York: McGraw-Hill, 1969

339.   Cazard, P.
       Interhemispheric synchronism of parieto-occipital
         alpha rhythm: Attention and conscious experience
       American Psychologist, 1974, 74:7-22

340.   Cerny, M. & Dolezalova, V.
       Biofeedback voluntary and hypnotic control of
         autonomic functions
       Activitas Nervosa Superior (Praha), 1975, 17:37-38

341.   Chaney, D.S. & Andreason, L.
       Relaxation and neuromuscular control and changes in
         mental performance under induced tension
       Perceptual and Motor Skills, 1972, 34:677-678

342.   Chapman, R.M., Shelbourne, S.A. & Bragdon, H.R.
       EEG alpha activity influenced by visual input and
         not by eye position
       Electroencephalography and Clinical Neurophysiology,
         1970, 28:183-189

343.   Chari, C.T.K.
       Psychophysiological issues about EEG alpha activity
         and ESP
       Journal of the American Society for Psychic Research,
         1970, 64:411-420

344.   Chase, M.H. & Harper, R.M.
       Somatomotor and vasomotor correlates of operantly
         conditioned 12-14 c/sec sensorimotor cortical
         activity
       Electroencephalography and Clinical Neurophysiology,
         1971, 31:85-92

345.   Chattergee, B.B. & Eriksen, C.W.
       Conditioning and generalization of GSR as a function
         of awareness
       Journal of Abnormal and Social Psychology, 1960,
         60:396-403

346.   Chattergee, B. & Eriksen, C.W.
       Cognitive factors in heart rate conditioning
       Journal of Experimental Psychology, 1962, 64:272-
         279

347.   Chaves, J.F.
        Hypnosis reconceptualized: An overview of Barber's
            theoretical and empirical work
        Psychological Reports, 1968, 22:587-608

348.   Cherry, C. & Sayers, B. McA.
        Experiments upon the total inhibition of stammering
            by external control and some clinical results
        Journal of Psychosomatic Research, 1956, 1:233-246

349.   Chesney, M.A. & Shelton, J.L.
        A comparison of muscle relaxation and electro-
            myogram biofeedback treatments for muscle con-
            traction headache
        Journal of Behavior Therapy and Experimental
            Psychiatry, 1976, 7:221-226

350.   Childers, C.A.
        Modification of social behavior problems by alpha
            biofeedback training
        Proceedings of the Biofeedback Research Society
            Sixth Annual Meeting
        Monterey, 1975, 60   (Abst.)

351.   Chisholm, R.C., DeGood, D. & Hartz, M.A.
        Effects of alpha feedback training on occipital
            EEG, heart rate and experimental reactivity to a
            laboratory stressor
        Psychophysiology, 1977, 14:157-163

352.   Chisholm, R.C., Valle, R.S., Adams, A.S., et al.
        Effects of occipital alpha training on EEG response
            to a laboratory stressor
        Proceedings of the Biofeedback Research Society
            Sixth Annual Meeting
        Monterey, 1975, 37   (Abst.)

353.   Christie, D.J. & Kotses, H.
        Bidirectional operant conditioning of the cephalic
            vasomotor response
        Journal of Psychosomatic Research, 1973, 17:167-170

354.   Church, R.M.
        Systematic effect of random error in the yoked
            control design
        Psychological Bulletin, 1964, 62:122-131

355.   Clark, R.E. & Forgione, A.G.
       Gingival and digital vasomotor response to thermal
           imagery in hypnosis
       Journal of Dental Research, 1974, 53:792-796

356.   Clarke, N.G. & Kardachi, B.J.
       Treatment of myofascial pain-dysfunction syndrome
           using biofeedback principle
       Journal of Periodontology, 1977, 48:643-645

357.   Clayman, K. & Simkins, L.
       The relationship between EMG and mood correlates of
           the menstrual cycle
       Proceedings of the Biofeedback Research Society
           Fifth Annual Meeting
       Colorado Springs, 1974, 42   (Abst.)

358.   Clayman, K.K. & Simkins, L.
       The relationship of temperature control to menstrual
           distress
       Proceedings of the Biofeedback Research Society
           Sixth Annual Meeting
       Monterey, 1975, 58 (Abst.)

359.   Cleaves, C.M.
       The control of muscle tension through psycho-
           physiological information feedback
       Dissertation Abstracts, 1971, 31B:4331

360.   Cleeland, C.S.
       Behavioral techniques in the modification of
           spasmodic torticollis
       Neurology, 1973, 23:1241-1247

361.   Cleeland, C.S., Booker, H.E. & Hosokawa, K.
       Alpha enhancement: Due to feedback or the nature
           of the task
       Psychophysiology, 1971, 8:262-263

362.   Clemens, W.J.
       Procedures for studying the discrimination of heart
           beats
       Psychophysiology, 1977, 14:98 (Abst.)

363.   Clemens, W.J. & MacDonald, D.F.
        Relationship between heart beat discrimination and
            heart rate control
        Psychophysiology, 1976, 13:176 (Abst.)

364.   Clippinger, F.W., Avery, R. & Titus, B.R.
        A sensory feedback system for an upper limb am-
            putation prosthesis
        Bulletin of Prosthetic Research, 1974, 247-258

365.   Coffman, M. & Kimmel, H.D.
        Instrumental conditioning of the GSR: A comparison
            of light deprivation and monotony hypothesis
        Journal of Experimental Psychology, 1971, 89:410-
            413

366.   Coger, R. & Werbach, M.
        Attention, anxiety and the effects of learned
            enhancement of EEG alpha in chronic pain: A
            pilot study in biofeedback
        In B. L. Crue (Ed.), Pain: Research and Treatment
        New York: Academic Press, 1975

367.   Cohen, D.H.
        Analysis of the final common path for heart rate
            conditioning
        In P. A. Obrist, A.H. Black, J. Brener & L. V.
            DiCara (Eds.), Cardiovascular Psychophysiology
        Chicago: Aldine Publishing Co., 1974

368.   Cohen, D.H. & MacDonald, R.L.
        A selective review of central visual pathways
            involved in cardiovascular control
        In P. A. Obrist, A.H. Black, J. Brener & L. V.
            DiCara (Eds.), Cardiovascular Psychophysiology
        Chicago: Aldine Publishing Co., 1974

369.   Cohen, H.D., Graham, C., Fotopoulos, S.S., et al.
        A double-blind methodology for biofeedback research
        Psychophysiology, 1977, 14:99 (Abst.)

370.   Cohen, H.D., Graham, C., Fotopoulos, S., et al.
        A double-blind methodology for biofeedback research
        Psychophysiology, 1977, 14:603-608

371.   Cohen, M.J.
       The relation between heart rate and electromyo-
           graphic activity in a discriminated escape-
           avoidance paradigm
       Psychophysiology, 1973, 10:8-20

372.   Cohen, M.J., Levee, J.R., McArthur, D.L. et al.
       Physiological and psychological dimensions of
           migraine headache and biofeedback training
       Biofeedback and Self-Regulation, 1976, 1:348 (Abst.)

373.   Colgan, M.
       Effects of binary and proportional feedback on
           bidirectional control of heart rate
       Psychophysiology, 1977, 14:187-197

374.   Conger, J.C., Conger, A.J. & Brehm, S.S.
       Fear level as a moderator of false feedback effects
           in snake phobics
       Journal of Consulting and Clinical Psychology,
           1976, 44:135-141

375.   Conner, W.H.
       Effects of brief relaxation training of autonomic
           response to anxiety-evoking stimuli
       Psychophysiology, 1974, 11:591-599

376.   Connor, W.H. & Phares, R.
       Heart rate control and awareness of heart rate
           change
       Proceedings of the Biofeedback Research Society
           Fourth Annual Meeting
       Boston, 1972, 21   (Abst.)

377.   Cook, M.R.
       Psychophysiology of peripheral vascular changes
       In P. A. Obrist, A.H. Black, J. Brener & L. V.
           DiCara (Eds.), Cardiovascular Psychophysiology
       Chicago: Aldine Publishing Co, 1974

378.   Cook, S.W. & Harris, R.E.
       The verbal conditioning of the galvanic skin reflex
       Journal of Experimental Psychology, 1937, 21:202-
           210

379. Cornsweet, T.N. & Crane, H.D.
Training the visual accommodation system
Vision Research, 1973, 13:713-715

380. Cotton, D.W.
Yoga and biofeedback in hypertension
Lancet, 1973, 2:1274-1275

381. Coursey, R.D.
Electromyograph feedback as a relaxation technique
Journal of Consulting and Clinical Psychology,
     1975, 43:825-834

382. Coursey, R.D. & Chao, G.
Differential effectiveness of relaxation techniques
     in a posttraining nonfeedback session
Biofeedback and Self-Regulation, 1977, 2:319 (Abst.)

383. Coursey, R.D. & Frankel, B.L.
EMG feedback as a relaxation technique
Proceedings of the Biofeedback Research Society
     Fifth Annual Meeting
Colorado Springs, 1974, 43   (Abst.)

384. Coursey, R., Frankel, B. & Gaarder, K.
EMG biofeedback and autogenic training as relaxation
     techniques for chronic sleep-onset insomnia
Biofeedback and Self-Regulation, 1976, 1:353-354
     (Abst.)

385. Cox, D.E.
Extinction of an operantly conditioned autonomic
     response as a function of insight
Dissertation Abstracts, 1971, 32B:2997

386. Cox, D.J., Freundlich, A. & Meyer, R.G.
Differential effectiveness of electromyograph
     feedback, verbal relaxation instructions, and
     medication placebo with tension headaches
Journal of Consulting and Clinical Psychology,
     1975, 43:892-898

387. Cox, R.J. & McGuinness, D.
The effect of chronic anxiety level upon self-
     control of heart rate
Biological Psychology, 1977, 5:7-14

388.   Craighead, W.E.
        The role of muscular relaxation in systematic
           desensitization
        Dissertation Abstracts International, 1971, 31:7592

389.   Craighead, W.E.
        The role of muscular relaxation in systematic
           desensitization
        In R.D. Rubin, J.P. Brady, & J.D. Henderson (Eds.),
           Advances in Behavior Therapy (Vol 4)
        New York: Academic Press, 1973, 177-197

390.   Cram, J., Kohlenberg, R.J. & Singer, M.
        Operant control of alpha EEG and the effects of
           illumination and eye closure
        Psychosomatic Medicine, 1977, 34:11-18

391.   Crasilneck, H.B. & Hall, J.A.
        Physiological changes associated with hypnosis: A
           review of the literature since 1948
        International Journal of Clinical and Experimental
           Hypnosis, 1959, 7:9-50

392.   Crawford, D.G., Friesen, D.D. & Tomlinson-Keasey, C.
        Effects of cognitively induced anxiety on hand
           temperature
        Biofeedback and Self-Regulation, 1977, 2:139-146

393.   Crawford, D. & Tomlinson-Keasey, C.
        Effects of cognitively induced anxiety on hand
           temperature in nonclinical subjects
        Biofeedback and Self-Regulation, 1976, 1:313-314
        (Abst.)

394.   Crider, A., Schwartz, G. & Shapiro, D.
        Operant suppression of spontaneous skin potential
           responses
        Conditional Reflex, 1968, 3:131

395.   Crider, A., Schwartz, G.E. & Shapiro, D.
        Operant suppression of electrodermal response rate
           as a function of punishment schedule
        Journal of Experimental Psychology, 1970, 83:333-
           334

396. Crider, A., Schwartz, G.E. & Shnidman, S.
     On the criteria for instrumental autonomic con-
         ditioning: A reply to Katkin and Murray
     Psychology Bulletin, 1969, 71:455-461

397. Crider, A., Shapiro, D. & Tursky, B.
     Reinforcement of spontaneous electrodermal activity
     Journal of Comparative and Physiological Psychology,
         1966, 61:20-27

398. Crosson, B., Meinz, R., Laur, E. et al.
     Relationship of baseline techniques, hypnotic
         susceptibility and EEG alpha training
     Biofeedback and Self-Regulation, 1976, 1:337 (Abst.)

399. Crosson, B., Meinz, R., Laur, E., et al.
     EEG alpha training, hypnotic susceptibility, and
         baseline techniques
     International Journal of Clinical and Experimental
         Hypnosis, 1977, 25:348-360

400. Csaszar, G.
     Biofeedback and its therapeutic use
     Orv Hetil, 1977, 118:1213-1218 (Hungarian)

401. Culligan, M.J. & Sedlacek, K.
     How to Kill Stress Before it Kills You
     New York: Grosset and Dunlap, 1976

402. Curtis, W.D. & Wessberg, H.W.
     A comparison of heart rate, respiration and galvanic
         skin response among meditators, relaxers and
         controls
     Journal of Altered States of Consciousness, 1976,
         2:319-324

403.   Dalal, A.S.
          An empirical approach to hypnosis: An overview
             of Barber's work
          Archives of General Psychiatry, 1966, 15:151-157

404.   Dalal, A.S. & Barber, T.X.
          Yoga, "Yogic feats", and hypnosis in the light
             of empirical research
          American Journal of Clinical Hypnosis, 1969,
             11:155-166

405.   Dale, A. & Anderson, D.E.
          Feedback variables (field dependence, heart rate
             perception, shock sensitivity, and analog
             biofeedback) in the experimental control of
             human heartrate
          Proceedings of the Biofeedback Research Society
             Sixth Annual Meeting
          Monterey, 1975, 44   (Abst.)

406.   Dalessio, D.J. & Sternbach, R.A.
          Biofeedback techniques in the treatment of
             chronic headache
          In J. I. Martin (Ed.), Proceedings of the San
             Diego Biomedical Symposium, 1976 - Vol. 15
          New York: Academic Press, 1976

407.   Dalton, A.J.
          Discriminative conditioning of hippocampal
             electrical activity in curarized dogs
          Communications in Behavioral Biology, 1969,
             3:283-287

408.   Daniels, L.K.
          The effects of automated hypnosis and hand
             warming on migraine: A pilot study
          The American Journal of Clinical Hypnosis, 1976,
             19:91-94

409.   Danker, P.S., Miklich, D.R., Pratt, C. et al.
          An unsuccessful attempt to instrumentally con-
             dition peak expiratory flow rates in asthmatic
             children
          Journal of Psychosomatic Research, 1975, 19:209-
             213

53

410.   Danskin, D.G. & Walters, E.D.
        Biofeedback and voluntary self-regulation:
          Counseling and education
        Personnel and Guidance Journal, 1973, 51:633-638

411.   Darley, S.A.
        Cognitive and personality factors in emotional
          expression under conditions of false heart-
          rate feedback
        Dissertation Abstracts, 1970, 31A:1370-1371

412.   Darrow, C.W.
        The galvanic skin reflex and finger volume
          changes
        American Journal of Physiology, 1929, 88:219

413.   Das, N.N. & Gastaut, H.
        Variations de l'activite' electrique, du cerveau,
          du coeur et des muscles squelettiques au cours
          de la meditation et de l'extase yogique
        Electroencephalography and Clinical Neuro-
          physiology, 1955, 6:211-219

414.   Datey, K.K.
        Effect of relaxation using biofeedback in-
          struments in systematic hypertension
        Proceedings of the Biofeedback Research Society
          Sixth Annual Meeting
        Monterey, 1975, 13   (Abst.)

415.   Datey, K.K.
        Temperature regulation in the management of
          hypertension
        Biofeedback and Self-Regulation, 1976, 1:308
          (Abst.)

416.   Datey, K.K.
        Biofeedback training and Shavasan in the manage-
          ment of hypertension
        Biofeedback and Self-Regulation, 1977, 2:303
          (Abst.)

REFERENCES

417.   Datey, K.K., Deshmukh, S.N., Dalvi, C.P. &
           Vinekar, S.L.
         "Shavasan": A yogic exercise in the management
         of hypertension
         Angiology, 1969, 20:325-333

418.   Davidson, P.O. & Hiebert, S.F.
         Relaxation training, relaxation instruction and
           repeated exposure to a stressor film
         Journal of Abnormal Psychology, 1971, 78:154-159

419.   Davidson, P.O. & Neufeld, R.W.J.
         Response to pain and stress: A multivariate
           analysis:
         Journal of Psychosomatic Research, 1974, 18:25-
         32

420.   Davidson, R.J. & Goleman, D.J.
         The role of attention in meditation and hypnosis:
           A psychobiological perspective on transfor-
           mations of consciousness
         International Journal of Clinical and Experi-
           mental Hypnosis, 1977, 25:291-308

421.   Davidson, R., McAllister, H. & Hale, D.
         Control of cardiac rate and variability using
           computer produced averaged digital feedback
         IRCS Medical Science, 1975, 3:137

422.   Davidson, R.J.& Schwartz, G.E.
         Sex differences in cerebral lateralization
           during cardiac self-regulation versus affect
           self generation
         Proceedings of the Biofeedback Research Society
           Sixth Annual Meeting
         Monterey, 1975, 43   (Abst.)

423.   Davidson, R.J. & Schwartz, G.E.
         Psychobiology of relaxation and related states:
           A multi-process theory
         In D. Mostofsky (Ed.). Behavior Control and
           Modification of Physiological Activity
         Englewood Cliffs: Prentice-Hall, 1976

424.   Davidson, R.J. & Schwartz, G.E.
        Patterns of cerebral lateralization during
           cardiac biofeedback versus self-regulation of
           emotion: Sex differences
        Psychophysiology, 1976, 13:62-68

425.   Davidson, R.J. & Schwartz, G.E.
        The influence of musical training on patterns of
           EEG asymmetry during musical and nonmusical
           self-generation tasks
        Psychophysiology, 1977, 14:58-63

426.   Davidson, R.J. & Schwartz, G.E.
        Brain mechanisms subserving self-generated
           imagery: Electrophysiological specificity
           and patterning.
        Psychophysiology, 1977, 14:598-602

427.   Davidson, R.J., Schwartz, G.E., Pugash, E., et al.
        Sex differences in patterns of EEG asymmetry
        Biological Psychology, 1976, 4:119-138

428.   Davidson, R.J., Schwartz, G.E. & Rothman, L.P.
        Attentional style and the self-regulation of
           mode-specific attention: An electroencephalo-
           graphic study
        Journal of Abnormal Psychology, 1976, 85:611-621

429.   Davis, J.D., Collins, B.J. & Levine, M.W.
        Peripheral control of drinking: Gastrointestinal
           feeling as a negative feedback signal, a
           theoretical and experimental analysis
        Journal of Comparative and Physiological
           Psychology, 1975, 89:985-1002

430.   Davis, M.H., Saunders, D.R., Creer, T.L. et al.
        Relaxation training facilitated by biofeedback
           apparatus as a supplemental treatment in
           bronchial asthma
        Journal of Psychosomatic Research, 1973, 17:121-
           128

431.   Davis, R.C. & Kantor, J.R.
        Skin resistance during hypnotic states
        Journal of General Psychology, 1935, 13:62-81

432.   Davison, G.S.
         Anxiety under total curarization: Implication
           for the role of muscular relaxation in the
           desensitization of neurotic fears
         Journal of Nervous and Mental Disease, 1966,
           143:443-448

433.   Deabler, H.L., Fidel, E., Dillenkoffer, R.L., et
           al.
         The use of relaxation and hypnosis in lowering
           high blood pressure
         American Journal of Clinical Hypnosis, 1973,
           16:75-83

434.   Dean, S.J., Martin, R.B. & Streiner, D.
         Mediational control of the GSR
         Journal of Experimental Research in Personality,
           1968, 3:71-76

435.   Deane, G.E.
         Human heart-rate responses during experimentally
           induced anxiety: Effects of instructions on
           acquisition
         Journal of Experimental Psychology, 1966,
           71:771-772

436.   Deane, G.E.
         Cardiac activity during experimentally induced
           anxiety
         Psychophysiology, 1969, 6:17-30

437.   DeBacher, G.A.
         Operant shaping of local muscular relaxation in
           normal children
         Dissertation Abstracts, 1973, 33B:3338-3339

438.   DeBacher, G. & Basmajian, J.V.
         Two systems for EMG biofeedback treatment of
           spasticity and paresis
         In Kwatney, E., Zuckerman, E. (Eds.), Devices
           and Systems for Disabled
         Philadelphia: Temple University Health Sciences
           Center, 1975, 26-30

439.   DeBacher, G. & Basmajian, J.V.
         EMG feedback strategies in rehabilitation of
         neuromuscular disorders
         In J. Beatty & H. Legewie (Eds.), Biofeedback
         and Behavior
         New York: Plenum Press, 1977.

440.   Decaria, M.D., Proctor, S. & Malloy, T.E.
         The effect of false heart rate feedback on self-
         reports of anxiety and on actual heart rate
         Behavior Research and Therapy, 1974, 12:251-253

441.   Defares, P.B., van Enkevort, G.M., van Gelderen,
         M.H. & Schendelaar, J.K.
         Pseudoheart beat - feedback and the reduction of
         anxiety
         Nederlands Tijdschrift voor de Psychologie en
         haar Grenegebieden, 1969, 24:117-135

442.   Defran, R.H., Badia, P. & Lewis, P.
         Stimulus control over operant galvanic skin
         responses
         Psychophysiology, 1969, 6:101-106

443.   DeGood, D.
         Comparison of training period and generalization
         to a laboratory stressor as criteria for
         evaluating heart rate biofeedback and pro-
         gressive muscle relaxation effects
         Biofeedback and Self-Regulation, 1976, 1:319
         (Abst.)

444.   DeGood, D.
         A multiple-response comparison of parietal EEG
         and frontalis EMG biofeedback
         Biofeedback and Self-Regulation, 1977, 2:307
         (Abst.)

445.   DeGood, D. & Adams, A.
         Control of cardiac response under aversive
         stimulation: Superiority of a heart rate
         feedback condition
         Biofeedback and Self-Regulation, 1976, 1:373-385

446.   DeGood, D.E. & Chisholm, R.C.
        The independence of occipital EEG, heart rate,
        and self-reports during stress testing of
        alpha training effects
        Psychophysiology, 1977, 14:84 (Abst.)

447.   DeGood, D. & Chisholm, R.C.
        Multiple response comparison of parietal EEG and
        frontalis EMG feedback
        Psychophysiology, 1977, 14:258-265

448.   DeGood, D.E., Chisholm, R.C. & Valle, R.S.
        The interrelationships of parietal alpha and
        frontalis muscle activity during biofeedback
        training
        Psychophysiology, 1976, 13:164 (Abst.)

449.   DeGood, D.E., Elkin, B, & Lessin, S., et al.
        Expectancy influence on self reported experience
        during alpha feedback training: Subject and
        situational factors
        Biofeedback and Self-Regulation, 1977, 2:183-194

450.   DeGood, D.E. & Redgate, E.S.
        Frontalis EMG biofeedback effects on plasma
        cortisol levels
        Psychophysiology, 1977, 14:84 (Abst.)

451.   Deikman, A.J.
        Experimental meditation
        Journal of Nervous and Mental Disease, 1963,
        136:329-343

452.   Deikman, A.J.
        Implication of experimentally induced contem-
        plative meditation
        Journal of Nervous and Mental Disease, 1966,
        142:101-116

453.   Deikman, A.J.
        Bimodal consciousness
        Archives of General Psychiatry, 1971, 25:481-489

454.   Delgado, J.M.R. Johnston, V., Wallace, J.D.,
          et al.
       Operant conditioning of amygdala spindling in
          the free chimpanzee
       Brain Research, 1970, 22:347-362

455.   Delman, R.P. & Johnson, H.J.
       Biofeedback and progressive muscle relaxation:
          A comparison of psychophysiological effects
       Psychophysiology, 1976, 13:181 (Abst.)

456.   Delse, F.C. & Feather, B.W.
       The effect of augmented sensory feedback on the
          control of salivation
       Psychophysiology, 1968, 5:15-21

457.   Dengerink, H.A. & Taylor, S.P.
       Multiple responses with differential properties
          in delayed galvanic skin response condition-
          ing: A review
       Psychophysiology, 1971, 8:348-360

458.   DeSousa, C. & Wallace, R.B.
       Pain: A review and interpretation
       International Journal of Neuroscience, 1977,
          7:81-101

459.   deVries, H.A., Burke, R.K., Hopper, R.T. et al.
       Relationship of resting EMG level to total body
          metabolism with reference to the origin of
          "tissue noise"
       American Journal of Physical Medicine, 1976,
          55:139-147

460.   deVries, H.A., Burke, R.K., Hopper, R.T. et al.
       Efficacy of EMG biofeedback in relaxation train-
          ing
       American Journal of Physical Medicine, 1977,
          56:75-81

461.   Dewan, E.
       Communication by voluntary control of the electro-
          encephalogram
       Proceedings of the Symposium on Biomedical
          Engineering, 1966, 1:349-351

462.   Dewan, E.M.
Occipital alpha rhythm eye position and lens
   accommodation
Nature, 1967, 214:975-977

463.   DeWitt, D.J. & Greenwald, L.
A treatment approach involving EMG feedback of
   motor disability resulting from conversion
   reaction
Biofeedback and Self-Regulation, 1977, 2;313
   (Abst.)

464.   Diamond, S. & Franklin, M.
Indications and contraindications for the use of
   biofeedback therapy in headache patients
Proceedings of the Biofeedback Research Society
   Fifth Annual Meeting
Colorado Springs, 1974, 22 (Abst.)

465.   Diamond, S. & Franklin, M.
Intensive biofeedback therapy in the treatment
   of headache
Proceedings of the Biofeedback Research Society
   Sixth Annual Meeting
Monterey, 1975, 52 (Abst.)

466.   Diamond, S. & Franklin, M.
Biofeedback--choice of treatment in childhood
   migraine
Biofeedback and Self-Regulation, 1976, 1:349
   (Abst.)

467.   DiCara, L.V.
Plasticity in the autonomic nervous system:
   Instrumental learning of visceral and glandular
   responses
In F. O. Schmitt (Ed.), The Neurosciences Second
   Study Program
New York: Rockefeller University Press, 1970

468.   DiCara, L.V.
Learning in the autonomic nervous system
Scientific American, 1970, 222:30-39

469. DiCara, L.V.
Learning of cardiovascular responses: A review
and a description of physiological and bio-
chemical consequences
Transactions of the New York Academy of Sciences,
1971, 33:411-422

470. DiCara, L.V.
Learning mechanisms
In E. Frohlich (Ed.), Pathophysiology: Altered
Regulatory Mechanisms in Disease, Lippincott,
1972

471. DiCara, L.V.
Some critical methodological variables involved
in instrumental visceral learning
In: P. A. Obrist, et al (Eds.), Contemporary
Trends in Cardiovascular Psychology
Chicago: Aldine Publishing Co., 1974, 276-294

472. DiCara, L. V. (Ed.)
Limbic and Autonomic Nervous Systems Research
New York: Plenum Press, 1974

473. DiCara, L.V., Barber, T.X., Miller, N.E.,
Shapiro, D., Stoyva, J. & Kamiya, J. (Eds.)
Biofeedback and Self-Control, 1974: An Aldine
Annual on the Regulation of Bodily Processes
and Consciousness
Chicago: Aldine Publishing Co., 1974

474. DiCara, L.V., Braun, J.J. & Pappas, B.A.
Classical conditioning and instrumental learning
of cardiac and gastrointestinal responses
following removal of neocortex in the rat
Journal of Comparative and Physiological
Psychology, 1970, 73:209-216

475. DiCara, L.V. & Miller, N.E.
Instrumental learning of urine formation by
curarized rats
Psychonomic Bulletin, 1967, 1:23-24

476.   DiCara, L.V. & Miller, N.E.
          Transfer of instrumentally learned heart-rate
             changes from curarized to noncurarized state:
             Implications for a mediational hypothesis
          Journal of Comparative and Physiological
             Psychology, 1968, 68:159-162

477.   DiCara, L.V. & Miller, N.E.
          Long term retention of instrumentally learned
             heart-rate changes in the curarized rat
          Communications in Behavioral Biology. Part A,
             1968, 2:19-23

478.   DiCara, L.V. & Miller, N.E.
          Instrumental learning of vasomotor responses by
             rats: Learning to respond differentially in
             the two ears
          Science, 1968, 159:1485-1486

479.   DiCara, L.V. & Miller, N.E.
          Instrumental learning of systolic blood pressure
             responses by curarized rats: Dissociation of
             cardiac and vascular changes
          Psychosomatic Medicine, 1968, 30:489-494

480.   DiCara, L.V. & Miller, N.E.
          Instrumental learning of peripheral vasomotor
             responses by the curarized rat
          Communications in Behavioral Biology, 1968,
             1:209-212

481.   DiCara, L.V. & Miller, N.E.
          Changes in heart rate instrumentally learned by
             curarized rats as avoidance responses
          Journal of Comparative and Physiological
             Psychology, 1968, 65:8-12

482.   DiCara, L.V. & Miller, N.E.
          Heart rate learning in the noncurarized state,
             transfer to the curarized state, and subsequent
             retraining in the noncurarized state
          Physiology and Behavior, 1969, 4:621-624

483.   DiCara, L.V. & Stone, E.A.
        Effect of instrumental heart-rate training in
            rat cardiac and brain catecholamines
        Psychosomatic Medicine, 1970, 32:359-368

484.   DiCara, L.V. & Weiss, J.M.
        Effect of heart-rate learning under curare on
            subsequent noncurarized avoidance learning
        Journal of Comparative and Physiological
            Psychology, 1969,69:368-374

485.   Dickel, H.A., Dixon, H.H., Stoner, W. et al.
        Electromyographic studies on patients with
            chronic headaches
        Northwest Medicine, 1958, 57:1458-1462

486.   Dickinson, J.
        Proprioceptive Control of Human Movement
        Princeton, NJ: Princeton Book, 1974

487.   Diekhoff, G.M.
        Effects of feedback in a forced-choice GSR
            detection task
        Psychophysiology 1976, 13:22-26

488.   Dixon, C., deToledo, L. & Black, A.H.
        A technique for recording electromyographic
            activity in freely-moving rats using an all-
            purpose slip ring commutator
        Journal of the Experimental Analysis of Behavior,
            1969, 12:507-509

489.   Dohrmann, R.J. & Laskin, D.M.
        Treatment of myofascial pain dysfunction syndrome
            with EMG biofeedback
        IADR Abstracts, Journal of Dental Research,
            1976, 55:B249

490.   Don, N.S.
        Cortical activity changes during a psycho-
            therapeutic procedure: Implications for EEG
            biofeedback training
        Proceedings of the Biofeedback Research Society
            Sixth Annual Meeting
        Monterey, 1975, 68 (Abst.)

491.   Donelson, F.E.
       Discrimination and control of human heart rate
       Dissertation Abstracts, 1967, 27:B,4571

492.   Dorcus, R.M.
       Modification by suggestion of some vestibular
          and visual responses
       American Journal of Psychology, 1937, 49:82-87

493.   Dowdell, L.R., Clarke, N.G. & Kardachi, B.J.
       Biofeedback: Control of masticatory muscle
          spasm
       Medical and Biological Engineering, 1976,
          14:295-298

494.   Drost, R.
       (Autoregulation of cerebral blood flow)
       Munch Med Wochenschr, 1970, 112:318-321 (Ger.)

495.   Drury, R.
       The use of across-subjects multiple baseline
          design in biofeedback research
       Proceedings of the Biofeedback Research Society
          Fifth Annual Meeting
       Colorado Springs, 1974, 107   (Abst.)

496.   Drury, R.L., DiRisi, W., Liberman, R.
       Temperature feedback treatment for migraine
          headache: A controlled study
       Proceedings of the Biofeedback Research Society
          Sixth Annual Meeting
       Monterey, 1975, 29   (Abst.)

497.   Dugan, M. & Sheridan, C.
       Effects of instructed imagery on temperature of
          hands
       Perceptual and Motor Skills, 1976, 42:14

498.   Dumas, R.A.
       Operant control of EEG alpha and hypnotizability
       Doctoral dissertation, Stanford University, 1976

499.   Dumas, R.A.
         EEG alpha – hypnotizability correlations: A
           review
         Psychophysiology, 1977, 14:431–438

500.   Dunbar, P.W. & Baer, P.E.
         Performance of trained HR slowing: Effects of
           instructions, feedback, and stress
         Proceedings of the Biofeedback Research Society
           Fourth Annual Meeting
         Boston, 1972, 18 (Abst.)

501.   Dworkin, B. & Miller, N.
         Visceral learning in the curarized rat
         In G. E. Schwartz & J. Beatty (Eds.), Biofeed-
           back: Theory and Research
         New York: Academic Press, 1977

502.   Dykman, R.A., Ackerman, P.T., Galbrecht, P.T.,
           et al.
         Physiological reactivity to different stressors
           and methods of evaluation
         Psychosomatic Medicine, 1963, 25:37–59

503.   Eberlin, P. & Mulholland, T.
        Bilateral differences in parietal-occipital EEG
            induced by contingent visual feedback
        Psychophysiology, 1976, 13:212-218

504.   Eberlin, P. & Mulholland, T.
        Effects of alpha-stimulus contingency on the
            occipital EEG
        Biofeedback and Self-Regulation, 1976, 1:342
            (Abst.)

505.   Edelberg, R.
        Effect of vasoconstriction on galvanic skin
            response amplitude
        Journal of Applied Physiology, 1964, 19:427

506.   Edelman, R.
        Effects of differential afferant feedback in
            instrumental GSR conditioning
        Journal of Psychology, 1970, 74:3-14

507.   Edelman, R.
        Effects of progressive relaxation on autonomic
            processes
        Journal of Clinical Psychology, 1970, 26:421-425

508.   Edmonston, W.E. & Grotevant, W.R
        Hypnosis and alpha density
        American Journal of Clinical Hypnosis, 1975,
            17:221-232

509.   Elder, S.T. & Eustis, N.K.
        Instrumental blood pressure conditioning in
            outpatient essential hypertensives
        Behavior Research and Therapy, 1975, 13:185-188

510.   Elder, S.T., Frentz, K.G., Lewis, R.A. et al.
        Learned self-control of surface body temperature
        Biofeedback and Self-Regulation, 1977, 2:292
            (Abst.)

511.   Elder, S.T., Leftwich, D.A. & Wilkerson, L.
        The role of systolic versus diastolic contingent
            feedback in blood pressure conditioning
        Psychological Record, 1974, 24:171-176

512. Elder, S.T., Longacre, A., Welsh, D.M., et al.
     Apparatus and procedure for training subjects to
        control their blood pressure
     Psychophysiology, 1977, 14:68-72

513. Elder, S.T., Ruiz, R.Z., Deabler, H.J., et al.
     Instrumental conditioning of diastolic blood
        pressure in essential hypertensive patients
     Journal of Applied Behavioral Analysis, 1973,
        6:377-382

514. Elkin, B., Lessen, S., DeGood, D. et al.
     Subject and situational expectancy influences in
        self-reported experience during alpha feedback
        training
     Biofeedback and Self-Regulation, 1976, 1:342-
        343 (Abst.)

515. Elliott, C.H. & Denney, D.R.
     Weight control through covert sensitized and
        false feedback
     Journal of Consulting and Clinical Psychology,
        1975, 43:842-850

516. Ellsworth, R.B.
     Feedback: Asset or liability in improving
        treatment effectiveness
     Journal of Consulting and Clinical Psychology,
        1973, 40:383-393

517. Elmore, A.M. & Tursky, B.
     A model and improved methodology to enhance
        biofeedback's therapeutic success
     Psychophysiology, 1977, 14:118 (Abst.)

518. Engel, B.T.
     Operant conditioning of cardiac function: A
        status report
     Psychophysiology, 1972, 9:161-177

519. Engel, B.T.
     Clinical applications of operant conditioning
        techniques in the control of the cardiac
        arrhythmias
     Seminars in Psychiatry, 1973, 5:433-438

520.   Engel, B.T.
        Electroencephalographic and blood pressure
            correlates of operantly conditioned heart rate
            in the restrained monkey
        Pavlovian Journal of Biological Science, 1974,
            9:222-232

521.   Engel, B.T.
        Comment on self-control of cardiac functioning:
            A promise as yet unfulfilled
        Psychological Bulletin, 1974, 81:43

522.   Engel, B.T.
        Biofeedback as treatment for cardiovascular
            disorders: A critical review
        In J. Beatty & H. Legewie (Eds.), Biofeedback
            and Behavior
        New York: Plenum Press, 1977

523.   Engel, B.T. & Bleecker, E.R.
        Application of operant conditioning techniques
            to the control of cardiac arrhythmias
        In P. A. Obrist et al (Eds.), Cardiovascular
            Psychophysiology
        Chicago: Aldine Publishing Co., 1974, 456-476

524.   Engel, B.J. & Chism, R.A.
        Operant conditioning of heart rate speeding
        Psychophysiology, 1967, 3:418-426

525.   Engel, B.T. & Chism, R.A.
        Effect of increases and decreases in breathing
            rate on heart rate and finger pulse volume
        Psychophysiology, 1967, 4:83-89

526.   Engel, B.T. & Gottlieb, S.H.
        Differential operant conditioning of heart rate
            in the restrained monkey
        Journal of Comparative and Physiological
            Psychology, 1970, 73:217-225

527.   Engel, B.T., Gottlieb, S.H. & Hayhurst, V.F.
        Tonic and phasic relationships between heart
            rate and somato-motor activity in monkeys
        Psychophysiology, 1976, 13:288-295

69

528.   Engel, B.T. & Hansen, S.P.
        Operant conditioning of heart rate slowing
        Psychophysiology, 1966, 3:176-187

529.   Engel, B.T. & Melmon, K.L.
        Operant conditioning of heart rate in patients
          with cardiac arrhythmias
        Conditional Reflex, 1968, 3:130   (Abst.)

530.   Engel, B.T., Nikoomanesh, P.   & Schuster, M.M.
        Operant conditioning of rectosphincteric res-
          ponses in the treatment of fecal incontinence
        New England Journal of Medicine, 1974, 290:646-
          649

531.   Engel, R.R.
        Measurement and quantification of surface EMG
          signals in states of relaxation
        Proceedings of the Biofeedback Research Society
          Fourth Annual Meeting
        Boston, 1972, 35   (Abst.)

532.   Engel, R.
        Methodological and technological issues in
          biofeedback research
        In J. Beatty & H. Legewie (Eds.), Biofeedback
          and Behavior
        New York: Plenum Press, 1977

533.   Engel, R.R. & Schaefer, S.
        Operant control of forehead skin temperature
        Proceedings of the Biofeedback Research Society
          Fifth Annual Meeting
        Colorado Springs, 1974, 58   (Abst.)

534.   Engelhardt, L.
        Application of biofeedback techniques within a
          public school setting
        Biofeedback and Self-Regulation, 1976, 1:351
          (Abst.)

535.   Engel-Sittenfeld, P.
        Biofeedback and control of autonomic functions:
          Therapeutic use
        Medicine Klinische, 1977, 72:840-847   (German)

536.   Engel-Sittenfeld, P.
       Biofeedback in the treatment of neuromuscular
          disorders
       In J. Beatty & H. Legewie (Eds.), Biofeedback
       and Behavior
       New York: Plenum Press, 1977

537.   Engstrom, D.R.
       Hypnotic susceptibility, EEG-alpha and self-
          regulation
       In G. E. Schwartz, & D. Shapiro (Eds.), Con-
       sciousness and Self-Regulation
       New York: Plenum Press, 1976, 173-221

538.   Engstrom, D.R., London, P. & Hart, J. T.
       Hypnotic susceptibility increased by EEG alpha
          training
       Nature, 1970, 227:1261-1262

539.   Engstrom, D.R., London, P. & Hart, J.T.
       EEG alpha feedback training and hypnotic sus-
          ceptibility
       Dissertation Abstracts, 1971, 31B:4334

540.   Epstein, L.H. & Abel, G.G.
       An analysis of biofeedback training effects for
          tension headache patients
       Behavior Therapy, 1977, 8:37-47

541.   Epstein, L.H. & Blanchard, E.B.
       Biofeedback, self control and self-management:
          An integration and reappraisal
       Biofeedback and Self-Regulation, 1977, 2:201-212

542.   Epstein, L.H., Hersen, M. & Hemphill, D.P.
       Music feedback in the treatment of tension
          headaches: An experimental case study
       Journal of Behavior Therapy and Experimental
          Psychiatry, 1974, 5:59-63

543.   Epstein, L.H. & Stein, D.B.
       Feedback-influenced heart rate discrimination
       Journal of Abnormal Psychology, 1974, 83:585-588

544. Epstein, L.H. & Webster, G.S.
      Instructional, pacing, and feedback control of
        respiratory behavior
      Perceptual and Motor Skills, 1975, 41:895-900

545. Ericksen, R.A. & Huber, H.
      Elimination of hysterical torticollis through
        the use of a metronome in an operant con-
        ditioning paradigm
      Behavior Therapy, 1975, 6:405-406

546. Ernst, F.A. & Kordenat, R.K.
      A preliminary report of an attempt toward res-
        pondent and operant control of coronary artery
        blood flow
      Proceedings of the Biofeedback Research Society
        Sixth Annual Meeting
      Monterey, 1975, 9 (Abst.)

547. Ernst, F.A. & Kordenat, R.K.
      Coronary biofeedback: A challenge to bioengineer-
        ing
      In J. Beatty & H. Legewie (Eds.), Biofeedback
        and Behavior
      New York: Plenum Press, 1977

548. Evans, C. & Mulholland, T.
      Attention as a concept in neurophysiology
      Science, 1969, 158:495-496

549. Evans, C.R. & Mulholland, T.B. (Eds.)
      Attention in Neurophysiology
      London: Butterworths, 1969

550. Evans, F.J.
      The placebo response in pain reduction
      In J. J. Bonica (Ed.), Pain (Advances in Neurology),
        Vol 4.
      New York: Raven Press, 1974

551. Evarts, E.F.
      Central control of movement: Feedback and
        corollary discharge: A merging of the concepts
      Neuroscience Research Program Bulletin, 1971,
        9:86-112

552. Evarts, E.V.   & Thatch, W.T.
      Strategies and tactics in research on central
         control of movement
      Neuroscience Research Program Bulletin, 1971,
         9:113-139

553. Eversaul, G.
      Psycho-physiology training and the behavioral
         treatment of premature ejaculation: Pre-
         liminary findings
      Proceedings of the Biofeedback Research Society
         Fifth Annual Meeting
      Colorado Springs, 1974, 8   (Abst.)

554. Eversaul, G.A.
      The treatment of arthritis and other functional
         disorders resulting from circulatory dysponesis,
         by feedback thermometer training and nutrition
      Proceedings of the Biofeedback Research Society
         Sixth Annual Meeting
      Monterey, 1975, 80   (Abst.)

555.   Farr, S.P., Smith, R.P. & Meyer, R.G.
       Promise and problems in biofeedback research
       Psychologia, 1975, 18:212-220

556.   Farrar, W.B.
       Using electromyographic biofeedback in treating
         orofascial dyskinesia
       Journal of Prosthetic Dentistry, 1976, 35:384-
         387

557.   Fehmi, L.G.
       The effects of EEG biofeedback training on
         middle management executives
       Proceedings of the Biofeedback Research Society
         Fifth Annual Meeting
       Colorado Springs, 1974, 52   (Abst.)

558.   Fehmi, L.G., Ancoli, S. & Selzer, F.
       Tactile and auditory feedback in the autoregula-
         tion of frontal lobe EEG
       Proceedings of the Biofeedback Research Society
         Fourth Annual Meeting
       Boston, 1972, 29   (Abst.)

559.   Fehmi, L.G., Schlossman, A. & Saltaformaggio, L.
       Directional bias of conjugate lateral eye move-
         ment in the autoregulation of frontal lobe EEG
         activity
       Proceedings of the Biofeedback Research Society
         Fourth Annual Meeting
       Boston, 1972, 30   (Abst.)

560.   Fehmi, L. & Selzer, F.
       The effects of feedback signal delay upon alpha
         production and subjective experience
       Biofeedback and Self-Regulation, 1976, 1:343-
         344   (Abst.)

561.   Feil, H., Green, H.D. & Eiber, D.
       Voluntary acceleration of the heart in a subject
         showing the Wolff-Parkinson-White Syndrome
       American Heart Journal, 1947, 34:334-348

562.   Feinstein, B. & Sterman, M.B.
       Effects of sensorimotor rhythm biofeedback
         training on insomnia
       Proceedings of the Biofeedback Research Society
         Fifth Annual Meeting
       Colorado Springs, 1974, 101   (Abst.)

563.   Feldman, G.M.
       The effect of biofeedback training on respira-
         tory resistance of asthmatic children
       Psychosomatic Medicine, 1976, 38:27-34

564.   Fenton, G.W. & Scotton, L.
       Personality and the alpha rhythm
       British Journal of Psychiatry, 1967, 113:1283-
         1289

565.   Fenwick, P.B.C., Donaldson, S., Bushman, J., et
         al.
       EEG and metabolic changes during Transcendental
         Meditation
       Electroencephalography and Clinical Neuro-
         physiology, 1975, 39:220-221

566.   Fenz, W.D.
       The effect of augmented feedback on cardiac
         conditioning in the rhesus monkey
       Conditional Reflex, 1972, 7:164-169

567.   Fenz, W.D.
       Stress and its mastery: Predicting from labo-
         ratory to real life
       Canadian Journal of Behavioral Sciences, 1973,
         5:332-346

568.   Fenz, W.D. & Jones, G.B.
       Cardiac conditioning in a reaction time task and
         heart rate control during real life stress
       Journal of Psychosomatic Research, 1974, 18:199-
         204

569.   Fenz, W.D. & Plapp, J.M.
       Voluntary control of heart rate in a practitioner
         of yoga: Negative findings
       Perceptual and Motor Skills, 1970, 30:493-494

570.   Fetz, E.E.
       Operant conditioning of cortical unit activity
       Science, 1969, 163:955-957

571.   Fetz, E.E.
       Biofeedback and differential conditioning of
          response patterns in skeletal motor system
       In J. Beatty & H. Legewie (Eds.), Biofeedback
          and Behavior
       New York: Plenum Press, 1977

572.   Fetz, E.E. & Baker, M.A.
       Operantly conditioned patterns of perceptual
          unit activity and correlated responses in
          adjacent cells and contralateral muscles
       Journal of Neurophysiology, 1973, 36:179-204

573.   Fetz, E.E. & Finocchio, D.V.
       Operant conditioning of specific patterns of
          neural and muscular activity
       Science, 1971, 174:431-435

574.   Fetz, E.E. & Finocchio, D.V.
       Operant conditioning of isolated activity in
          specific muscles and pre central cells
       Brain Research, 1972, 40:19-23

575.   Fetz, E.E. & Wyler, A.R.
       Operantly conditioned firing patterns of epilep-
          tic neurons in the monkey motor cortex
       Experimental Neurology, 1973, 40:587-607

576.   Feuerstein, M. & Adams, H.E.
       Cephalic vasomotor feedback in the modification
          of migraine headache
       Biofeedback and Self-Regulation, 1977, 2:241-254

577.   Feuerstein, M., Adams, H.E. & Beiman, I.
       Cephalic vasomotor and electromyographic feedback
          in the treatment of combined muscle contraction
          and migraine headaches in a geriatric case
       Headache, 1976, 16:232-237

578.   Feuerstein, M. & Schwartz, G.E.
        Training in clinical psychophysiology
        American Psychologist, 1977, 32:560-567

579.   Fey, S.G. & Lindholm, E.
        Systolic blood pressure and heart rate changes
            during three sessions involving biofeedback or
            no feedback
        Psychophysiology, 1975, 12:513-519

580.   Fields, C.
        Instrumental conditioning of the rat cardiac
            control system
        Proceedings of the National Academy of Science,
            1970, 65:293-299

581.   Finley, W.W.
        The effect of feedback and instructional set on
            the control of cardiac rate and variability
        Dissertation Abstracts, 1969, 30B:1920

582.   Finley, W.W.
        The effect of feedback on the control of cardiac
            rate
        The Journal of General Psychology, 1971, 77:43-
            54

583.   Finley, W.W.
        Reduction of seizures and normalization of the
            EEG in a severe epileptic following sensori-
            motor biofeedback training
        Proceedings of the Biofeedback Research Society
            Fifth Annual Meeting
        Colorado Springs, 1974, 15   (Abst.)

584.   Finley, W.W.
        Seven weeks noncontingent feedback after one
            year of SMR BFT in a severe epileptic: Follow-
            up study
        Proceedings of the Biofeedback Research Society
            Sixth Annual Meeting
        Monterey, 1975, 48   (Abst.)

585. Finley, W.W.
      Effects of sham feedback following successful
         SMR training in an epileptic: Follow-up study
      Biofeedback and Self-Regulation, 1976, 1:227-235

586. Finley, W.W.
      Effects of mysoline and dilantin on the EEG
         during SMR biofeedback training of a psycho-
         motor epileptic: Single case study
      Biofeedback and Self-Regulation, 1977, 2:286
         (Abst.)

587. Finley, W.W.
      Operant conditioning of the EEG in two patients
         with epilepsy: Methodologic and clinical
         considerations
      Pavlovian Journal of Biological Science, 1977,
         12:93-111

588. Finley, W.W., Besserman, R.L., Bennett, L.F., et al.
      The effect of continuous, intermittent, and "placebo"
         reinforcement on the effectiveness of the con-
         ditioning treatment for enuresis nocturna
      Behavior Research and Therapy, 1973, 11:289-297

589. Finley, W.W. & Niman, C.
      EMG biofeedback and cerebral palsy
      Proceedings of the Biofeedback Research Society
         Sixth Annual Meeting
      Monterey, 1975, 61 (Abst.)

590. Finley, W.W., Niman, C., Standley, J., et al.
      Frontal EMG-biofeedback training of athetoid
         cerebral palsy patients: A report of six cases
      Biofeedback and Self-Regulation, 1976, 1:169-182

591. Finley, W.W., Niman, C., Standley, J., et al.
      Frontal EMG training of cerebral palsy children
      Biofeedback and Self-Regulation, 1976, 1:332-
         333 (Abst.)

592. Finley, W.W., Niman, C.A., Standley, J., et al.
      Electrophysiologic behavior modification of
         frontal EMG in cerebral-palsied children
      Biofeedback and Self-Regulation, 1977, 2:59-79

593.   Finley, W.W., Smith, H.A. & Etherton, M.D.
        Reduction of seizures and normalization of the
           EEG in a severe epileptic following sensori-
           motor biofeedback training: Preliminary study
        Biological Psychology, 1975, 2:189-203

594.   Fischer, R.
        A cartography of the ecstatic and meditation
           states
        Science, 1971, 174:897-904

595.   Fitzsimmons, C.I., Peiffer, A.L.
        Autononetic sensitization in the treatment of
           acute, chronic alcoholism
        Proceedings of the Biofeedback Research Society
           Fifth Annual Meeting
        Colorado Springs, 1974, 6 (Abst.)

596.   Fletcher, E.G., Hall, J.F. & Shaub, H.G.
        The skin temperature of an extremity as a measure
           of its blood flow
        Science, 1949, 110:422-423

597.   Flom, R.P., Quast, J.E., Boller, J., et al.
        Biofeedback training to overcome post stroke
           foot-drop
        Geriatrics, 1976, 31:47-52

598.   Ford, M., Sheer, D.E., Newton, F., et al
        Follow-up on voluntary control of 40Hz EEG,
           maintenance of control during problem solving,
           and generalization of effect
        Biofeedback and Self-Regulation, 1977, 2:287
           (Abst.)

599.   Ford, W.L., & Yeager, C.L.
        Changes in electroencephalogram in subjects
           under hypnosis
        Diseases of the Nervous System, 1948, 9:190-192

600.   Fordyce, W.E.
        Operant conditioning as a treatment method in
           management of selected chronic pain problems
        Northwest Medicine, 1970, 69:580-581

601.   Fordyce, W.E.
        Behavioral Methods for Chronic Pain and Illness
        St. Louis: Mosby, 1976

602.   Fotopoulos, S.
        Internal vs external control: Increase of heart
           rate by thinking under feedback and no-feedback
           conditions
        Dissertation Abstracts, 1970, 31B:3703-3704

603.   Fotopoulos, S.S.   & Binegar, G.A.
        Differences in baseline and volitional control
           of EEG (8-12 Hz and 13-20 Hz) EMG and skin
           temperature. Internal vs external orientation
        Biofeedback and Self-Regulation, 1976. 1:357-
           358 (Abst.)

604.   Fotopoulos, S.F., Cook, M.R. & Larsen, L.S.
        Skin temperature baselines and internal vs
           external locus of control
        Psychophysiology, 1976, 13:165-166 (Abst.)

605.   Fotopoulos, S.F., Graham, C. & Cook, M.R.
        Biofeedback and cancer pain
        In J. J. Bonica (Ed.), Proceedings of the Inter-
           national Symposium on Cancer Pain
        Department H.E.W. (In Press)

606.   Fowler, J. & Budzynski, T.H.
        The effects of an EMG biofeedback relaxation
           program on the control of diabetes in one
           patient
        Proceedings of the Biofeedback Research Society
           Fifth Annual Meeting
        Colorado Springs, 1974, 9 (Abst.)

607.   Fowler, J.E., Budzynski, T.H. & VandenBergh,R.L.
        Effects of an EMG biofeedback relaxation program
           on the control of diabetes
        Biofeedback and Self-Regulation, 1976, 1:105-112

608.   Fowler, R.S., Fordyce, W.E. & Berne, R.
        Operant conditioning in chronic illness
        American Journal of Nursing, 1969, 69:1226-1228

80

609. Fowler, R.L. & Kimmel, H.D.
Operant conditioning of the GSR
Journal of Experimental Psychology, 1962,
63:563-567

610. Fox, S.S. & Rudell, A.P.
Operant controlled neural event: Formal and
systematic approach to electrical coding
behavior in brain
Science, 1968, 126:1299-1302

611. Fox, S.S. & Rudell, A.P.
Operant controlled neural event: Functional
independence in behavioral coding by early and
late components of visual cortical evoked
response in cats
Journal of Neurophysiology, 1970, 33:548-561

612. Frank, C., Norris, P., Lebow, K.E., et al.
Applications research of biofeedback in rehab-
ilitation programs in prison settings
Proceedings of the Biofeedback Research Society
Sixth Annual Meeting
Monterey, 1975, 96 (Abst.)

613. Frankel, B. L., Patel, D.J., Horwitz, D., et al.
Clinical ineffectiveness of a combination of
psychophysiologic therapies in essential
hypertension
Biofeedback and Self-Regulation, 1977, 2:304
(Abst.)

614. Frazier, L.M.
Using biofeedback to aid relaxation during
childbirth
Birth and Family Journal, 1974, 1:4

615. Frazier, L.M.
Second generation electromyographic measurements:
A new approach to accurate recording and
reporting of neuromuscular activity
Biofeedback and Self-Regulation, 1976, 1:362
(Abst.)

616. Frederick, A.B.
Tension control in the physical education class-
room
Journal of Health, Education and Recreation,
1967, 38:42-44

617. Frederick, A.B.
Biofeedback and tension control
Journal of Physical Education and Recreation,
1975, 46:25-28

618. Frederick, A.N.D. & Barber, T.X.
Yoga, hypnosis and self-control of cardiovascular
functions
Proceedings, 80th Annual Conventions, APA, 1972,
859-860

619. Freedman, R.& Papsdorf, J.
Biofeedback and progressive relaxation treatment
of sleep onset insomnia: A controlled, all
night investigation
Proceedings of the Biofeedback Research Society
Sixth Annual Meeting
Monterey, 1975, 22 (Abst.)

620. Freedman, R. & Papsdorf, J.
Biofeedback and progressive relaxation treatment
of sleep-onset insomnia: A controlled, all-
night investigation
Biofeedback and Self-Regulation, 1976, 1:253-271

621. Freedman, R. & Papsdorf, J.
Generalization of frontal EMG biofeedback train-
ing to other muscles
Biofeedback and Self-Regulation, 1976, 1:333
(Abst.)

622. Freeman, G.L.
The galvanic phenomenon and conditioned responses
Journal of General Psychology, 1930, 3:529-539

623. Freeman, G.L., & Simpson, R.M.
The effect of the experimentally induced mus-
cular tension upon palmar skin resistance
Journal of General Psychology, 1938, 18:319-326

624.   French, D., Fahrion, S. & Leeb, C.
        Self-induced scrotal hyperthemia: An extension
        Proceedings of the Biofeedback Research Society
            Fifth Annual Meeting
        Colorado Springs, 1974, 62   (Abst.)

625.   French, D.J., Leeb, C.S. & Boerner, G.L.
        Theoretical application of biofeedback hand
            temperature training to prepared (Lamaze)
            childbirth training
        Perceptual and Motor Skills, 1973, 37:326

626.   French, D.J., Leeb, C.S. & Fahrion, S.
        Biofeedback hand temperature training in the
            mentally retarded
        Proceedings of the Biofeedback Research Society
            Sixth Annual Meeting
        Monterey, 1975, 59   (Abst.)

627.   French, D.J., Leeb, C.S., Fahrion, S.L., et al.
        Self-induced scrotal hyperthermia in man followed
            by decrease in sperm output. A preliminary
            report
        Andrologie, 1973, 5:311-316

628.   Frezza, D.A. & Holland, J.G.
        Operant conditioning of the human salivary
            response
        Psychophysiology, 1971, 8:581-587

629.   Friar, L.R. & Beatty, G.T.
        Migraine: Management by trained control of
            vasoconstriction
        Journal of Consulting and Clinical Psychology,
            1976, 44:46-53

630.   Friedman, H.
        Biofeedback I. Current status of its clinical
            application
        Acta Psychiatrica Belgica, 1977, 77:117-133

631.   Friedman, H.
        Biofeedback II. Reflections, perspectives
        Acta Psychiatrica, Belgica, 1977, 77:134-144

632. Friedman, H. & Taub, H.A.
The use of hypnosis and biofeedback procedures
for essential hypertension
International Journal of Clinical and Experimental
Hypnosis, 1977, 25:335-347

633. Friedman, M. & Roseman, R.H.
Type A Behavior and Your Heart
New York: Knopf, 1974

634. Fromm, E.
Altered states of consciousness and hypnosis:
A discussion
International Journal of Clinical and Experi-
mental Hypnosis, 1977, 25:325-334

635. Fruhling, M., Basmajian, J.V., & Simard, T.B.
A note on the conscious controls of motor units
by children under six
Journal of Motor Behavior, 1969, 1:65-68

636. Frumkin, L.R. & Pagano, R.R.
Meditation and right hemisphere functioning
Biofeedback and Self-Regulation, 1976, 1:357
(Abst.)

637. Fuller, G.
Biofeedback -- Methods and Procedures in Clinical
Practice
San Francisco: Biofeedback Institute, 1977

638. Furedy, J.J.
Pavlovian and operant biofeedback procedures
combined produce large-magnitude conditional
heart-rate decelerations
In J. Beatty & H. Legewie (Eds.), Biofeedback
and Behavior
New York: Plenum Press, 1977

639. Furedy, J.J. & Poulos, C.X.
Heart-rate decelerative Pavlovian conditioning
with tilt as UCS: Towards behavioral control
of cardiac dysfunction
Biological Psychology, 1976, 4:93-106

640.   Furman, S.
         Intestinal biofeedback in functional diarrhea:
         A preliminary report
         Journal of Behavior Therapy and Experimental
         Psychiatry, 1973, 4:317-321

641. Gaarder, K.
Control of states of consciousness - I. Attain-
ment through control of psychophysiological
variables
Archives of General Psychiatry, 1971, 25:429-435

642. Gaarder, K.
Control of states of consciousness II. Attain-
ment through external feedback augmenting
control of psychophysiological variables
Archives of General Psychiatry, 1971, 25:436-441

643. Gaarder, K. Gormley, J., Montgomery, P., et al.
Clinical closure on effective methods of treat-
ing essential hypertension
Biofeedback and Self-Regulation, 1977, 2:304-305
(Abst.)

644. Gaarder, K.R. & Montgomery, P.S.
Clinical Biofeedback
Baltimore: William & Wilkins Co., 1977

645. Galbraith, G. et al.
EEG and hypnotic susceptibility
Journal of Comparative and Physiological
Psychology, 1970, 72:125-131

646. Gallon, R. & Padnes, S.
EMG biofeedback and the relaxation response
Biofeedback and Self-Regulation, 1976, 1:325
(Abst.)

647. Gannon, L.
The role of interoception in learned visceral
control
Biofeedback and Self-Regulation, 1977 2:337-347

648. Gannon, L. & Sternbach, R.A.
Alpha enchancement as a treatment for pain: A
case study
Behavior Therapy and Experimental Psychiatry,
1971, 2:209-213

649.   Gans, B.M. & Noordergraaf, A.
       Voluntary skeletal muscles: A unifying theory of
          the relationship of their electrical and
          mechanical activities
       Archives of Physical Medicine and Rehabili-
          tation, 1975, 56:194-199

650.   Gardner, E.T. & Keefe, F.J.
       The effect of knowledge of response on temper-
          ature biofeedback training
       Biofeedback and Self-Regulation, 1976, 1:314
          (Abst.)

651.   Garfinçkel, P.E., Kline, S.A. & Stancer, H.C.
       Treatment of anorexia nervosa using operant
          conditioning techniques
       Journal of Nervous and Mental Disease, 1973,
          157:428-433

652.   Gastaut, H.
       Comments on "Biofeedback in epileptics: Equi-
          vocal relationship of reinforced EEG frequency
          to seizure reduction," by B. J. Kaplan
       Epilepsia, 1975, 16:477-485 and 487-490

653.   Garcia, J. & Rusiniak, K.W.
       Visceral feedback and the taste signal
       In J. Beatty & H. Legewie (Eds.), Biofeedback
          and Behavior
       New York: Plenum Press, 1977

654.   Gatchel, R.J.
       Frequency of feedback and learned heart rate
          control
       Journal of Experimental Psychology, 1974,
          103:274-283

655.   Gatchel, R.J.
       Change over training sessions of relationship
          between locus of control and voluntary heart-
          rate control
       Perceptual and Motor Skills, 1975, 40:424-426

656. Gatchel, R.J.
      The effect of voluntary control of heart rate
         deceleration on skin conductance level: An
         example of response fractionation
      Biological Psychology, 1976, 4:241-248

657. Gatchel, R.J.
      Effectiveness of voluntary heart rate control in
         reducing speech anxiety
      Psychophysiology, 1976, 13:175   (Abst.)

658. Gatchel, R.J.
      Therapeutic effectiveness of voluntary heart
         rate control in reducing anxiety
      Journal of Consulting and Clinical Psychology,
         1977, 45:689-691

659. Gatchel, R.J. & Hatch, J.P.
      Comparative effectiveness of voluntary heart
         rate control and muscular relaxation in re-
         ducing speech anxiety
      Psychophysiology, 1977, 14:87-88 (Abst.)

660. Gatchel, R.J. & Proctor, J.D.
      Effectiveness of voluntary heart rate control in
         reducing speech anxiety
      Journal of Consulting and Clinical Psychology,
         1976, 44:381-389

661. Gaupp, L.A., Stern, R.M. & Galbraith, G.G.
      False heart-rate feedback and reciprocal in-
         hibition by aversion relief in the treatment
         of snake avoidance behavior
      Behavior Therapy, 1972, 3:7-20

662. Gavalas, R.J.
      Operant reinforcement of an autonomic response:
         Two studies
      Journal of Experimental Analysis of Behavior,
         1967, 10:119-130

663. Gavalas, R.J.
      Operant reinforcement of a skeletally mediated
         autonomic response: Uncoupling of the two
         responses
      Psychonomic Science, 1968, 11:195-196

664.   Gavalas-Medici, R.
        Uses and abuses of the mediation construct: The
           case of operant reinforcement of autonomic and
           neural responses
        Behaviorism, 1972, 1:103-117

665.   Gavin, J. & Stephen, K.
        Biofeedback muscle reeduction: A clinical
           review of ten cases
        Biofeedback and Self-Regulation, 1976, 1:330-331
           (Abst.)

666.   Geddes, L.A.
        Electrodes and the Measurement of Bioelectric
           Events
        New York: Wiley & Sons, 1972

667.   Gelder, M.G. & Matthews, A.M.
        Forearm blood flow and phobic anxiety
        British Journal of Psychiatry, 1968, 114:1371-
           1376

668.   Gellhorn, E. & Kiely, W.F.
        Mystical states of consciousness: Neurophysiologi-
           cal and clinical aspects
        Journal of Nervous and Mental Diseases, 1972,
           154:399-405

669.   Gershman, L. & Clouser, R.A.
        Treating insomnia with relaxation and desensiti-
           zation in a group setting by an automated
           approach
        Journal of Behavior Therapy and Experimental
           Psychiatry, 1974, 5:31-35

670.   Gersten, C.D. & Pope, A.T.
        EMG feedback gain as a determinant of muscle
           tension reduction
        Biofeedback and Self-Regulation, 1976, 1:333-
           334 (Abst.)

671.   Gessel, A.
        Biofeedback-enhanced training in therapeutic
            muscular relaxation: A clinician's view
        Proceedings of the First Meeting of the American
            Association for the Advancement of Tension
            Control
        1974, 97-103

672.   Gessel, A.H.
        Electromyographic biofeedback and tricyclic
            antidepressants in myofascial pain-dysfunction
            syndrome: Psychological predictors of outcome
        Journal of the American Dental Association,
            1975, 91:1048-1052

673.   Gessel, A.H. & Alderman, M.M.
        Management of myofascial pain dysfunction syn-
            drome of the temporomandibular joint by
            tension control training
        Psychosomatics, 1971, 12:302-309

674.   Gessel, A.H. & Harrison, S.
        Case report: Bilateral EMG feedback in the
            treatment of chronic dislocation
        Proceedings of the Biofeedback Research Society
            Fifth Annual Meeting
        Colorado Springs, 1974, 44 (Abst.)

675.   Gibb, J.D. & MacDougall, A.B.
        Biofeedback: An operational definition and
            control of dissonance
        Proceedings of the Biofeedback Research Society
            Fifth Annual Meeting
        Colorado Springs, 1974, 45 (Abst.)

676.   Gibb, J.D., Stephan, E. & Rohm, C.E.T.
        Belief in biofeedback: A tentative method for
            the control of short term stress
        Proceedings of the Biofeedback Research Society
            Sixth Annual Meeting
        Monterey, 1975, 6 (Abst.)

677.   Gibb, J.D., Stephan, E., & Rohm C.E.T., Jr.
        Belief in biofeedback for the control of short
          term stress
        Behavioral Engineering, 1975, 3:79-84

678.   Gibson, R.C. & Papsdorf, J.D.
        Counselor anxiety: Biofeedback-assisted stress
          inoculation therapy
        Biofeedback and Self-Regulation, 1977, 2:319-320
          (Abst.)

679.   Ginsberg, S.
        The effect of instructions and heart rate per-
          ceptability on cardiac control
        Psychophysiology, 1971, 8:268 (Abst.)

680.   Girton, D.G. & Kamiya, J.
        A simple on-line technique for removing eye
          movement artifacts from the EEG
        Proceedings of the Biofeedback Research Society
          Fourth Annual Meeting
        Boston, 1972, 42 (Abst.)

681.   Gladman, A.E. & Estrada, N.
        Biofeedback, some clinical applications
        Proceedings of the Biofeedback Research Society
          Fifth Annual Meeting
        Colorado Springs, 1974, 7 (Abst.)

682.   Glaros, A.G.
        Comment on "Alcoholism, alpha production and
          biofeedback"
        Journal of Consulting and Clinical Psychology,
          1977, 45:698-699

683.   Glaros, A.G.
        Subjective reports in alpha feedback training
        Biofeedback and Self-Regulation, 1977, 2:280-281
          (Abst.)

684.   Glaros, A.G., Freedman, R. & Foureman, W.C.
        Effects of perceived control on subjective
          reports in alpha feedback training
        Biofeedback and Self-Regulation, 1977, 2:281
          (Abst.)

685. Glass, D.C.
Stress, behavior patterns and coronary disease
American Scientist, 1977, 65:177-187

686. Glaus, K.D. & Kotses, H.
Generalization of frontalis muscle tension
Biofeedback and Self-Regulation, 1977, 2:307-308
(Abst.)

687. Gliner, J.A., Horvath, S.N. & Wolfe, R.R.
Operant conditioning of heart rate in curarized
rats: Hemodynamic changes
American Journal of Physiology, 1975, 228:870-
874

688. Glueck, B.C. & Stroebel, C.F.
Biofeedback and meditation in the treatment of
psychiatric illness
Comprehensive Psychiatry, 1975, 16:303-321

689. Goesling, W.J. & Brener, J.
Effect of activity and immobility conditioning
upon subsequent heart-rate conditioning in
curarized rats
Journal of Comparative and Physiological
Psychology, 1972, 8:311-317

690. Goesling, W., May, C., Lavond, D. et al.
Relationship between internal and external locus
of control and the operant conditioning of
alpha through biofeedback training
Perceptual and Motor Skills, 1974, 39:1339-1343

691. Goldberg, R.J., et al.
Alpha conditioning as an adjunct treatment for
drug dependence: Part I
International Journal of Addiction, 1976,
11:1085-1089

692. Goldberg, R.J., et al.
Alpha conditioning as an adjunct treatment for
drug dependence: Part II
International Journal of Addiction, 1977,
12:195-204

693.   Goldfried, M.P.
        Systematic desensitization as training in self-
           control
        Journal of Consulting and Clinical Psychology,
           1971, 37:228-234

694.   Goldiamond, I.
        Self-control procedures in personal behavior
           problems
        Psychological Reports, 1965, 17:851-868

695.   Goldman, H., Kleinman, K.M., Snow, M.Y., et al.
        Relationship between essential hypertension and
           cognitive functioning: Effects of biofeedback
        Psychophysiology, 1975, 12:569-573

696.   Goldstein, D.S., Harris, A.H. & Brady, J.V.
        Sympathetic adrenergic blockade effects upon
           operantly conditioned blood pressure elevations
           in baboons
        Biofeedback and Self-Regulation, 1977, 2:93-105

697.   Goldstein, D.S., Harris, A.H. & Brady, J.V.
        Baroreflex sensitivity during operant blood
           pressure conditioning
        Biofeedback and Self-Regulation, 1977, 2:127-138

698.   Goldstein, D.S., Harris, A.H., Gilliam, W.J., et
           al.
        Baroreflex sensitivity during operant cardio-
           vascular conditioning in baboons
        Proceedings of the Biofeedback Research Society
           Fifth Annual Meeting
        Colorado Springs, 1974, 91 (Abst.)

699.   Goldstein, D.S., Ross, R.S. & Brady, J.V.
        Biofeedback heart rate training during exercise
        Biofeedback and Self-Regulation, 1977, 2:107-126

700.   Goldstein, I.B.
        Electromyography. A measure of skeletal muscle
           response
        In N. S. Greenfield & R. A. Sternbach (Eds.),
           Handbook of Psychophysiology
        New York: Holt, Rinehart and Winston, 1972

701. Goldstein, I.B.
      The relationship of muscle tension and autonomic
        activity to psychiatric disorders
      Psychosomatic Medicine, 1965, 27:39-52

702. Goldstein, I.B., Grinker, R.R., Heath, H.A., et
        al.
      Study in psychophysiology of muscle tension: I.
        Response specificity
      Archives of General Psychiatry, 1964, 11:322-330

703. Goleman, D.
      Meditation as meta-therapy: Hypothesis toward a
        proposed fifth state of consciousness
      Journal of Transpersonal Psychology, 1971, 3:1-
        25

704. Goleman, D.
      Meditation and consciousness: An Asian approach
        to mental health
      American Journal of Psychotherapy, 1976, 30:41-
        53

705. Goleman, D.J. & Schwartz, G.E.
      Meditation as an intervention in stress reactivity
      Journal of Consulting and Clinical Psychology,
        1976, 44:456-466

706. Golla, F., Hutton, E. & Walter, W.
      The objective study of mental imagery: I.
        Physiological concomitants
      Journal of Mental Science, 1943, 89:216-223

707. Good, R.
      Frontalis muscle tension and sleep latency
      Psychophysiology, 1975, 12:465-467

708. Goodman, D.
      Collection of EEG alpha under feedback control
        using time series analysis
      Psychophysiology, 1973, 10:437-440

709.   Goodman, D.
        The effect of oculomotor activity on alpha
            blocking in the absence of visual stimuli
        Psychophysiology, 1976, 13:462-465

710.   Gorman, P.J.
        Biofeedback and the regulation of human gastric
            acid
        Proceedings of the Biofeedback Research Society
            Sixth Annual Meeting
        Monterey, 1975, 92 (Abst.)

711.   Gorton, B.E.
        The physiology of hypnosis
        Psychiatric Quarterly, 1949, 23:317-343 and 457-
        485

712.   Gorton, B.E.
        Autogenic training
        American Journal of Clinical Hypnosis, 1959,
            2:31-41

713.   Gotestam, K.G., Melin, L. & Ost, L.
        Behavioral techniques in the treatment of drug
            abuse: An evaluative review
        Addictive Behaviors, 1976, 1:205-225

714.   Gottschalk, L.A.
        A study of conditioned vasomotor responses in
            ten human subjects
        Psychosomatic Medicine, 1946, 8:16-27

715.   Gracenin, C.T. & Cook, J.E.
        Alpha biofeedback and children
        Academic Therapy, 1977, 12:275-280

716.   Graham, C., Fotopoulos, S.S., Cohen, H.D., et
            al.
        The use of biofeedback during acute opiate
            withdrawal: A double blind evaluation
        Biofeedback and Self-Regulation, 1976, 1:355
            (Abst.)

717.   Graham, C.,   Fotopoulos, S.S.,   Cook, M.R., et al.
        Psychophysiological aspects of opiate withdrawal:
        A double-blind biofeedback study
        Psychophysiology, 1977, 14:99 (Abst.)

718.   Graham, C. & Evans, F.J.
        Hypnotizability in the deployment of waking
           attention
        Journal of Abnormal Psychology, 1977 (in press)

719.   Graham, C. & Leibowitz, H.W.
        The effect of suggestion on visual acuity
        International Journal of Clinical and Experimen-
           tal Hypnosis, 1972, 20:169-186

720.   Graham, L.A., Cohen, S.E. & Shmavonian, B.M.
        Physiologic discrimination and behavioral re-
           lationships in human instrumental conditioning
        Psychosomatic Medicine, 1964, 26:321-336

721.   Graham, W.K.
        Effects of simulated biofeedback and human
           monitoring in brainstorming performance
        Journal of Social Psychology, 1977, 101:139-144

722.   Grant, R.T. & Pearson, R.S.B.
        The blood circulation in the human limb: Ob-
           servations on the differences between the
           proximal and distal parts and remarks on the
           regulation of body temperature
        Clinical Science, 1938, 3:119-139

723.   Gray, E.R.
        Conscious control of motor units in a neuro-
           muscular disorder
        Electromyography, 1971, 11:515-517

724.   Gray, E.
        Conscious control of motor units in a tonic
           muscle
        American Journal of Physical Medicine, 1971,
           50:34-40

725.   Green, A.M.
        Brainwave training, imagery, creativity and
           integrative experiences
        Proceedings of the Biofeedback Research Society
           Fifth Annual Meeting
        Colorado Springs, 1974, 98 (Abst.)

726.   Green, E.
        Biofeedback for mind-body self-regulation:
           Healing and creativity
        In D. Shapiro et al (Eds.), Biofeedback and
           Self-Control
        Chicago: Aldine Publishing Co., 1973, 152-166

727.   Green, E. & Green, A.
        Conference on voluntary control of internal
           states
        Psychologia, 1969, 12:107-108

728.   Green, E. & Green, A.
        On the meaning of transpersonal: Some meta-
           physical perspectives
        Journal of Transpersonal Psychology, 1971, 3:27-
           46

729.   Green, A. & Green, E.
        Biofeedback: Research and therapy
        In N. Jacobson (Ed.), Being Well is a Respon-
           sibility
        London: Turnstone Brooks, 1975

730.   Green, E.F., Green, A.M. & Walters, E.D.
        Self-regulation of internal states
        In J. Rose (Ed.), Progress of Cybernetics:
           Proceedings of the International Congress of
           Cybernetics, London, 1969
        London: Gordon and Breach, 1970, 1299-1317

731.   Green, E.E., Green, A.M. & Walters, E.D.
        Voluntary control of internal states: Psycho-
           logical and physiological
        Journal of Transpersonal Psychology, 1970, 2:1-
           26

732.   Green, E., Green, A. & Walters, E.D.
        Biofeedback for mind-body self-regulation:
        Healing and creativity
        Fields Within Fields. . . Within Fields 1972,
        25:131-144

733.   Green, E.E., Green, A.M. & Walters, E.D.
        Biofeedback training for anxiety tension reduc-
        tion
        Annals of the New York Academy of Sciences,
        1974, 233:157-161

734.   Green, E.E., Green, A.M., Walters, R.D., et al.
        Autogenic feedback training
        Psychotherapy and Psychosomatics, 1975, 25:88-98

735.   Green, E.F., Walters, E.D., Green, A.M. &
        Murphy, G.
        Feedback technique for deep relaxation
        Psychophysiology 1969, 6:371-377

736.   Greenbaum, H.H. & White, N.D.
        Biofeedback at the organizational level: The
        communication audit
        The Journal of Business Communications, 1976,
        13:3-15

737.   Greene, W.A.
        Operant conditioning of the GSR using partial
        reinforcement
        Psychological Reports, 1966, 19:571-578

738.   Greene, W.A.
        Operant conditioning of spontaneous GSR's;
        negative results
        Journal of Experimental Psychology, 1967,
        75:128-130

739.   Greene, W.A. & Nielson, T.C.
        Operant GSR conditioning of high and low auto-
        nomic perceivers
        Psychonomic Science, 1966, 6:359-360

740.   Greene, W.A. & Slosser, J.
        The influence of different schedules of music
          reinforcement on the operant skin resistance
          response and a comparison with a skeletal
          operant
        Proceedings of the Biofeedback Research Society
          Sixth Annual Meeting
        Monterey, 1975, 90 (Abst.)

741.   Greene, W.A. & Sutor, L.T.
        Stimulus control of skin resistance responses on
          an escape-avoidance schedule
        Journal of Experimental Analysis of Behavior,
          1971, 16:269-274

742.   Greene, W.A. & Wirth, H.G.
        Operant conditioning of the skin resistance
          response with afferent intensities of light
          flashes
        Bulletin of the Psychonomic Society, 1974,
          4:177-179

743.   Greenspan, S.I.
        The clinical use of operant learning approaches:
          Some complex issues
        American Journal of Psychiatry, 1974, 131:852-
          857

744.   Greenstadt, L., Schuman, M. & Shapiro, D.
        Differential effects of left versus right mon-
          aural biofeedback for heart rate increase
        Psychophysiology, 1977, 14:82 (Abst.)

745.   Gregg, R.H., Frazier, L.M. & Nesbit, R.A.
        Effects of techniques of biofeedback on re-
          laxation during childbirth
        Biofeedback and Self-Regulation, 1976, 1:325-326
          (Abst.)

746.   Greiner, J.
        Relaxation in the physical education program
        Physical Education, 1972, 29:152-153

747.   Grim, P.F.
        Anxiety change produced by self-induced muscle
           tension and by relaxation with respiration
           feedback
        Behavior Therapy, 1971, 2:11-17

748.   Grim, P.F.
        Relaxation, meditation, and insight
        Psychologia, 1975, 18:125-133

749.   Grinberg, M.
        Analog vs. digital feedback modalities: Com-
           parison of efficacy in conditioning penile
           erections
        Proceedings of the Biofeedback Research Society
           Sixth Annual Meeting
        Monterey, 1975, 91 (Abst.)

750.   Grings, W.W. & Carlin, S.
        Instrumental modification of autonomic behavior
        Psychological Record, 1966, 16:153-159

751.   Grings, W.W., Lockhart, R.A. & Dameron, L.E.
        Conditioning of autonomic responses in mentally
           subnormal individuals
        Psychological Monographs, 1962, 76 (Whole #558)

752.   Grings, W.W. & Schandler, S.L.
        Interaction of learned relaxation and aversion
        Psychophysiology, 1977, 14:275-280

753.   Gross, S.N.
        Biofeedback technique in treating myofascial
           pain dysfunction syndrome
        Journal of the New Jersey Dental Association,
           1975, 46:26-27

754.   Grossan, M.
        A brief introduction to biofeedback for oto-
           laryngologists
        O.R.L. Digest, 1975, 37:15-19

755.   Grossan, M.
        Treatment of subjective tinnitus with biofeed-
            back
        Ear, Nose and Throat Journal, 1976, 55:22-30

756.   Grossan, M.
        Biofeedback Treatment
        In D. Morgan (Ed.), Diseases of Temporomandib-
            ular Joint
        New York: C. V. Mosby, 1977

757.   Grossberg, J.M.
        Brainwave feedback experiments and the concept
            of mental mechanisms
        Journal of Behavior Therapy and Experimental
            Psychiatry, 1972, 3:245-251

758.   Grossberg, J.M. & Wilson, H.K.
        Physiological changes accompanying the visuali-
            zation of fearful and neutral situations
        Journal of Personality and Social Psychology,
            1968, 10:124-133

759.   Grossman, W.I. & Weiner, H.
        Some factors affecting the reliability of sur-
            face electromyography
        Psychosomatic Medicine, 1966, 28:78-83

760.   Grove, R.N. & Denver, D.R.
        Differential sensitivy of forearm and sterno-
            mastoid muscle activity to biofeedback after
            prolonged baselines: A microanalysis
        Biofeedback and Self-Regulation, 1977, 2:308-309
            (Abst.)

761.   Grynbaum, B.B., Brudny, J., Korein, J., et al.
        Sensory feedback therapy for stroke patients
        Geriatrics, 1976, 31:43-47

762.   Grynol, E. & Jamieson, J.
        Alpha feedback and relaxation: A cautionary note
        Perceptual and Motor Skills, 1975, 40:58

763. Grzesiak, R.C.
Relaxation techniques in treatment of chronic
pain
Archives of Physical Medicine and Rehabilitation,
1977, 58:270-272

764. Guenther, C.R. & McFarland, R.A.
Effects of motivation upon performance of an
operant heart rate control task
Psychological Reports, 1973, 32:659-663

765. Guitar, B.
Reduction of stuttering frequency using analog
electromyographic feedback
Journal of Speech and Hearing Research, 1975,
18:672-685

766. Guralnick, M.J. & Mott, D.E.
Biofeedback training with a learning disabled
child
Perceptual and Motor Skills, 1976, 42:27-30

767. Gutmann, M.C. & Benson, H.
Interaction of environmental factors and systemic
arterial blood pressure: A review
Medicine, 1971, 50:543-553

768.   Hager, J.L. & Surwit, R.S.
       Hypertension, self-control with a portable feed-
          back unit or relaxation
       Psychophysiology, 1977, 14:97-98 (Abst.)

769.   Haggendal, E., Nilsson, N.J. & Norback, B.
       Aspects of the autoregulation of cerebral blood
          flow
       International Anesthesiology Clinics, 1969,
          7:353-367

770.   Hahn, W.W.
       Physiological state of the curarized rat:
          Implications for the learned control of auto-
          nomic responses
       Psychophysiology, 1973, 10:197 (Abst.)

771.   Hahn, W.W.
       The learning of autonomic responses by curarized
          animals
       In P. A. Obrist et al (Eds.), Contemporary
          Trends in Cardiovascular Psychophysiology
       Chicago: Aldine Publishing Co., 1974, 295-311

772.   Haight, M., Jampolsky, G. & Irvine, A.
       The response of hyperkinesis to EMG biofeedback
       Biofeedback and Self-Regulation, 1976, 1:326
          (Abst.)

773.   Hall, S.M.
       Self-control and therapist control in the be-
          havioral treatment of overweight women
       Behavior Research and Therapy, 1972, 10:59-69

774.   Hall, S.M. & Hall, R.G
       Outcome and methodological considerations in
          behavioral treatment of obesity
       Behavior Therapy, 1974, 5:352-364

775.   Halpern, D., Kottke, F.J., Burrill, C., et al
       Training of control of head posture in children
          with cerebral palsy
       Developmental Medicine and Child Neurology,
          1970, 12:290-305

776.   Hamano, K.
       Studies on modification of spontaneous autonomic
          activity: I. Preliminary report on habitua-
          tion of spontaneous heart rate with concomitant
          measurement of three autonomic variables
       Japanese Psychological Research, 1969, 11:110-
          116

777.   Hamano, K. & Miyake, S.
       Studies on modification of spontaneous autonomic
          activity: II. Modification of heart rate
          change through training procedure of instru-
          mental conditioning
       Japanese Psychological Research, 1971, 13:19-25

778.   Hamano, K. & Miyoke, S.
       Studies on modification of spontaneous autonomic
          activity: III. The relation of strength of
          reinforcers to instrumental modifiability of
          autonomic response
       Japanese Psychological Research, 1972, 14:38-42

779.   Hamano, K., Okita, T. & Miyata, Y.
       (Instrumental conditioning of autonomic responses)
       Japanese Psychological Review, 1970, 13:244-264

780.   Hamano, K. & Okita, T.
       Some experiments on instrumental modification of
          autonomic responses
       Psychologia, 1972, 15:101-109

781.   Hammel, H.T.
       Regulation of internal body temperature
       Annual Reviews of Physiology, 1968, 30:641-710

782.   Hanna, R., Wilfling, F. & McNeil, B.
       A biofeedback treatment for stuttering
       Journal of Speech and Hearing Disorders, 1975,
          40:270-273

783.   Hardt, J.V.
       Alpha EEG responses of low and high anxiety
          males to respiration and relaxation training
          and to auditory feedback of occipital alpha
       Dissertation Abstracts International, 1974,
          35:#74-19309

784.   Hardt, J.V.
        A predictive "dual process" theory for alpha
           enhancement
        Biofeedback and Self-Regulation, 1977, 2:282-283
           (Abst.)

785.   Hardt, J.V.
        Relaxation during breathing feedback, yogic
           breathing, and alpha feedback: Effects on
           alpha EEG activity in low and high anxiety
           males
        Proceedings of the Biofeedback Research Society
           Sixth Annual Meeting
        Monterey, 1975, 72 (Abst.)

786.   Hardt, J.V. & Kamiya, J.
        A comparison of percent time and amplitude
           integration measures of EEG alpha
        Psychophysiology, 1975, 12:228 (Abst.)

787.   Hardt, J.V. & Kamiya, J.
        Some comments on Plotkin's self-regulation of
           EEG alpha
        Journal of Experimental Psychology: General,
           1976, 105:100-108

788.   Hardt, J.V. & Kamiya, J.
        Conflicting results in EEG alpha feedback studies
        Biofeedback and Self-Regulation, 1976, 1:63-75

789.   Hardt, J.V. & Kamiya, J.
        The ups and downs of learning alpha feedback,
           Part 2: Differential early-late correlation
           with drug use, sleep records, and mood scales
        Biofeedback and Self-Regulation, 1976, 1:344
           (Abst.)

790.   Hardt, J.V. & Kamiya, J.
        Predicting alpha enhancement from baseline
           physiology: Differences in high and low
           anxiety subjects
        Psychophysiology, 1977, 14:108 (Abst.)

791.   Hardt, J.V., Timmons, B.H., Yeager, C.L., et al.
        Studying power and coherence relationships in
          6-channel EEGs: A McLuhanistic technique
          applied to Zen meditation
        Biofeedback and Self-Regulation, 1976, 1:362-
          363 (Abst.)

792.   Hardt, J.V. & Witmer, N.T.
        Baseline respiration components predict per-
          formance at alpha enhancement feedback
        Biofeedback and Self-Regulation, 1977, 2:281-282
          (Abst.)

793.   Hardyck, C.
        The elimination of sub-vocal speech activity
          during reading by continuous feedback
        Psychophysiology, 1969, 5:564 (Abst.)

794.   Hardyck, C. & Petrinovich, L.
        Treatment of subvocal speech during reading
        Journal of Reading, 1969, 1:1-11

795.   Hardyck, C.D., Petrinovich, L.F. & Ellsworth, D.W.
        Feedback of speech muscle activity during silent
          reading: Rapid extinction
        Science, 1966, 154:1467-1468

796.   Hardyck, C.D., Petrinovich, L.F. & Ellsworth, D.W.
        A reply on two comments by McGuigan and Camacho
        Science, 1967, 157:581

797.   Hare, R.D.
        Response requirements and directional fractionation
          of autonomic responses
        Psychophysiology, 1972, 9:419-427

798.   Hare, R. & Quinn, M.
        Psychopathy and autonomic conditioning
        Journal of Abnormal Psychology, 1971, 77:223-235

799.   Hare, R., Wood, K., Britain, S., et al.
        Autonomic responses to affective visual stimulation
        Psychophysiology, 1970, 7:408-417

800. Harmatz, M.G. & Lupuc, P.S.
      A technique for employing a yoked control in
         free operant verbal conditioning experiments
      Behavior Research and Therapy, 1968, 6:483

801. Harrell, J.P. & Coles, M.G.H.
      Attention and the use of progressive relaxation
         under stress
      Psychophysiology, 1977, 14:110 (Abst.)

802. Harris, A.H. & Brady, J.V.
      Instrumental (operant) conditioning of visceral
         and autonomic functions
      In L. Birk (Ed.), Biofeedback: Behavioral Medicine
      New York: Grune & Stratton, 1973

803. Harris, A.H. & Brady, J.V.
      Animal learning-visceral and autonomic conditionin
      Annual Review of Psychology, 1974, 25:107-133

804. Harris, A.H. & Brady, J.V.
      Long term studies of cardiovascular control in
         primates
      In G.E. Schwartz & J. Beatty (Eds.), Biofeedback:
         Theory and Research
      New York: Academic Press, 1977

805. Harris, A.H. & Brady, J.V.
      The effects of food presentation upon blood
         pressure and heart rate in the "hypertensive"
         baboon
      Biofeedback and Self-Regulation, 1977, 2:305
         (Abst.)

806. Harris, A.H., Findley, G.D. & Brady, J.V.
      Instrumental conditioning of blood pressure
         elevations in the baboon
      Conditional Reflex, 1971, 6:215-226

807. Harris, A.H., Gilliam, W.J. & Brady, J.V.
      Operant conditioning of large magnitude, 12 hour
         duration, heart rate elevations in the baboon
      Pavlovian Journal of Biological Science, 1976,
         11:86-92

808. Harris, A.H., Gilliam, W.J. & Findley, J.D., et al.
Instrumental conditioning of large magnitude 12-hour blood pressure elevations in the baboon
Science, 1973, 182:175-177

809. Harris, A.H., Goldstein, D. & Brady, J.V.
Conditioned blood pressure elevations in the baboon: An update
Biofeedback and Self-Regulation, 1976, 1:308-309 (Abst.)

810. Harris, A.H., Goldstein, D.S. & Brady, J.V.
Visceral learning: Cardiovascular conditioning in primates.
In J. Beatty & H. Legewie (Eds.), Biofeedback and Behavior
New York: Plenum Press, 1977

811. Harris, F.A.
Inapproprioception: A possible sensory basis for athetoid movements
Physical Therapy, 1971, 51:761-770

812. Harris, F.A., Spelman, F.A. & Hymer, J.W.
Electronic sensory aids as treatment for cerebral-palsied children
Physical Therapy, 1974, 54:354-365

813. Harris, M.B. & Bruner, C.G.
A comparison of a self-control and a contract procedure for weight control
Behavior Research and Therapy, 1971, 9:347-354

814. Harris, V.A. & Katkin, E.S.
Primary and secondary emotional behavior: An analysis of the role of autonomic feedback on affect, arousal and attribution
Psychological Bulletin, 1975, 82:904-916

815. Harris, V.A., Katkin, E.S., Lick, J.R., et al.
Paced respiration as a technique for the modification of autonomic response to stress
Psychophysiology, 1976, 13:386-391

816.   Harrison, A.
        Augmented feedback training of motor control in
           cerebral palsy
        Developmental Medicine and Child Neurology,
           1977, 19:75-78

817.   Harrison, A. & Connolly, K.
        The conscious control of five levels of neuro-
           muscular firing in spastic and normal subjects
        Developmental Medicine and Child Neurology,
           1971, 13:762-771

818.   Harrison, R.S. & Raskin, D.C.
        Learned control of HR variability during feed-
           back and no-feedback conditions
        Psychophysiology, 1973, 10:207 (Abst.)

819.   Harrison, R.S., & Raskin, D.C.
        The role of feedback in control of heart rate
           variability
        Psychophysiology, 1976, 13:135-139

820.   Harrison, V.F.
        Voluntary control of low threshold motor unit
           potentials in the neuromuscularly skilled
           individual
        Anatomical Record, 1963, 145:237

821.   Harrison, V.F. & Kock, W.B.
        Voluntary control of single motor unit activity
           in the extensor digitorum muscle
        Physical Therapy, 1972, 52:267-272

822.   Harrison, V.F. & Mortenson, O.A.
        Identification and voluntary activation of low
           threshold motor units
        Anatomical Record, 1960, 136:207 (Abst.)

823.   Harrison, V.F. & Mortenson, O.A.
        Identification and voluntary control of single
           motor unit activity in the tibialis anterior
           muscle
        Anatomical Record, 1962, 144:109-116

824.   Hart, J.D. & Wilson, A.E.
        The effect of relaxation training on physiolog-
          ical responses to single stimuli
        Psychophysiology, 1973, 10:208 (Abst.)

825.   Hart, J.T.
        Autocontrol of EEG alpha
        Psychophysiology, 1968, 4:506 (Abst.)

826.   Hartje, J.C.
        The evolution of a university headache program
        Biofeedback and Self-Regulation, 1977, 2:297
          (Abst.)

827.   Hartman, C.H.
        Group relaxation training for control of im-
          pulsive behavior in alcoholics
        Behavior Therapy, 1973, 4:173-174

828.   Harwood, C.W.
        Operant heart rate conditioning
        The Psychological Record, 1962, 12:279-284

829.   Hassett, J. & Schwartz, G.E.
        Relationships between heart rate and occipital
          alpha-A biofeedback approach
        Psychophysiology, 1975, 12:228 (Abst.)

830.   Hastings, L.O., Christie, D.J. & Kotses, H.
        Instructional influences in operant conditioning
          of cardiac deceleration in humans
        Psychophysiology, 1974, 11:241 (Abst.)

831.   Hauri, P.
        Biofeedback and self-control of physiolgical
          functions: Clinical applications
        International Journal of Psychiatry in Medicine,
          1975, 6:255-265

832.   Hauri, P., Phelps, P.J. & Jordan, J.B.
        Biofeedback as a treatment for insomnia
        Biofeedback and Self-Regulation, 1976, 1:354
          (Abst.)

833. Havelick, R.J.
The use of biofeedback and twilight learning in
the treatment of migraine headache, valium
dependency and cigarette smoking
Biofeedback and Self-Regulation, 1977, 2:297-298
(Abst.)

834. Haynes, M. & Blanchard, E.
The effects of the distribution of training on
learning feedback-assisted cardiac acceleration
Biofeedback and Self-Regulation, 1977 2:427-434

835. Haynes, S.N.
Application of operant feedback techniques in
the control of diastolic blood pressure of
essential hypertensives
Dissertation Abstracts, 1972, 32B:7311

836. Haynes, S.N.
Assessment of the comparative effectiveness of
electromyographic biofeedback and relaxation
training in laboratory and clinical settings
Proceedings of the Biofeedback Research Society
Fifth Annual Meeting
Colorado Springs, 1974, 46 (Abst.)

837. Haynes, S.N.
Electromyographic biofeedback treatment of a
woman with chronic dysphagia
Biofeedback and Self-Regulation, 1976, 1:121-126

838. Haynes, S.N., Griffin, R., Mooney, D., et al.
Relaxation instructions and biofeedback in the
treatment of muscle-contraction headaches
Behavior Therapy, 1975, 6:672-678

839. Haynes, S.N., Moseley, D. & McGowan, W.T.
Relaxation training and biofeedback in the
reduction of frontalis muscle tension
Psychophysiology, 1975, 12:547-552

840. Haynes, S.N., Woodward, S., Moran, R., et al.
Relaxation treatment of insomnia
Behavior Therapy, 1974, 5:555-558

841.   Headrick, M.W., Feather, B.W. & Wells, D.T.
        Voluntary changes from baseline heart rate with
           augmented sensory feedback
        Psychophysiology, 1970, 6:636 (Abst.)

842.   Headrick, M.W., Feather, B.W. & Wells, D.T.
        Undirectional and large magnitude heart rate
           changes with augmented sensory feedback
        Psychophysiology, 1971, 8:132-142

843.   Heath, H.A.,Oken, D. & Shipman, W.G.
        Muscle tension and personality. A serious
           second look
        Archives of General Psychiatry, 1967, 16:720-726

844.   Hefferline, R.F.
        The role of proprioception in the control of
           behavior
        Transactions of the New York Academy of Sciences,
           1958, 20:739-764

845.   Hefferline, R. & Bruno, L.
        The psychophysiology of private events
        In A. Jacobs & L. Sachs (Eds.), The Psychology
           of Private Events
        New York: Academic Press, 1971

846.   Hefferline, R.F., Bruno, L.J.J. & Davidowitz,
           J.E.
        Feedback control of covert behavior
        In K. Connolly (Ed.), Mechanisms of Motor Skill
           Development
        New York: Academic Press, 1970

847.   Hefferline, R.F. & Perera, B.
        Proprioceptive discrimination of covert operant
           without its observation by the subject
        Science, 1963, 139:834-835

848.   Hefferman, M.S.
        The effects of self-initiated control of brain
           waves on digit recall
        Dissertation Abstracts, 1971, 31:6404

849.   Hein, P.L
        Heart rate conditioning in the cat and its
            relationship to other physiological responses
        Psychophysiology, 1969, 5:455-464

850.   Heinemann, L.G. & Emrich, H.
        Alpha activity during inhibitory brain processes
        Psychophysiology, 1971, 7:442-450

851.   Heller, R.F. & Forgione, A.G.
        An evaluation of bruxism control: Massed nega-
            tive practice and automated relaxation training
        Journal of Dental Research, 1975, 54:1120-1123

852.   Helmer, R.J.
        Modulator and filter circuits for EEG biofeed-
            back
        Behavior Research Methods and Instrumentation,
            1975, 7:15-18

853.   Helmer, J.E. & Furedy, J.J.
        Operant conditioning of GSR amplitude
        Journal of Experimental Psychology, 1968,
            78:463-467

854.   Hendler, N., Derogatis, L., Avella, J., et al.
        EMG biofeedback in patients with chronic pain
        Diseases of the Nervous System, 1977, 38:505-514

855.   Hendrick, C., Giesen, M. & Borden, R.
        False physiological feedback and persuasion:
            Effect of fear and arousal vs. fear reduction
            in attitude change
        Journal of Personality, 1975, 43:196-214

856.   Henning, D.
        Some clinical applications of biofeedback EMG
            training
        American Corrective Therapy Journal, 1976,
            30:145-149

857.   Henry, J.P., Junas, R. & Smith, K.U.
        Experimental cybernetic analysis of delayed
            feedback of breath pressure control
        American Journal of Physical Medicine, 1967,
            46:1317-1331

858.   Henry, J.P., Smith, K.U. & Rosenstein, R.
        Visual feedback and voluntary control in patients
          with chronic pulmonary disease
        Federation Proceedings, 1966, 25:396

859.   Henschen, T.
        Biofeedback-induced reverie: A counseling tool
        Personnel and Guidance Journal, 1976, 54:327-328

860.   Henson, D.E. & Rubin, H.B.
        Voluntary control of eroticism
        Journal of Applied Behavior Analysis, 1971,
          4:37-44

861.   Herman, R.
        Augmented sensory feedback in control of limb
          movement
        In W. S. Field (Ed.), Neural organization and
          its Relevance to Prosthetics
        New York: Intercontinental Medical Corporation,
          1973

862.   Herring, M. & Richlin, M.
        Effectiveness of self-relaxation training in
          reducing the severity of recurrent angina
          pectoris
        Psychophysiology, 1977, 14:101 (Abst.)

863.   Hersen, M. & Barlow, D.H.
        Single-Case Experimental Designs: Strategies
          for Studying Behavior Change
        New York: Pergamon Press, 1976

864.   Herzfeld, G.M. & Taub, E.
        Effect of suggestion on feedback-aided self-
          regulation of hand temperature
        Biofeedback and Self-Regulation, 1976, 1:315
          (Abst.)

865.   Hilgard, E.R.
        Altered states of awareness
        Journal of Nervous and Mental Disease, 1969,
          149:68-79

866.   Hilgard, E.R., Macdonald, H., Marshall, G., et
        al.
        Anticipation of pain and of pain control under
        hypnosis
        Journal of Abnormal Psychology, 1974, 83:561-568

867.   Hinman, A., Engel, B. & Bickford, A.
        A portable blood pressure recorder: Accuracy
        and preliminary use in evaluating intradaily
        variations in pressure
        American Heart Journal, 1962, 63:663-668

868.   Hirai, H.
        (Biofeedback)
        Japanese Journal of Medical Electronics, 1976,
        14:279-388 (English Abst.)

869.   Hirai, H., Ikeda, Y. & Watanabe, S.
        Biofeedback and electrodermal self-regulation in
        a Zen meditator
        Psychophysiology, 1977, 14:103 (Abst.)

870.   Hirai, T.
        Electroencephalographic study on the Zen medi-
        tation (Zazen) - EEG changes during the con-
        centrated relaxation
        Psychiatria et Neurologia Japonica, 1960, 62:76-
        105

871.   Hirai, T., Izawa, S. & Koga, E.
        EEG and Zen Buddhism. EEG changes in the course
        of meditation
        Electroencephalography and Clinical Neuro-
        physiology, Suppl, 18, 1959, 52-53

872.   Hirschman, R.
        Effects of anticipatory bogus heart rate feed-
        back in a negative emotional context
        Psychophysiology, 1973, 10:208 (Abst.)

873.   Hirschman, R.
        Cross-modal effects of anticipatory bogus heart
        rate feedback in a negative emotional context
        Journal of Personality and Social Psychology,
        1975, 31:13-19

874. Hirschman, R., Clark, M. & Hawk, G.
      Relative effects of bogus physiological feedback
        and control stimuli on autonomic and self-
        report indicants of emotional attribution
      Personality and Social Psychology Bulletin,
        1977, 3:270-275

875. Hirschman, R. & Favaro, L.
      Relationship between imagery and voluntary heart
        rate control
      Psychophysiology, 1977, 14:120 (Abst.)

876. Hnatiow, M.
      Learned control of heart rate and blood pressure
      Perceptual and Motor Skills, 1971, 33:219-226

877. Hnatiow, M. & Lang, P.J.
      Learned stabilization of heart rate
      Psychophysiology, 1965, 1:330-336

878. Hoffman, E.
      Biofeedback training: A new therapy in the
        treatment of migraine and tension headache
      Danish Medical Bulletin, 1975, 22:97-99

879. Hoffman, E. & Willanger, R.
      Proceedings: Low arousal induced by EMG and EEG
        feedback in various patient groups: Descrip-
        tion of the methodology in a pilot study
      Electroencephalography and Clinical Neurophysiol-
        ogy, 1975, 39:557 (Abst.)

880. Hokanson, J.E., DeGood, D.E., Forrest, M.S. et
        al.
      Availability of avoidance behaviors in modulat-
        ing vascular stress responses
      Journal of Personality and Social Psychology,
        1971, 19:60-68

881. Holmes, D.S.
      Reply to "A comment on alcoholism, alpha pro-
        duction and biofeedback
      Journal of Consulting and Clinical Psychology,
        1977, 45:700-701

882.   Holmes, D.S. & Frost, R.O.
        Effect of false autonomic feedback on self
           reported anxiety, pain perception and pulse
           rate
        Behavior Therapy, 1976, 7:330-334

883.   Holmes, D..S., Frost, R.O. & Bennett, D.H.
        Influence of adaptation period length on the
           ability of humans to increase and decrease
           heart rate with instructions and biofeedback
        Behavioral Biology, 1977, 20:261-279

884.   Honorton, C. & Carbone, M.
        A preliminary study of feedback augmented EEG-
           alpha, shifts in subjective state, and ESP
           card guessing performance
        Journal of American Society for Psychical Re-
           search, 1971, 65:66-74.

885.   Honorton, C., Davidson, R. & Bendler, P.
        Feedback-augmented EEG alpha, shifts in subjective
           state, and ESP card - guessing performance
        Journal of the American Society of Psychic
           Research, 1971, 65:308-321

886.   Honorton, C., Davidson, R. &   Bendler, P.
        Shifts in subjective state associated with
           feedback-augmented EEG alpha
        Psychophysiology, 1972, 9:269 (Abst.)

887.   Hoon, P.W., Wincze, J.P. & Hoon, E.F.
        The effect of biofeedback and cognitive mediation
           upon vaginal blood volume
        Behavior Therapy, 1977, 8:694-702

888.   Hoover, E.
        Alpha, the first step to a new level of reality
        Human Behavior, 1972, 3:8-15

889.   Hord, D. & Barber, J.
        Autonomic activity levels during "tone on" and
           "tone off" alpha feedback
        Psychophysiology, 1971, 8:269 (Abst.)

890.   Hord, D. & Barber, J.
        Alpha control: Effectiveness of two kinds of
           feedback
        Psychonomic Science, 1971, 25:151-154

891.   Hord, D. & Johnson, L.C.
        Recuperative effects of self-regulated alpha
           during long waking vigils
        Proceedings of the Biofeedback Research Society
           Fifth Annual Meeting
        Colorado Springs, 1974, 77 (Abst.)

892.   Hord, D.J., Lubin, A., Tracy, M.L., et al.
        Feedback for high EEG alpha does not maintain
           performance or mood during sleep
        Psychophysiology, 1976, 13:58-61

893.   Hord, D.J., Naitoh, P., Johnson, L.C., et al.
        Intra-hemispheric phase relationships during
           self-regulated alpha activity
        Proceedings of the Biofeedback Research Society
           Fourth Annual Meeting
        Boston, 1972, 27 (Abst.)

894.   Hord, D., Naitoh, P. & Johnson, L.
        EEG spectral features of self-regulated high
           alpha states
        Psychophysiology, 1972, 9:278 (Abst.)

895.   Hord, D., Naitoh, P. & Johnson, L.C.
        Intensity and coherence contours during self-
           regulated high alpha activity
        Electroencephalography and Clinical Neuro-
           physiology, 1972, 32:429-433

896.   Hord, D.J., Tracy, M.L., Lubin, A., et al.
        Effect of self-enhanced EEG alpha on performance
           and mood after two nights of sleep loss
        Psychophysiology, 1975, 12:585-590

897.   Hord, D., Tracy, M. & Naitoh, P.
        Intrahemispheric phase relationships during
           self-regulated alpha activity
        Electroencephalography and Clinical Neuro-
           physiology, 1974, 37:133-136

898.   Hoshiko, M.
        Electromyographic investigation of the intercostal
            muscles during speech
        Archives of Physical Medicine and Rehabilitation,
            1962, 43:115-119

899.   Hoshiko, M. & Grandstaff, H.L.
        An electromyographic investigation of motor
            conflict
        Psychonomic Science, 1967, 9:87-88

900.   Hothersall, D. & Brener, J.
        Operant conditioning of changes in heart rate in
            curarized rats
        Journal of Comparative Physiology and Psychology,
            1969, 68:338-342

901.   Houk, J.C.
        On the significance of various command signals
            during voluntary control
        Brain Research, 1972, 40:4953

902.   Houk, J. & Henneman, E.
        Feedback control of skeletal muscles
        Brain Research, 1967, 5:433-451

903.   Houk, J. & Henneman, E.
        Feedback control of movement and posture
        In V.B. Mountcastle (Ed.), Medical Physiology
            Ed. 12
        St. Louis: Mosby, 1968, 1681-1696

904.   Houston, K.
        Control over stress, locus of control, and
            response to stress
        Journal of Personality and Social Psychology,
            1972, 21:249-255

905.   Howard, J.L., Turner, M.A., Gaebelein, C.J., et al.
        Operant conditioning of heart rate in curarized
            rats
        Psychophysiology, 1974, 11:242-243 (Abst.)

906.   Howe, R.C. & Sterman, M.B.
        Cortical-subcortical EEG correlates of suppressed
          motor behavior during sleep and waking in the
          cat
        Electroencephalography and Clinical Neuro-
          physiology, 1972, 32:681-695

907.   Howe, R.C. & Sterman, M.B.
        Somatosensory system evoked potentials during
          waking behavior and sleep in the cat
        Electroencephalography and Clinical Neuro-
          physiology, 1973, 34:605-618

908.   Hubel, K.A.
        Voluntary control of gastrointestinal function:
          Operant conditioning and biofeedback
        Gastroenterology, 1974, 66:1085-1088

909.   Huber, H., Karlin, R. & Nathan, P.
        Blood alcohol level discrimination by non-
          alcoholics: The role of internal and external
          cues
        Journal of Studies on Alcohol, 1976, 37:27-39

910.   Hudgins, C.V.
        Conditioning and the voluntary control of the
          pupilary light reflex
        Journal of General Psychology, 1933, 8:3-51

911.   Hughes, W.G. & Shean, G.D.
        Ability to control GSR amplitude
        Psychonomic Science, 1971, 23:309-311

912.   Hukill, E.L.
        Uses and meta-uses of biofeedback in psycho-
          therapy and vice-versa
        Proceedings of the Biofeedback Research Society
          Sixth Annual Meeting
        Monterey, 1975, 32 (Abst.)

913.   Hukill, E.L. & Turner, A.
        Feedback of respiratory patterns
        Proceedings of the Biofeedback Research Society
          Sixth Annual Meeting
        Monterey, 1975, 73 (Abst.)

914.   Hume, W.I.
       Electrodermal measures in behavioral research
       Journal of Psychosomatic Research, 1966, 9:383-
       391

915.   Hume, W.I.
       Biofeedback: Research and Therapy
       Montreal: Eden Press, 1976

916.   Hume, W.
       Biofeedback Vol. 2
       Montreal: Eden Press, 1977

917.   Hunter, S., Russell, H., Russell, E., et al.
       Control of fingertip temperature increases via
          biofeedback in learning disabled and normal
          children
       Perceptual and Motor Skills, 1976, 43:743-755

918.   Hunter, W.S. & Hudgins, C.V.
       Voluntary activity from the standpoint of
          behavior
       Journal of General Psychology, 1934, 10:198-204

919.   Hutchings, D., Morgret, M., Reinking. R.
       Tension headaches: What type of therapy is most
          effective?
       Proceedings of the Biofeedback Research Society
          Sixth Annual Meeting
       Monterey, 1975, 99 (Abst.)

920.   Hutchings, D.F. & Reinking, R.H.
       Tension headaches: What form of therapy is most
          effective
       Biofeedback and Self-Regulation, 1976, 1:183-190

921.   Hutchinson, J.M. & Burk, K.W.
       An investigation of the effects of temporal
          alterations in auditory feedback upon stutter-
          ers and clutterers
       Journal of Communication Disorders, 1973, 6:193-
          205

922.   Hyman, E.T.   & Gale, E.N.
        Galvanic skin response and reported anxiety
          during systematic desensitization
        Journal of Consulting and Clinical Psychology,
          1973, 40:108-114

923.   Ikeda, Y. & Hirai, H.
        Voluntary control of electrodermal activity in
           relation to imagery and internal perception
           scores
        Psychophysiology, 1976, 13:330-333

924.   Ince, L.P.
        The use of relaxation training and a conditioned
           stimulus in the elimination of epileptic
           seizures in a child: A case study
        Journal of Behavior Therapy and Experimental
           Psychiatry, 1976, 7:39-42

925.   Ingham, R.J. & Andrews, G.
        Behavior therapy and stuttering: A review
        Journal of Speech and Hearing Disorders, 1973,
           38:405-441

926.   Inglis, J., Campbell, D. & Donald, M.W.
        Electromyographic biofeedback and neuromuscular
           rehabilitation
        Canadian Journal of Behavioral Science, 1976,
           8:299-323

927.   Ivanenkova, E.D., Ivanenkov, V.V., Kolichko,
           B.A., et al.
        Use of feedback devices during training in
           standing and walking of patients with dis-
           orders of the function of the musculo-skeletal
           apparatus
        Ortop. Travmatol Protez, 1973, 34:27-31

928.   Jacobs, A. & Felton, G.S.
        Visual feedback of myoelectric output to facil-
          itate muscle relaxation in normal persons and
          patients with neck injuries
        Archives of Physical Medicine and Rehabilita-
          tion, 1969, 50:34-39

929.   Jacobs, D.W. & Smith, G.
        Personality changes as a function of EMG train-
          ing in a group of marijuana users
        Proceedings of the Biofeedback Research Society
          Sixth Annual Meeting
        Monterey, 1975, 95 (Abst.)

930.   Jacobson, A.M., Hackett, T.P., Surman, O.S., et al.
        Raynaud phenomenon. Treatment with hypnotic and
          operant technique
        Journal of the American Medical Association,
          1973, 225:739-740

931.   Jacobson, E.
        Use of relaxation in hypertensive states
        New York Medical Journal, 1920, 111:419

932.   Jacobson, E.
        Voluntary relaxation of the esophagus
        American Journal of Physiology, 1925, 72:387-394

933.   Jacobson, E.
        Electrical measurements of neuromuscular states
          during mental activities: I. Imagination of
          movement involving skeletal muscles
        American Journal of Physiology, 1930, 91:567-708

934.   Jacobson, E.
        Electrical measurements of neuromuscular states
          during mental activities: II. Imagination
          and recollection of various muscular acts
        American Journal of Physiology, 1930, 94:22-34

935.   Jacobson, E.
        Electrical measurements of neuromuscular states
          during mental activities: III. Visual
          imagination and recollection
        American Journal of Physiology, 1930, 95:694-702

936.   Jacobson, E.
        Electrical measurements of neuromuscular states
            during mental activities: IV. Evidence of
            contraction of specific muscles during imagina-
            tion
        American Journal of Physiology, 1930, 95:703-712

937.   Jacobson, E.
        Electrical measurements of neuromuscular states
            during mental activities: V. Variation of
            specific muscles contracting during imagination
        American Journal of Physiology, 1931, 96:115-
        121

938.   Jacobson, E.
        Electrical measurements of neuromuscular states
            during mental activities: VI. A note on
            mental activities concerning an amputated limb
        American Journal of Physiology, 1931, 96:122-125

939.   Jacobson, E.
        Electrical measurements of neuromuscular states
            during mental activities: VII. Imagination,
            recollection and abstract thinking involving
            the speech musculature
        American Journal of Physiology, 1931, 97:200-209

940.   Jacobson, E.
        Electrical measurements concerning muscular
            contraction (tonus) and the cultivation of
            relaxation in man
        American Journal of Physiology, 1934, 107:230-
        248

941.   Jacobson, E.
        Electrical measurements concerning muscular
            contractions (tonus) and the cultivation of
            relaxation in man: Relaxation times of indi-
            viduals
        American Journal of Physiology, 1934, 108:573-
        580

942.   Jacobson, E.
        The course of relaxation in muscles of athletes
        American Journal of Psychology, 1936, 48:98

943.   Jacobson, E.
        The influence of skeletal muscle tension and
            relaxation on blood pressure
        American Journal of Physiology, 1936, 116:86

944.   Jacobson, E.
        Progressive Relaxation, (Second Edition)
        Chicago: University of Chicago Press, 1938

945.   Jacobson, E.
        Variation of blood pressure with skeletal muscle
            tension and relaxation
        Annals of Internal Medicine, 1939, 12:1194-1212

946.   Jacobson, E.
        Variations of blood pressure with brief volun-
            tary muscular contractions
        Journal of Laboratory and Clinical Medicine,
            1940, 25:1029-1037

947.   Jacobson, E.
        Variation of blood pressure with skeletal muscle
            tension and relaxation. The heart beat
        Annals of Internal Medicine, 1940, 13:1619-1625

948.   Jacobson, E.
        Cultivated relaxation in "essential" hypertension
        Archives of Physical Therapy, 1940, 21:645-654

949.   Jacobson, E.
        The effect of daily rest without training to
            relax on muscular tonus
        American Journal of Physiology, 1942, 55:248-254

950.   Jacobson, E.
        The cultivation of physiological relaxation
        Annals of Internal Medicine, 1943, 19:965-972

951.   Jacobson, E.
        Innervation and tonus of striated muscle in man
        Journal of Nervous and Mental Diseases, 1943,
            97:197-203

952.   Jacobson, E.
        Neuromuscular controls in man: Methods of self
           direction in health and disease
        American Journal of Physiology, 1955, 68:549-561

953.   Jacobson, E.
        You Must Relax
        New York: McGraw Hill,1934

954.   Jacobson, E.
        Modern Treatment of Tense Patients
        New York: C. C. Thomas, 1963

955.   Jacobson, E.
        Self-operations Control
        Philadelphia: Lippincott, 1964

956.   Jacobson, E.
        Anxiety and Tension Control
        Philadelphia: Lippincott, 1964

957.   Jacobson, E (Ed.)
        Tension in Medicine
        Springfield, IL: Charles C. Thomas, 1967

958.   Jacobson, E.
        Modern Treatment of Tense Patients
        Springfield: Charles C. Thomas, 1970

959.   Jacobson, E. & Carlson, A.J.
        The influence of relaxation upon the knee jerk
        American Journal of Physiology, 1925, 73:224-328

960.   Jacobson, G.R., Wilson, A. & LaRocca, L.
        Perceptual field dependence and biofeedback
           training (EEG alpha) among male alcoholics
        In F. A. Seixas (Ed.), Currents in Alcoholism,
           Vol. 2
        New York: Grune & Stratton, 1977

961.   Jaffe, P., Haynes, S. & Wilson, C.
        Biofeedback training in atopic dermatitis
        Southern Medical Journal, 1977, 70:1249

962.   Jankel, W.R.
        EMG feedback in Bell's palsy
        Biofeedback and Self-Regulation, 1977, 2:313-314
          (Abst.)

963.   Jasper, H. & Shagass, C.
        Conditioning of the occipital alpha rhythm in
          man
        Journal of Experimental Psychology, 1941,
          28:373-387

964.   Jasper, H. & Shagass, C.
        Conscious time judgments related to conditioned
          time intervals and voluntary control of the
          alpha rhythm
        Journal of Experimental Psychology, 1941,
          28:503-508

965.   Javel, A.F. & Denholtz, M.S.
        Audible GSR feedback and systematic desensitiza-
          tion. A case report
        Behavior Therapy, 1975, 6:251-253

966.   Jeffrey, D.B.
        Self-control: Methodological issues and research
          trends
        In J. J. Mahoney and C.E. Thoresen (Eds.), Power
          to the Person: Self-control
        Monterey: Brooks-Cole, 1974

967.   Jenks, R.S. & Deane, H.E.
        Human heart rate responses during experimentally
          induced anxiety: A follow-up
        Journal of Experimental Psychology, 1963,
          65:109-112

968.   Jernstedt, G.C. & Newcomer, J.P.
        Blood pressure and pulse wave velocity measure-
          ment for operant conditioning of autonomic
          responding
        Behavior Research Methods Instrumentation, 1974,
          6:393-397

128 REFERENCES

969. Jessup, B.A. & Neufeld, R.W.J.
      Effects of biofeedback and "autogenic relaxa-
      tion" techniques on physiological and sub-
      jective responses in psychiatric patients: A
      preliminary analysis
      Behavior Therapy, 1977, 8:160-167

970. Jevning, R., Smith, R., Wilson, A.F., et al.
      Alterations in blood flow during transcendental
      meditation
      Psychophysiology, 1976, 13:168 (Abst.)

971. Jevning, R. & Wilson, A.F.
      Altered red cell metabolism in TM
      Psychophysiology, 1977: 14:94 (Abst.)

972. Johns, T.R.
      Heart rate control in humans under paced respira-
      tion and restricted movement: The effect of
      instructions and exteroceptive feedback
      Dissertation Abstracts, 1970, 30B:5712-5713

973. Johnson, C.P.
      Analysis of five tests commonly used in deter-
      mining the ability to control single motor
      units
      American Journal of Physical Medicine, 1976,
      55:113-121

974. Johnson, H.E. & Garton, W.H.
      Muscle re-education in hemiplegia by use of
      electromyographic device
      Archives of Physical Medicine and Rehabili-
      tation, 1973, 54:320-323

975. Johnson, H.J. & Schwartz, G.E.
      Suppression of GSR activity through operant
      reinforcement
      Journal of Experimental Psychology, 1967,
      75:307-312

976. Johnson, L.C.
      A psychophysiology for all states
      Psychophysiology, 1970, 6:501-516

977.   Johnson, L.C.
        Learned control of brain wave activity
        In J. Beatty & H. Legewie (Eds.), Biofeedback
           and Behavior
        New York: Plenum Press, 1977

978.   Johnson, L.C., Lubin, A., Naitoh, P., et al.
        Spectral analysis of the EEG of dominant and
           non-dominant alpha subjects during waking and
           sleeping
        Electroencephalography and Clinical Neuro-
           physiology, 1966, 26:361-370

979.   Johnson, R.J.
        Operant reinforcement of an autonomic response
        Dissertation Abstracts, 1963, 24B:1255-1256

980.   Johnson, R.K. & Meyer, R.G.
        The locus of control construct in EEG alpha
           rhythm feedback
        Journal of Consulting and Clinical Psychology,
           1974, 42:913

981.   Johnson, R.K. & Meyer, R.G.
        Phased biofeedback approach for epileptic
           seizure control
        Journal of Behavior Therapy and Experimental
           Psychiatry, 1974, 5:185-187

982.   Johnson, W.G. & Turin, A.
        Biofeedback treatment of migraine headache: A
           systematic case study
        Behavior Therapy, 1975, 6:394-397

983.   Johnston, D.
        Criterion level and instructional effects in the
           voluntary control of heart rate
        Biological Psychology, 1976, 4:1-17

984.   Johnston, D.
        Feedback and instructional effects in the
           voluntary control of digital pulse amplitude
        Biological Psychology, 1977, 5:159-171

985.   Johnston, D.
        Biofeedback, verbal instructions and the motor
           skills analogy
        In J. Beatty & H. Legewie (Eds.), Biofeedback
           and Behavior
        New York: Plenum Press, 1977

986.   Johnston, R. & Lee, K.
        Myofeedback: A new method of teaching breathing
           exercises in emphasematous patients
        Physical Therapy, 1976, 56:826-831

987.   Jonas, Gerald.
        Visceral Learning
        New York: Viking Press, 1973

988.   Jones, B.
        Is there any proprioceptive feedback? Comments
           on Schmidt (1971)
        Psychological Bulletin, 1973, 79:386-388

989.   Jones, F.P.
        Body Awareness in Action: A Study of the
           Alexander Technique
        New York: Schocken Books, 1976

990.   Jones, F.W. & Holmes, D.S.
        Alcoholism, alpha production and biofeedback
        Journal of Consulting and Clinical Psychology,
           1976, 44:224-228

991.   Jones, G.B. & Fenz, W.D.
        Relationships between cardiac conditionability
           in the laboratory and autonomic control in
           real life stress
        Psychophysiology, 1972, 9:267 (Abst.)

992.   Jones, R.W.
        Principles of Biological Regulation: An Intro-
           duction to Feedback Systems
        New York: Academic Press, 1973

993.   Jordan, C. & Schallow, J.R.
        The role of locus of control in electromyo-
          graphic feedback and brief progressive
          relaxation
        Proceedings of the Biofeedback Research Society
          Sixth Annual Meeting
        Monterey, 1975, 5 (Abst.)

994.   Jurriaans, J.H.
        (Anxiety and pseudo-heartrate feedback)
        Ned Tijdschr Psychol, 1972, 27:91-112 (Dut)
          English Abst.

995. Kahn, M., Baker, B.L. & Weiss, J.M.
      Treatment of insomnia by relaxation training
      Journal of Abnormal Psychology, 1968, 73:556-558

996. Kahn, S.D., Swint, E.B. & Bowne, G.W.
      A film demonstration of biofeedback technology in
        which covert operants control the visual environment
      Psychophysiology, 1973, 10:197 (Abst.)

997. Kamiya, J.
      Conditioned discrimination of the EEG alpha rhythm
        in humans
      Abstract of a paper presented at the Western Psycho-
        logical Association, 1962

998. Kamiya, J.
      Conscious control of brain waves
      Psychology Today, 1968, 1(11):55-60

999. Kamiya, J.
      A fourth dimension of consciousness
      Experimental Medicine and Surgery, 1969, 27:13-18

1000. Kamiya, J.
      Operant control of the EEG alpha rhythm and some of
        its reported effects on consciousness
      In C. Tart (Ed.), Altered States of Consciousness
      New York: John Wiley & Sons, 1969, 489-501

1001. Kamiya, J.
      Training of the left-right alpha amplitude ratio
      Proceedings of the Biofeedback Research Society
        Fourth Annual Meeting
      Boston, 1972, 28 (Abst.)

1002. Kamiya, J.
      Autoregulation of the EEG alpha rhythm: A program
        for the study of consciousness
      In M. H. Chase (Ed.), Operant Control of Brain
        Activity
      Los Angeles: UCLA Brain Research Institute, 1974

1003. Kamiya, J., Barber, T.X., DiCara, L.V., Miller,
N.E., Shapiro, D. & Stoyva, J. (Eds.).
Biofeedback and Self-Control: An Aldine Reader on
the Regulation of Bodily Processes and Conscious-
ness
Chicago: Aldine, 1971

1004. Kanfer, F.H. & Karoly, P.
Self-regulation: Research, issues and speculations
In C. Neuringer & J. L. Michael (Eds.), Behavior
Modification and Clinical Psychology
New York: Appleton-Century-Crofts, 1970

1005. Kanfer, F.H. & Karoly, P.
Self-regulation and its clinical application: Some
additional conceptualizations
In R. C. Johnson, P.R. Dolecki, & O. H. Mowrer,
(Eds.), Conscience, Contract and Social Reality
New York: Holt, Rinehart, & Winston, 1972; 428-
438

1006. Kantor, R.E.
On-line computer augmentation of biofeedback processes
International Journal of Biomedical Computers, 1970,
1:265-275

1007. Kaplan, B.E., Corby, J.C. & Liederman, P.H.
Attention and verbalization: Differential responsivity of cardiovascular and electrodermal
systems
Journal of Psychosomatic Research, 1971, 15:323-328

1008. Kaplan, B.
EEG biofeedback and epilepsy
Proceedings of the Biofeedback Research Society
Fifth Annual Meeting
Colorado Springs, 1974, 16 (Abst.)

1009. Kaplan, B.J.
Biofeedback in epileptics: Equivocal relationship
of reinforced EEG frequency to seizure reduction
Epilepsia, 1975, 16:477-485

1010. Kaplan, B.J.
Reply to Professor Gastaut's comments on "Biofeed-
back in epileptics"
Epilepsia, 1975, 16:488-489

1011. Kardachi, B.J. & Clarke, N.G.
Use of biofeedback to control bruxism
Journal of Periodontology, 1977, 48:639-642

1012. Karlins, M. & Andrews, L.
Biofeedback, Turning on the Power of Your Mind
New York: Lippincott, 1972

1013. Kasamatsu, A. & Hirai, T.
Science of Zazen
Psychologia, 1963, 6:86-91

1014. Kasamatsu, A. & Hirai, T.
An electroencephalograhic study of the Zen meditation (Zazen)
Folia Psychiatrica et Neurologica Japonica, 1966,
20:315-336

1015. Kasamatsu, A., Hirai, T. & Ando, N
EEG responses to click stimulation in Zen meditation
Proceedings of the Japanese EEG Society, 1962, 77-78

1016. Kasamatsu, A., Okuma, T., et al.
The EEG of Zen and Yoga practitioners
Electroencephalography and Clinical Neurophysiology,
1957, Suppl. 9, 51-52

1017. Katkin, E.S.
Relationship between manifest anxiety and two indices
of autonomic response to stress
Journal of Personality and Social Psychology, 1965,
2:324-333

1018. Katkin, E.S.
The relationship between a measure of transitory
anxiety and spontaneous autonomic activity
Journal of Abnormal Psychology, 1966, 71:142-146

1019. Katkin, E.S. & Murray, E.N.
Instrumental conditioning of autonomically mediated
behavior: Theoretical and methodological issues
Psychological Bulletin, 1968, 70:52-68

1020. Katkin, E.S., Murray, E.N. & Lachman, R.
Concerning instrumental autonomic conditioning: A
rejoinder.
Psychological Bulletin, 1969, 71:462-466

1021. Katkin, E.S. & Rappaport, H.
Relationship among manifest anxiety, response to stress
and the perception of autonomic activity
Psychophysiology, 1970, 6:646 (Abst.)

1022. Kato, M. & Tanji, J.
Cortical motor potentials accompanying volitionally
controlled single motor unit discharges in human
finger muscles
Brain Research, 1972, 47:103-111

1023. Kato, M. & Tanji, J.
Volitionally controlled single motor units in human
finger muscles
Brain Research, 1972, 40:345-357

1024. Kato, M. & Tanji, J.
Conscious control of motor unit of human finger
muscles
In G. G. Somjen (Ed.), Neurophysiology Studied in
Man
Amsterdam: Excerpta Medica, 1972, 330-344

1025. Katz, D.
Voluntary control of skin conductance response:
Some paradoxical findings
Proceedings of the Biofeedback Research Society
Fifth Annual Meeting
Colorado Springs, 1974, 72 (Abst.)

1026. Kazden, A.E.
Statistical analyses for single-case experimental
designs
In M. Hersen & D. H. Barlow (Eds.), Single-Case
Experimental Designs: Strategies for Studying
Behavior Change
New York: Pergamon Press, 1976

1027. Kazniak, A.W.
       Dichotic auditory vigilance during feedback-enhanced
          EEG alpha
       Psychophysiology, 1973, 10:203 (Abst.)

1028. Keefe, F.J.
       The effect of instructions upon the conditioning of
          changes in absolute skin temperature
       Proceedings of the Biofeedback Research Society
          Fifth Annual Meeting
       Colorado Springs, 1974, 59 (Abst.)

1029. Keefe, F.J.
       Conditioning changes in differential skin temper-
          ature
       Perceptual and Motor Skills, 1975, 40:283-288

1030. Keefe, F.J. & Gardner, E.T.
       Learned control of skin temperature: Effects of short
          and long-term biofeedback training
       Psychophysiology, 1976, 13:187 (Abst.)

1031. Kelly, D.H.W.
       Measurement of anxiety by forearm blood flow
       British Journal of Psychiatry, 1966, 112:789-798

1032. Kelly, D.H.W.
       The technique of forearm plethysmography for assessing
          anxiety
       Journal of Psychosomatic Research, 1967, 10:373-382

1033. Kelly, D.H.W. & Walter, C.J.S.
       The relationship between clinical diagnosis and
          anxiety, assessed by forearm blood flow and other
          measurements
       British Journal of Psychiatry, 1968, 114:611-626

1034. Kelly, D., Brown, C.C. & Shaffer, J.W.
       A comparison of physiological and psychological
          measurements on anxious patients and normal
          controls
       Psychophysiology, 1970, 6:429-441

1035. Kent, R.N., Wilson, G.T. & Nelson, R.
Effects of false heart rate feedback on avoidance
behavior: An investigation of "cognitive desensitization."
Behavior Therapy, 1972, 3:1-6

1036. Kentsmith, D.K.
Psychosomatic illnesses and biofeedback, unlocking
answers
Nebraska Medical Journal, 1974, 59:380-382

1037. Kentsmith, D., Strider, F., Copenhaver, J., et al.
Effects of biofeedback upon suppression of migraine
symptoms and plasma dopamine-B-hydroxylase activity
Headache, 1976, 16:173-177

1038. Kerber, K.W. & Coles, M.G.H.
Attractiveness and false heart rate feedback: Cog-
nitive and physiological effects
Psychophysiology, 1977, 14:110 (Abst.)

1039. Kerr, M.E.
Aspects of biofeedback physiology and its relation-
ship to family systems theory
American Journal of Psychoanalysis, 1977, 37:23-36

1040. Khan, A.U.
Effectiveness of biofeedback and counterconditioning
in the treatment of bronchial asthma
Journal of Psychosomatic Research, 1977, 21:97-104

1041. Khan, A.U., Staerck, M. & Bonk, C.
Role of counterconditioning in the treatment of
asthma
Journal of Psychosomatic Research, 1973, 17:389-392

1042. Khan, A.U., Staerk, M. & Bonk, C.
Role of counter conditioning in the treatment of asthma
Journal of Asthma Research, 1973, 11:57-62

1043. Kiefer, D.
EEG alpha feedback and subjective states of conscious-
ness
Psychologia, 1971, 14:3-14

1044. Kiefer, D.
Meditation and biofeedback
In White, J. (Ed.), Highest State of Consciousness
New York: Doubleday, 1972

1045. Kimble, G.A.   & Perlmutter, L.C.
The problem of volition
Psychological Review, 1970, 77:361-384

1046. Kimm, J.
On the specification of control in single motor
units
Dissertation Abstracts, 1969, 30:869

1047. Kimm, J.   & Sutton, D.
Foreperiod effects on human single motor unit reactio
times
Physiology and Behavior, 1973, 10:539-542

1048. Kimmel, H.D.
Equating stimulus intensities by means of the GSR
Psychonomic Science, 1967, 7:77-78

1049. Kimmel, H.D.
Instrumental conditioning of autonomically mediated
behavior
Psychological Bulletin, 1967, 67:337-345

1050. Kimmel, H.D.
Instrumental conditioning
In W. Prokasy & D. Raskin, (Eds.), Electrodermal
Behavior
New York: Academic Press, 1973

1051. Kimmel, H.D.
Instrumental conditioning of autonomically mediated
responses in human beings
American Psychologist, 1974, 29:325-335

1052. Kimmel, H.D.   & Baxter, R.
Avoidance conditioning of the GSR
Journal of Experimental Psychology, 1964, 68:482-485

1053. Kimmel, H.D. & Burns, R.A.
      Inter-effector influences on operant autonomic
         control
      In J. Beatty & H. Legewie (Eds.), Biofeedback and
         Behavior
      New York: Plenum Press, 1977

1054. Kimmel, H.D. & Hill, F.A.
      Operant conditioning of the GSR
      Psychological Reports, 1960, 7:555-562

1055. Kimmel, H.D. & Hill, F.A.
      A comparison of two electrodermal measures of response
         to stress
      Journal of Comparative and Physiological Psychology,
         1961, 54:395-397

1056. Kimmel, E. & Kimmel, H.D.
      A replication of operant conditioning of the GSR
      Journal of Experimental Psychology, 1963, 65:212-213

1057. Kimmel, H.D. & Kimmel, E.
      Sex differences in adaptation of the GSR under
         repeated applications of a visual stimulus
      Journal of Experimental Psychology, 1965, 70:536

1058. Kimmel, H.D. & Kimmel, E
      Inter-effector influences in operant autonomic
         conditioning
      Psychonomic Science, 1967, 9:191-192

1059. Kimmel, E. & Kimmel, H.D.
      Instrumental conditioning of the GSR: Serendipitous
         escape and punishment training
      Journal of Experimental Psychology, 1968, 77:48-51

1060. Kimmel, H.D., Pendergrass, V.E. & Kimmel, E.B.
      Modifying childrens orienting reactions instrumentally
      Conditional Reflex, 1967, 2:227-235

1061. Kimmel, H.D. & Sternthal, H.S.
      Replication of GSR avoidance conditioning with
         concomitant EMG measurement and subjects matched
         in responsivity and conditionability
      Journal of Experimental Psychology, 1967, 74:144-146

1062. Kimmel, H.D., Sternthal, H.S. & Strub, H.
      Two replications of avoidance conditioning of the GSR
      Journal of Experimental Psychology, 1966, 72:151-152

1063. King, J.T., Jr.
      An instance of voluntary acceleration of the pulse
      Johns Hopkins Hospital Bulletin, 1920, September,
      303-305

1064. Kinsman, R.A., O'Banion, K., Robinson, S., et al.
      Continuous biofeedback and discrete posttrial verbal
         feedback in frontalis muscle relaxation training
      Psychophysiology, 1975, 12:30-35

1065. Kirschbaum, J. & Gistl, E.
      EEG alpha percentage, alpha feedback, anxiety and
         relaxation in clinically inconspicuous students
      Archives of Psychology (Frankfurt), 1973, 125:263-
      272

1066. Kleinman, A.M.
      A neuromuscular evaluation of oral facial tension:
         A pilot study
      New York Journal of Dentistry, 1976, 46:189-195

1067. Kleinman, A.M.
      Biofeedback: An innovative approach to dental
         problems:
      New York Journal of Dentistry, 1977, 47:42-44

1068. Kleinman, A. & Lidsky, A.
      Biofeedback training and rest position in denture
         subjects
      IADR Abstracts, Journal of Dental Research, 1976,
      55:B100

1069. Kleinman, K.M. & Goldman, H.
      Effects of biofeedback on the physiological and
         cognitive consequences of essential hypertension
      Proceedings of the Biofeedback Research Society
         Fifth Annual Meeting
      Colorado Springs, 1974, 37 (Abst.)

1070. Kleinman, K.M., Goldman, H. & Snow, M.Y.
      Effects of stress and motivation on effectiveness of
         biofeedback training in essential hypertensives
      Psychophysiology, 1976, 13:187 (Abst.)

1071. Kleinman, K.M., Goldman, H., Snow, M.Y., et al.
      Effects of stress and motivation on effectiveness
         of biofeedback training in essential hypertensives
      Biofeedback and Self-Regulation, 1976, 1:309 (Abst.)

1072. Kleinman, K.M., Goldman, H., Snow, M.Y., et al.
      Relationship between essential hypertension and
         cognitive functioning II. Effects of biofeedback
         training generalize to nonlaboratory environment
      Psychophysiology, 1977, 14:192-197

1073. Kleinman, K.M., Keister, M., Riggin, C.S., et al.
      Use of EMG feedback to inhibit flexor spasicity and
         increase active extension in stroke patients
      Psychophysiology, 1976, 13:165 (Abst.)

1074. Kleinman, K.M., Riggin, C.S., Keister, M.E., et al.
      Use of EMG feedback to inhibit flexor spasticity and
         increase active extension in stroke patients
      Biofeedback and Self-Regulation, 1976, 1:327 (Abst.)

1075. Klinge, V.
      Effects of exteroceptive feedback and instructions
         in control of spontaneous galvanic skin response
      Psychophysiology, 1972, 9:305-317

1076. Klug, J.W. & Brown, B.B.
      Learned control of EEG theta activity
      Proceedings of the Biofeedback Research Society
         Fifth Annual Meeting
      Colorado Springs, 1974, 99 (Abst.)

1077. Knapp, T. & Lubar, J.F.
      Affective behavior changes in cats following operant
         conditioning of 40 Hz amygdaloid activity
      Physiology and Behavior, 1976, 17:137-142

1078. Kobayashi, H., et al.
      (Feedback control of the alpha waves)
      Japanese Journal of Medical Electronics, 1976,
         14:314-318 (English Abst.)

1079. Koenig, K.P.
       False emotional feedback and the modification of
           anxiety
       Behavior Therapy, 1973, 4:193-202

1080. Koenig, K.P. & del Castello, D.
       False feedback and longevity of the conditioned GSR
           during extinction: Some implications for aversion
           therapy
       Journal of Abnormal Psychology, 1969, 74:505-510

1081. Koepke, J.E. & Pribram, K.H.
       Habituation of the vasoconstrictive response as a
           function of stimulus duration and anxiety
       Journal of Comparative and Physiological Psychology,
           1967, 64:502-504

1082. Kohlenberg, R.J.
       Operant-conditioning of human anal sphincter pressure
       Journal of Applied Behavior Analysis, 1973, 6:201-
           208

1083. Kohli, D.R.
       The physiopathology of functional disorders. Circuits
           and mechanisms affected by neuromuscular bio-
           feedback training
       Proceedings of the Biofeedback Research Society
           Fifth Annual Meeting
       Colorado Springs, 1974, 26 (Abst.)

1084. Kohli, D.R.
       The physiopathology of fatigue and the necessity for
           thorough neuromuscular biofeedback training
       Proceedings of the Biofeedback Research Society
           Sixth Annual Meeting
       Monterey, 1975, 82 (Abst.)

1085. Kondo, C. & Canter, A.
       True and false electromyographic feedback: Effect
           on tension headache
       Journal of Abnormal Psychology, 1977, 86:93-95

1086. Kondo, C.Y., Canter, A. & Bean, J.A.
       Intersession interval and reductions in frontalis
           EMG during biofeedback training
       Psychophysiology, 1977, 14:15-17

1087. Kondo, C., Canter, A. & Knott, J.R.
       Relaxation training as a method of reducing anxiety
         associated with depression
       Proceedings of the Biofeedback Research Society
         Sixth Annual Meeting
       Monterey, 1975, 87 (Abst.)

1088. Kondo, C., Knott, J.R. & Travis, T.A.
       The effects of varying levels of motivation on
         performance in alpha enhancement training
       Proceedings of the Biofeedback Research Society
         Fifth Annual Meeting
       Colorado Springs, 1974, 78 (Abst.)

1089. Kondo, C.Y., Travis, T.A. & Knott, J.A.
       Integrated alpha: Comparison with criterion or
         rewarded alpha
       Proceedings of the Biofeedback Research Society
         Fourth Annual Meeting
       Boston, 1972, 46 (Abst.)

1090. Kondo, C.Y., Travis, T.A., Knott, J.R., et al.
       Effects of true and inverted feedback on integrated
         occipital alpha
       Biofeedback and Self-Regulation, 1976, 1:344-345 (Abst.)

1091. Kondo, F.
       The effects of feedback signal and model signal on
         heart rate changes
       Japanese Journal of Psychology, 1975, 46:216-221

1092. Konigsberg, R.L.
       Electromyographic sensor design for use with an
         externally powered prosthetic arm
       Journal of the Association for the Advancement of
         Medical Instrumentation, 1972, 6:347-351

1093. Koppman, J.W., McDonald, R.D. & Kunzel, M.G.
       Voluntary regulation of temporal artery diameter by
         migraine patients
       Headache, 1974, 14:133-138

1094. Korein, J. & Brudny, J.
       Integrated EMG feedback in the management of spas-
         modic torticollis and focal dystonia
       In M. D. Yahr (Ed.), Basal Ganglia
       New York: Raven Press, 1976

1095. Korein, J., Brudny, J., Grynbaum, B., et al
       Sensory feedback therapy in spasmodic torticollis
           and dystonia: Results in treatment of 55 patients
       In R. Eldridge, S. Fahn, (Eds.), Advances in
           Neurology
       New York: Raven Press, 1976

1096. Korein, J., Levidow, L. & Brudny, J.
       Self-regulation of EEG and EMG activity using bio-
           feedback as therapeutic tool
       Electroencephalography and Clinical Neurophysiology,
           1974, 36:222 (Abst.)

1097. Korn, R.R.
       Vasomotor conditioning and the vascular headache:
           Toward a therapeutic synthesis (preliminary
           report)
       Intercollegiate Psychology Association Journal,
           1949, 1:51-67

1098. Korner, P.I.
       Central nervous system control of autonomic function
       Possible implications in the pathogenesis of hyper-
           tension
       Circulation Research, 1970, 27:159-168

1099. Kornfeld, C.M. & Beatty, J.T.
       Discriminant aversive control of human EEG rhythms
       Psychophysiology, 1974, 11:227 (Abst.)

1100. Kosbabs, P.A.
       Imagery techniques in psychiatry
       Archives of General Psychiatry, 1974, 31:283-290

1101. Koslovskaya, I.B., Verter, R.P., & Miller, N.E.
       Instrumental learning without proprioceptive feedback
       Physiology and Behavior, 1973, 10:101-107

1102. Kothare, U.
       Application of yoga, autohypnosis and biofeedback
           training in the modification of smoking and over-
           eating behaviors - a pilot study
       Proceedings of the Biofeedback Research Society
           Sixth Annual Meeting
       Monterey, 1975, 25 (Abst.)

1103. Kotses, H., Glaus, K.D. & Bricel, S.K.
       Muscle relaxation effects on peak expiratory flow
          rate in asthmatic children
       Biofeedback and Self-Regulation, 1977, 2:314 (Abst.)

1104. Kotses, H., Glaus, K.D., Crawford, P.L., et al
       The effect of operant conditioning of the frontalis
          muscle on peak expiratory flow in asthmatic
          children
       Biofeedback and Self-Regulation, 1976, 1:332 (Abst.)

1105. Kotses, H., Glaus, K.D., Crawford, P.L., et al.
       Operant reduction of frontalis EMG activity in the
          treatment of asthma in children
       Journal of Psychosomatic Research, 1976, 20:453-460

1106. Krantz, D.L.
       The separate worlds of operant and nonoperant
          psychology
       Journal of Applied Behavior Analysis, 1971, 4:61-70

1107. Krippner, S.
       Research on creativity and psychedelic drugs
       International Journal of Clinical and Experimental
          Hypnosis, 1977, 25:274-290

1108. Kristt, D.A. & Engel, B.T.
       Learned control of blood pressure in patients with
          high blood pressure
       Circulation, 1975, 51:370-378

1109. Kubie, L.S. & Margolin, S.
       An apparatus for the use of breath sounds as a
          hypnogogic stimulus
       American Journal of Psychiatry, 1944, 100:610

1110. Kuhlman, W.N.
       Topography and long term feedback training of
          sensoromotor area EEG activity in normal human
          subjects
       Proceedings of the Biofeedback Research Society
          Fifth Annual Meeting
       Colorado Springs, 1974, 17 (Abst.)

1111. Kuhlman, W.N.
EEG feedback training in epileptic patients:
Clinical and neurophysiological analysis
Biofeedback and Self-Regulation, 1976, 1:345-346
(Abst.)

1112. Kuhlman, W.N. & Allison, T.
EEG feedback training in the treatment of epilepsy:
Some questions and answers
The Pavlovian Journal of Biological Science, 1977,
12:112

1113. Kuhlman, W.N. & Klieger, D.M.
Alpha enhancement: Effectiveness of two feedback
contingencies
Psychophysiology, 1975, 12:456-460

1114. Kukulka, C.G. & Basmajian, J.V.
Assessment of an audio-visual feedback device used
in motor training
American Journal of Physical Medicine, 1975, 54:194-
208

1115. Kukulka, C.G., Brown, D.M. & Basmajian, J.V.
A preliminary report on biofeedback training for
early finger joint mobilization
American Journal of Occupational Therapy, 1975,
29:469-470

1116. Kuna, D.J.
Biofeedback and severe disability
Journal of Rehabilitation, 1977, 43:20-26

1117. Kuna, D.J., Salkin, W. & Weinberger, K.
Biofeedback, relaxation training and methadone
clients: An inquiry
Contemporary Drug Problems, 1976, 5:565-572

1118. Kurtz, P.S.
Treating chemical dependency through biofeedback
Hospital Progress, 1974, 55:68-85

1119. Lacey, J. I.
Individual differences in somatic response patterns
Journal of Comparative and Physiological Psychology,
1950, 43:338

1120. Lacey, J.I.
The evaluation of autonomic response: Toward a
general solution
Annals of the New York Academy of Sciences, 1956,
67:123-164

1121. Lacey, J.I.
Somatic response patterning and stress: Some re-
visions of activation theory
In M. H. Appley & R. Trumball (Eds.), Psychological
Stress: Issues in Research
New York: Appleton-Century Crofts, 1967

1122. Lacey, J.I., Kagan, J., Lacey, B.C., et al.
The visceral level: Situational determinants and
behavioral correlates of autonomic response
patterns
In P. Knapp (Ed.), Expression of the Emotions in Man
New York: International University Press, 1963

1123. Lacey, J.I. & Lacey, B.C.
Verification and extension of the principle of
autonomic response stereotype
American Journal of Psychology, 1958, 71:50-73

1124. Lacey, J.I. & Lacey, B.C.
The law of initial value in the longitudinal study
of autonomic constitution: Reproducibility of
autonomic responses and response patterns over a
four year interval
Annals of the New York Academy of Sciences, 1962,
98:1257-1290

1125. Lacey, B.C. & Lacey, J.I.
Studies of heart rate and other bodily processes in
sensorimotor behavior
In P. A. Obrist et al (Eds.), Cardiovascular Psycho-
physiology
Chicago: Aldine Publishing Co., 1974

1126. Lacroix, J.M.
      Self-control of skin conductance and heart rate in
         the same subjects
      Psychophysiology, 1977, 14:90 (Abst.)

1127. Lacroix, J.M.
      Effects of biofeedback on the discrimination of
         electrodermal activity
      Biofeedback and Self-Regulation, 1977, 2:393-406

1128. Lacroix, J.M. & Mignault, F.B.
      Effects of feedback training on the discrimination
         of skin potential responses
      Psychophysiology, 1977, 14:90 (Abst.)

1129. Lacroix, J.M. & Roberts, L.E.
      Determinants of learned electrodermal and cardiac
         control: a comparative study
      Psychophysiology, 1976, 13:175 (Abst.)

1130. Ladd, H., Jansson, B. & Lindegren, U.
      The learning process for fine neuromuscular controls
         in skeletal muscles of man
      Electromyography and Clinical Neurophysiology, 1972,
         12:213-223

1131. Ladd, H. & Simard, T.G.
      Bilaterally controlled neuromuscular activity in
         congenitally malformed children -- an electro-
         myographic study
      Inter-Clinic Information Bulletin, 1972, 11:9-16

1132. Lader, M.H.
      Psychophysiology of clinical anxiety
      British Journal of Hospital Medicine, 1969, 2:1448-
         1451

1133. Lader, M.H. & Mathews, A.M.
      A physiological model of phobic anxiety and desen-
         sitization
      Behavior Research and Therapy, 1968, 6:411-421

1134.   Lader, M. & Mathews, A.
        Comparison of methods of relaxation using physiological
            measures
        Behavior Research and Therapy, 1970, 8:331-337

1135.   Lader, M.H. & Mathews, A.M.
        Electromyographic studies of tension
        Journal of Psychosomatic Research, 1971, 15:479-486

1136.   Lamontagne, Y., Hand, I., Annable, L., et al.
        Physiological and psychological effects of alpha and
            EMG feedback training with college drug users: A
            pilot study
        Canadian Psychiatric Association Journal, 1975,
            20:337-349

1137.   Lang, P.J.
        The on-line computer in behavior therapy research
        American Psychologist, 1969, 24:236-239

1138.   Lang, P.J.
        Autonomic control or learning to play the internal
            organs
        Psychology Today, 1970, 4:37

1139.   Lang, P.
        The application of psychophysiological methods to
            the study of psychotherapy and behavior modification
        In A. E. Bergen & S. L. Garfield (Eds.), Handbook of
            Psychotherapy and Behavior Change
        New York: Wiley & Sons, 1971

1140.   Lang, P.
        Learned control of human heart rate in a computer-
            directed environment
        In P. Obrist et al (Eds.), Cardiovascular Psycho-
            physiology
        Chicago: Aldine Publishing Co., 1974

1141.   Lang, P.J.
        Research on the specificity of feedback training:
            Implications for the use of biofeedback in the
            treatment of anxiety and fear
        In J. Beatty & H. Legewie (Eds.), Biofeedback and
            Behavior
        New York: Plenum Press, 1977

1142. Lang, P.J., Sroufe, L.A. & Hastings, J.E.
       Effects of feedback and instructional set on the
          control of cardiac rate variability
       Journal of Experimental Psychology, 1967, 75:425-431

1143. Lang, P.J., Troyer, W.G., Twentyman, C.T. et al.
       Differential effects of heart rate modification
          training on college students, older males, and
          patients with ischemic heart disease
       Psychosomatic Medicine, 1975, 37:429-446

1144. Lang, P.J. & Twentyman, C.T.
       Learning to control heart rate: Binary vs. analogue
          feedback
       Psychophysiology, 1974, 11:616-629

1145. Lang, P.J. & Twentyman, C.T.
       Learning to control heart rate: Effects of varying
          incentive and criterion of success on task per-
          formance
       Psychophysiology, 1976, 13:378-385

1146. Lanyon, R.I.
       Effect of biofeedback-based relaxation on stuttering
          during reading and spontaneous speech
       Journal of Consulting and Clinical Psychology, 1977,
          45:860-866

1147. Lanyon, R.I., Barrington, C.C. & Newman, A.C.
       Modification of stuttering through EMG biofeedback:
          A preliminary study
       Behavior Therapy, 1976, 7:96-103

1148. Lavallee, Y.J. & Lamontagne, Y.
       Therapeutic applications of biological feedback
       Union Med Canada, 1974, 103:264-271

1149. Lavallee, Y., Lamontagne, Y., Pinard, G., et al
       Effects of EMG feedback, diazepam and their combina-
          tion on chronic anxiety
       Journal of Psychosomatic Research, 1977, 21:65-71

1150. Lawrence, G.H. & Johnson, L.C.
       Biofeedback and performance
       In G.E. Schwartz & J. Beatty (Eds.), Biofeedback:
         Theory and Research
       New York: Academic Press, 1977

1151. Laye, R.C.
       Acquisition and control of occipital alpha: Indi-
         vidual differences and the effects of contingent
         immediate and delayed feedback
       Biofeedback and Self-Regulation, 1976, 1:345 (Abst.)

1152. Laws, D.R. & Pawlowski, A.V.
       The application of a multi-purpose biofeedback
         device to penile plethysmography
       Journal of Behavior Therapy and Experimental
         Psychiatry, 1973, 4:339-343

1153. Laws, D.R. & Rubin, H.B.
       Instructional control of an autonomic sexual response
       Journal of Applied Behavioral Analysis, 1969, 2:93-
         99

1154. Lazarus, R.
       A cognitively oriented psychologist looks at biofeed-
         back
       American Psychologist, 1975, 30:553-561

1155. Lazarus, R.S.
       A cognitive analysis of biofeedback control
       In G. E. Schwartz & J. Beatty (Eds.) Biofeedback:
         Theory and Research
       New York: Academic Press, 1977

1156. Leaf, B. & Gaarder, K.R.
       A simplified electromyograph feedback apparatus for
         relaxation training
       Journal of Behavior Therapy and Experimental
         Psychiatry, 1971, 2:39-43

1157. LeBoeuf, A.
       The importance of individual differences in the
         treatment of chronic anxiety by EMG feedback
         technique
       Proceedings of the Biofeedback Research Society
         Fifth Annual Meeting
       Colorado Springs, 1974, 47 (Abst.)

1158. LeBoeuf, A.
       The treatment of a severe tremor by electromyogram
          feedback
       Journal of Behavior Therapy and Experimental
          Psychology, 1976, 7:59-63

1159. LeBoeuf, A.
       The effects of EMG feedback training on state
          anxiety in introverts and extroverts
       Journal of Clinical Psychology, 1977, 33:251-253

1160. LeBoeuf, A. & Hurrell, M.
       EMG feedback training: Increasing resistance to
          extinction
       Proceedings of the Biofeedback Research Society
          Sixth Annual Meeting
       Monterey, 1975, 7 (Abst.)

1161. LeBow, M.D.
       Operant conditioning-based behavior modification:
          One approach to treating somatic disorders
       Psychiatry in Medicine, 1975, 6:241-254

1162. Ledberg, L., Schalling, D. & Levander, S.E.
       Some characteristics of digital vasomotor activity
       Psychophysiology, 1972, 9:402-411

1163. Lee, K.H., et al.
       Myofeedback for muscle retraining in hemiplegic
          patients
       Archives of Physical Medicine and Rehabilitation,
          1976, 57:588-591

1164. Lee, R.M., Caldwell, J.R. & Lee, J.A.
       Blood pressure teaching systems and their applica-
          tion to biofeedback
       Biofeedback and Self-Regulation, 1977, 2:435-447

1165. Leeb, C., Fahrion, S. & French, D.
       Instructional set, deep relaxation and growth en-
          hancement: A pilot study
       Journal of Humanistic Psychology, 1976, 16:71-78

1166. Leeb, C., Fahrion, S., French, D., et al.
       Shifts in internalization-externalization following
         a massed practice multi-modality biofeedback
         training period
       Proceedings of the Biofeedback Research Society
         Fifth Annual Meeting
       Colorado Springs, 1974, 10 (Abst.)

1167. Leeb, C., French, D. & Fahrion, S.
       The effect of instructional set on autogenic
         biofeedback hand temperature training
       Proceedings of the Biofeedback Research Society
         Fifth Annual Meeting
       Colorado Springs, 1974, 60 (Abst.)

1168. Leeb, C., French, D., Fahrion, S., et al.
       Voluntary control of hand temperature: Increase and
         decrease
       Proceedings of the Biofeedback Research Society
         Fifth Annual Meeting
       Colorado Springs, 1974, 61 (Abst.)

1169. Lefcourt, H.
       Locus of Control
       Hillsdale, NJ: Lawrence Erlbaum, 1976

1170. Leff, H.S.
       A case study of scientists' opinions about the
         regulations of their work: Opinions of the
         members of the Society for Psychophysiological
         Research about the regulation of biofeedback
         research and technology
       Psychophysiology, 1973, 10:536-543

1171. Legalos, C.N.
       Biofeedback and psychotherapy
       Seminars in Psychiatry, 1973, 5:529-533

1172. Legewie, H.
       Subjective correlates of EEG feedback: Discrimination
         learning or superstition?
       Proceedings of the Biofeedback Research Society
         Sixth Annual Meeting
       Monterey, 1975, 36 (Abst.)

1173. Legewie, H.
Clinical implications of biofeedback
In J. Beatty & H. Legewie (Eds.), Biofeedback and
Behavior
New York: Plenum Press, 1977

1174. Legewie, H., Cleary, P. & Rackensberger, W.
EMG recording and biofeedback in the diagnosis and
therapy of stuttering: A case study
European Journal of Behavioral Analysis and Modification, 1975, 1:137

1175. Legewie, H. & Nusselt, L.
Application of biofeedback in the therapy of
Parkinson's disease
Proceedings of the Biofeedback Research Society
Fourth Annual Meeting
Boston, 1972, 43 (Abst.)

1176. Legewie, H. & Nusselt, L.
Biofeedback-Therapie: Lernmethoden in der Psycho-
somatik, Neurologie und Rehabilitation, 6
Munchen, Germany: Urban and Schwartzenberg, 1975

1177. Legewie, H. & Probst, W.
On-line analysis of EEG with a small computer
(period-amplitude analysis)
Electroencephalography and Clinical Neurophysiology,
1969, 27:533-536

1178. Lehmann, D.
Topography of spontaneous alpha EEG fields in
humans
Electroencephalography and Clinical Neurophysiology,
1971, 30:161

1179. Lehmann, D.
Multichannel topography of human alpha EEG fields
Electroencephalography and Clinical Neurophysiology,
1971, 31:439-449

1180. Lehmann, D., Lang, W. & Debruyne, P.
Controlled EEG alpha feedback training in normals
and headache patients
Archives of Psychiatry Nervenkr, 1976, 221:331-343

1181. Lehrer, P.M.
       Physiological effects of relaxation in a double
          blind analogue of desensitization
       Behavior Therapy, 1972, 3:193-208

1182. Lehrer, P.M.
       The physiological effects of relaxation in anxiety
          neurotic patients and the physiological effects of
          relaxation and alpha‾feedback in "normal" subjects
       Psychophysiology, 1977, 14:93 (Abst.)

1183. Leib, W., Tryon, W.W. & Stroebel, C.S.
       Alpha biofeedback: Fact or artifact
       Psychophysiology, 1976, 13:541-545

1184. Leibrecht, B.C., Lloyd, A.J. & Pounder, S.
       Auditory feedback and conditioning of the single
          motor unit
       Psychophysiology, 1973, 10:1-7

1185. Leitenberg, H., et al.
       Feedback in behavior modification: An experimental
          analysis in two phobic cases
       Journal of Applied Behavior Analysis, 1968, 1:131

1186. Lesh, T.V.
       Zen meditation and the development of empathy in
          counselors
       Journal of Humanistic Psychology, 1970, 10:39-74

1187. Letourneau, J.E. & Ludlam, W.M.
       Biofeedback reinforcement in the training of limi-
          tation of gaze: a case report
       American Journal of Opthomology and Physiological
          Optometry, 1976, 53:672-676

1188. Levee, J.R., Cohen, M.J. & Rickles, W.H.
       Electromyographic biofeedback for relief of tension
          in the fascial and throat muscles of a woodwind
          musician
       Biofeedback and Self-Regulation, 1976, 1:133-120

1189. Levendusky, P. & Pankratz, L.
      Self-control techniques as an alternative to pain
         medication
      Journal of Abnormal Psychology, 1975, 84:165-168

1190. Levene, H.I., Engel, B.T. & Pearsen, J.A.
      Differential operant conditioning
      Psychosomatic Medicine, 1968, 30:837-845

1191. Levenson, R.W.
      Automated system for direct measurement and feedback
         of total respiratory resistance by the forced
         oscillation technique
      Psychophysiology, 1974, 11:86-90

1192. Levenson, R.W.
      Feedback effects and respiratory involvement in
         voluntary control of heart rate
      Psychophysiology, 1976, 13:108-114

1193. Levenson, R.W.
      Effects of subjects' anxiety on ability to control
         heart rate and utilize biofeedback
      Psychophysiology, 1976, 13:174 (Abst.)

1194. Levenson, R.W.
      Cardiac-somatic relationships and feedback effects
         in a multiple session heart rate control experiment
      Psychophysiology, 1977, 14:84-5 (Abst.)

1195. Levenson, R.W., Gross, G.H. & Doxas, G.
      Effects of biofeedback training on subjects differing
         in initial ability to control heart rate
      Biofeedback and Self-Regulation, 1976, 1:320 (Abst.)

1196. Levenson, R.W., Manuck, S.B., Strupp, H.H., et al.
      A biofeedback technique for bronchial asthma
      Proceedings of the Biofeedback Research Society
         Fifth Annual Meeting
      Colorado Springs, 1974, 11 (Abst.)

1197. Levenson, R.W. & Strupp, H.H.
      Simultaneous feedback and control of heart rate
         and respiration rate
      Proceedings of the Biofeedback Research Society
         Fourth Annual Meeting
      Boston, 1972, 19 (Abst.)

1198. Levenson, R.W. & Strupp, H.H.
      Simultaneous feedback and control of heart rate
        and respiration rate
      Psychophysiology, 1973, 10:200 (Abst.)

1199. Lewis, C.N. & McLaughlin, T.J.
      Baseline and feedback EEG correlates of interview
        behavior
      Psychophysiology, 1976, 13:302-306

1200. Lewis, T. & Pickering, G.W.
      Vasodilation in the limbs in response to warming the
        body
      Heart, 1931, 16:33-51

1201. Lewis, L. & Schmeidler, G.R.
      Alpha relations with nonintentional and purposeful
        extrasensory perception after feedback
      Journal of American Society for Psychical Research,
        1971, 65:455-467

1202. Libby, W.L., Lacey, B.C. & Lacey, J.I.
      Pupillary and cardiac activity during visual
        attention
      Psychophysiology, 1973, 10:270-294

1203. Libo, L.M. & Fehmi, L.
      Cognitive strategies in biofeedback training of
        peripheral skin temperature
      Biofeedback and Self-Regulation, 1977, 2:293 (Abst.)

1204. Lick, J.R.
      Expectancy, false GSR feedback and systematic desen-
        sitization in the modification of severe phobic
        behavior
      Dissertation Abstracts, 1972, 33B:2814-2815

1205. Lick, J.
      Expectancy, false galvanic skin response to feed-
        back, and systematic desensitization in the
        modification of phobic behavior
      Journal of Consulting and Clinical Psychology, 1975,
        43:557-567

1206. Lick, J.R. & Heffler, D.
      Relaxation training and attention placebo in the
          treatment of severe insomnia
      Journal of Consulting and Clinical Psychology, 1977,
          45:153-161

1207. Lidberg, L., Schalling, D. & Levander, S.
      Some characteristics of digital vasomotor activity
      Psychophysiology, 1972, 9:402-411

1208. Liebhart, E.H.
      Effects of false heart rate feedback and task
          instructions on information search, attributions
          and stimulus ratings
      Psychological Research, 1977, 39:185-201

1209. Linden, W.
      Practicing of meditation by school children and
          their levels of field dependence-independence,
          test anxiety, and reading achievement
      Journal of Consulting and Clinical Psychology, 1973,
          1:139-143

1210. Lindsley, D.B. & Sassaman, W.H.
      Autonomic activation and brain potentials associated
          with "voluntary" control of the pilomotors
      Journal of Neurophysiology, 1938, 1:343-349

1211. Lipowski, Z.J.
      Psychosomatic medicine in the seventies: An over-
          view
      American Journal of Psychiatry, 1977, 134:233-244

1212. Lippold, O.
      Electromyography
      In P.H. Venables & I. Martin (Eds.), A Manual of
          Psychophysiological Methods
      New York: John Wiley & Sons, 1967

1213. Lippold, O. & Novotny, G.
      Is alpha rhythm an artifact?
      Lancet, 1970, 1:976-979

1214. Lippold, O. & Shaw, J.
Alpha rhythm in the blind
Nature, 1971, 232:134

1215. Lisina, M.I.
The role of orientation in the transformation of
involuntary reactions into voluntary ones
In L. G. Voronin, A.N. Leontiev, A.R. Luria, E.N.
Sokolov, & O.S. Winogradova: Orienting Reflex and
Exploratory Behavior
Washington: American Institute of Biological
Sciences, 1965

1216. Lloyd, A.J.
Auditory EMG feedback during a sustained submaximum
isometric contraction
Research Quarterly of the American Association of
Health and Physical Education, 1972, 43:39-46

1217. Lloyd, A.J. & Leibrecht, B.C.
Conditioning of a single motor unit
Journal of Experimental Psychology, 1971, 88:391-395

1218. Lloyd, A.J. & Shurley, J.T.
The effects of sensory perceptual isolation on
single motor unit conditioning
Psychophysiology, 1976, 13:340-344

1219. Locke, S.E. & Heisel, J.S.
The influence of stress and emotions on the human
immune response
Biofeedback and Self-Regulation, 1977, 2:320 (Abst.)

1220. Lomont, J.F. & Edwards, J.E.
The role of relaxation in systematic desensitization
Behavior Research and Therapy, 1967, 5:11-25

1221. London, P., Hart, J.T. & Leibovitz, M.P.
EEG alpha rhythms and susceptibility to hypnosis
Nature, 1968, 219:71-72

1222. London, P., Cooper., L.M. & Engstrom, D.R.
Increasing hypnotic susceptibility by brain wave
feedback
Journal of Abnormal Psychology, 1974, 83:554-560

1223. London, P., Hart, J.T. & Liebovitz, M.P.
      EEG alpha rhythms and susceptibility to hypnosis
      Nature, 1968, 219:71-72

1224. Lopatto, D. & Williams, J.L.
      Self-control: A critical review and an alternative
         interpretation
      The Psychological Record, 1976, 26:3-12

1225. Love, W.A.
      Problems in therapeutic application of EMG feedback
      Proceedings of the Biofeedback Research Society
         Fourth Annual Meeting
      Boston, 1972, 41 (Abst.)

1226. Love, W.A., Jr., Hochman, N., Blanton, F., et al.
      EMG feedback and relaxation training as an ancillary
         treatment for elevated intracular pressure
      Biofeedback and Self-Regulation, 1976, 1:327-328
         (Abst.)

1227. Love, W.A., Montgomery, D.D. & Moeller, T.A.
      A post hoc analysis of correlates of blood pressure
         reduction
      Proceedings of the Biofeedback Research Society
         Fifth Annual Meeting
      Colorado Springs, 1974, 34 (Abst.)

1228. Love, W.A., Jr., Montgomery, D.D. & Weston, A.A.
      The treatment of essential hypertension with EMG
         feedback and blood pressure feedback
      Proceedings of the Biofeedback Research Society
         Sixth Annual Meeting
      Monterey, 1975, 15 (Abst.)

1229. Lowenstein, T.J.
      Multimodality feedback and relaxation training in
         desensitization of one client
      Biofeedback and Self-Regulation, 1977, 2:314-315 (Abst

1230. Lubar, J.F.
      Behavioral management of epilepsy through sensori-
         motor rhythm EEG biofeedback conditioning
      National Spokesman, 1975, 8:6-7

1231. Lubar, J.F.
Maintenance of seizure control in epileptics during
long-term sensorimotor rhythm training and post-
training follow-up
Biofeedback and Self-Regulation, 1976, 1:346-347 (Abst.)

1232. Lubar, J.F.
Electroencephalographic biofeedback methodology and
management of epilepsy.
Pavlovian Journal, 1977, 12:147-185

1233. Lubar, J.F. & Bahler, W.W.
Behavioral management of epileptic seizures following
EEG biofeedback training of the sensorimotor
rhythm
Biofeedback and Self-Regulation, 1976, 1:77-104

1234. Lubar, J.F. & Seifert, A.R.
Patient control of the sensorimotor rhythm in the
management of epilepsy
Proceedings of the Biofeedback Research Society
Sixth Annual Meeting
Monterey, 1975, 49 (Abst.)

1235. Lubar, J.F. & Shouse, M.N.
EEG and behavioral changes in a hyperkinetic child
concurrent with training of the sensorimotor
rhythm (SMR): A preliminary report
Biofeedback and Self-Regulation, 1976, 1:293-306

1236. Lubar, J.F. & Shouse, M.N.
Use of biofeedback in the treatment of seizure
disorders and hyperactivity
In Advances in Child Clinical Psychology
New York: Plenum Press, 1977 (in press)

1237. Luborsky, L., Brady, J.P., McClintock, M., et al.
Estimating ones own blood pressure: Effects of feed-
back training
Psychosomatic Medicine, 1976, 38:426-438

1238. Lubin, A., Johnson, L. & Austin, M.
Discrimination among states of consciousness using
EEG spectra
Psychophysiology, 1969, 6:122-132

1239. Lucas, E.A. & Sterman, M.B.
The polycyclic sleep-wake cycle in the cat: Effects
produced by SMR conditioning
Experimental Neurology, 1974, 42:347-368

1240. Luce, G. & Peper, E.
Biofeedback: Mind over body, mind over mind
New York Times Magazine, September 12, 1971

1241. Ludwig, A.M.
Altered states of consciousness
Archives of General Psychiatry, 1966, 15:225-234

1242. Lundervold, A.J.S.
Electromyographic investigations of tense and re-
laxed subjects
Journal of Nervous and Mental Disease, 1952, 115:512-
525

1243. Luparello, T., Lyons, H.A., Bleecker, E.R., et al.
Influences of suggestion on airway reactivity in
asthmatic patients
Psychosomatic Medicine, 1968, 30:819-825

1244. Luthe, W.
Autogenic training: Method, research and application
in medicine
American Journal of Psychotherapy, 1963, 17:174-195

1245. Luthe, W. (Ed.).
Autogenic training: Correlations Psychosomaticae
New York: Grune & Stratton, 1965

1246. Luthe, W. (Ed.).
Autogenic Therapy
New York: Grune & Stratton, 1969

1247. Luthe, W. & Schultz, J.H.
Autogenic therapy, medical applications
New York: Grune & Stratton, 1969

1248. Luthe, W., Jus, A. & Geissman, P.
Autogenic state and autogenic shift: Psychophysiologic
and neurophysiologic aspects
Acta Psychotherapeutica, 1963, 11:1-13

1249. Lutker, E.
Treatment of migraine headache by conditioned re-
laxation: A case study
Behavior Therapy, 1971, 2:592-593

1250. Lutzenberger, W., Birbaumer, N. & Steinmetz, P.
Simultaneous biofeedback of heart rate and frontal
EMG as a pretraining for the control of EEG theta
activity
Biofeedback and Self-Regulation, 1976, 1:395-410

1251. Lutzenberger, W., Birbaumer, N. & Wildgruber, C.
An experiment on the feedback of the theta activity
of the human EEG
European Journal of Behavioral Analysis and Modification, 1975, 2:119-126

1252. Lynch, J.J.
The stimulus-the ghost-the response: The carousel
of conditioning
Conditional Reflex, 1970, 5:133-139

1253. Lynch, J.J.
Biofeedback: Some reflections on modern behavioral
science
Seminars in Psychiatry, 1973, 5:555-562

1254. Lynch, J.J. & Paskewitz, D.A.
On the mechanisms of the feedback control of human
brain wave activity
Journal of Nervous and Mental Disease, 1971, 153:205-
217

1255. Lynch, J.J., Paskewitz, D.A., Gimbel, K.S., et al.
Psychological aspects of cardiac arrhythmia
American Heart Journal, 1977, 93:645-657

1256. Lynch, J.J., Paskewitz, D.A. & Orne, M.T.
Some factors in the feedback control of human alpha
rhythm
Psychosomatic Medicine, 1974, 36:399-410

1257. Lynch, J.J., Paskewitz, D.A. & Orne, M.T.
       Inter-session stability of human alpha rhythm
          densities
       Electroencephalography and Clinical Neurophysiology,
          1974, 36:538-540

1258. Lynch, J.J., Paskewitz, D.A., Orne, M.T. & Costello,
          J.
       An analysis of the feedback control of alpha activity
       Conditional Reflex, 1970, 5:185-186 (Abst.)

1259. Lynch, W.C., Hama, H., Kohn, S. & Miller, N.
       Instrumental learning of vasomotor responses: A
          progress report
       Proceedings of the Biofeedback Research Society
          Fifth Annual Meeting
       Colorado Springs, 1974, 68 (Abst.)

1260. Lynch, W.C., Hama, H., Kohn, S. & Miller, N.
       Instrumental control with peripheral vasomotor
          responses in children
       Psychophysiology, 1976, 13:219-221

1261. Lynch, W.C., Schuri, U. & D'Anna, J.
       Effects of isometric muscle tension on vasomotor
          activity and heart rate
       Psychophysiology, 1976, 13:222-230

1262. Lyndes, K.
       Application of biofeedback to functional dysphonia
       Proceedings of the Biofeedback Research Society
          Sixth Annual Meeting
       Monterey, 1975, 24 (Abst.)

1263. Lyndes, K.O.
       EMG biofeedback and its application to demonstrated
          laryngeal pathology
       Biofeedback and Self-Regulation, 1976, 1:328-329
          (Abst.)

1264. Lyon, C., Blankstein, K.R. & Darte, E.
       Long-term instructional and feedback control of
          heart rate slowing in good versus poor controllers
       Biofeedback and Self-Regulation, 1976, 1:320-321
          (Abst.)

✗1265. Macdonough, T.S.
       The relative effectiveness of a medical hospitaliza-
          tion program vs. a feedback-behavior modification
          program in treating alcohol and drug abusers
       International Journal of Addiction, 1976, 11:269-282

 1266. Machac, M.
       Vasomotor response to intentional autoregulative
          operations of the relaxation activation method
       Activitas Nervosa Superior (Praha), 1969, 11:42-45

 1267. Macpherson, E.L.R.
       Control of involuntary movement: EMG control of
          Huntingtons Chorea
       Behavior Research and Therapy, 1967, 5:143-145

 1268. Magnusson, E.
       The effects of controlled muscle tension on per-
          formance and learning of heart rate control
       Biological Psychology, 1976, 4:81-92

 1269. Mahoney, M.J.
       Research issues in self-management
       Behavior Therapy, 1972, 3:45-63

 1270. Mahoney, M.J.
       The behavioral treatment of obesity: A reconnaissance
       Biofeedback and Self-Regulation, 1976, 1:127-133

 1271. Mainardi, J.A., Victor, R. & Shapiro, D.
       Voluntary control of heart rate: Effects on heart
          rate and pain during the cold pressor test
       Psychophysiology, 1977, 14:81-82 (Abst.)

 1272. Malmo, R.
       Viseral learning: Learning to control the un-
          controllable
       Science News, 1970, 97:274-275

 1273. Malmo, R.B., Shagass, C. & Davis, J.F.
       Electromyographic studies of muscular tension in
          psychiatric patients under stress
       Journal of Clinical and Experimental Psychopathology,
          1951, 12:45-66

1274. Malmo, R.B. & Smith, A.A.
Forehead tension and motor irregularities in psycho-
neurotic patients under stress
Journal of Personality, 1955, 23:391-406

1275. Mandler, G. & Kremer, I.
Autonomic feedback: A correlational study
Journal of Personality, 1958, 26:388-399

1276. Mandler, G., Mandler, J.M. & Uviller, E.T.
Autonomic feedback: The perception of autonomic
activity
Journal of Abnormal and Social Psychology, 1958,
56:367-378

1277. Mandler, G., Previn, D.W. & Kuhlman, C.K.
Effects of operant conditioning on the GSR
Journal of the Experimental Analysis of Behavior,
1962, 5:317-321

1278. Manuck, S.B.
The voluntary control of heart rate under differential
somatic restraint
Biofeedback and Self-Regulation, 1976, 1:273-284

1279. Manuck, S.B., Levenson, R.W., Hinricksen, J.J., et al.
Role of feedback in voluntary control of heart rate
Perceptual and Motor Skills, 1975, 40:747-752

1280. Marcus, N. & Levin, G.
Clinical applications of biofeedback: Implications
for psychiatry
Hospital and Community Psychiatry, 1977, 28:21-25

1281. Marinacci, A.A.
Clinical Electromyography
Los Angeles: San Lucas Press, 1955

1282. Marinacci, A.A.
Lower motor neuron disorders superimposed on the
residuals of poliomyelitus. Value of the electromyogram in differential diagnosis
Bulletin of the Los Angeles Neurological Society,
1960, 25:18

1283. Marinacci, A.A.
Applied Electromyography
Philadelphia: Lea & Feabiger, 1968

1284. Marinacci, A.A.
The basic principles underlying neuromuscular re-
education
In D. Shapiro et al (Eds.), Biofeedback and Self-
Control, 1972: An Aldine Annual on the Regulation
of Bodily Processes and Consciousness
Chicago: Aldine Publishing Co., 1973

1285. Marinacci, A.A. & Horande, M.
Electromyogram in neuromuscular reeducation
Bulletin of the Los Angeles Neurological Society,
1960, 25:57-71

1286. Marsden, C., Meadows, J. & Hodgson, H.
Observations on the reflex response to muscle vibra-
tion in man and its voluntary control
Brain 1969, 92:829-846

1287. Marsden, C.D., Merton, P.A. & Morton, H.B.
Servo action in human voluntary movements
Nature, 1972, 238:140-143

1288. Marshall, M.S. & Bentler, P.M.
The effects of deep physical relaxation and low
frequency alpha brainwaves on alpha subjective
reports
Psychophysiology, 1976, 13:505-516

1289. Marston, A.R. & Feldman, S.E.
Toward the use of self-control in behavior modification
Journal of Consulting and Clinical Psychology, 1972,
39:429-433

1290. Martin, J.E. & Sachs, D.A.
The effects of visual feedback on the fine motor
behavior of a deaf cerebral palsied child
Journal of Nervous and Mental Disease, 1973, 157:59-
62

1291. Martindale, C. & Armstrong, J.
      The relationship of creativity to cortical activation
         and its operant control
      Journal of Genetic Psychology, 1974, 12:311-320

1292. Martindale, C. & Hines, D.
      Creativity and cortical activation during creative,
         intellectual and EEG feedback tasks
      Biological Psychiatry 1975, 3:91-100

1293. Masi, N. & Moore, R.
      A skeptical look at EMG training in the reduction of
         blood pressure in essential hypertensives
      Biofeedback and Self-Regulation, 1976, 1:310 (Abst.)

1294. Mason, J.W.
      A historical view of the stress field
      Journal of Human Stress, 1975, 1:6-12 and 22-35

1295. Massaro, D.W.
      The effects of feedback on psychophysical tasks
      Perception and Psychophysics, 1969, 6:89-91

1296. Masters, J.C. & Santrock, J.W.
      Studies in the self-regulation of behavior: Effects
         of contingent cognitive and affective events
      Developmental Psychology, 1976, 12:334-348

1297. Matheson, D.W., Edelson, R., Hiatrides, D., et al.
      Relaxation measured by EMG as a function of vibro-
         tactile stimulation
      Biofeedback and Self-Regulation, 1976, 1:285-292

1298. Mathews, A.M. & Gelder, M.G.
      Psychophysiologic investigations of brief relaxation
         training
      Journal of Psychosomatic Research, 1969, 13:1-12

1299. Matus, I.
      Internal awareness, muscle sense, and muscle re-
         laxation in bioelectric information feedback-
         training
      Dissertation Abstracts International 1972, 33:1309

1300. Matus, I.
    Select personality variables and tension in two
        muscle groups
    Psychophysiology, 1974, 11:91-92

1301. Matus, I., Stilson, D.W. & Ball, G.
    Subjective awareness of muscle activity as a
        correlate of tension levels
    Biofeedback and Self-Regulation, 1976, 1:358 (Abst.)

1302. Matyas, T.A. & King, M.G.
    Stable T wave effects during improvement of heart
        rate control with biofeedback
    Physiology and Behavior, 1976, 16:15-20

1303. Maupin, E.W.
    Individual differences in response to a Zen medi-
        tation exercise
    Journal of Consulting Psychology, 1965, 29:139-145

1304. May, D.S. & Weber, C.A.
    Temperature feedback training for symptom reduction
        in primary and secondary Raynauds Disease
    Biofeedback and Self-Regulation, 1976, 1:317 (Abst.)

1305. Mayr, O.
    The origins of feedback control
    Scientific American, 1970, 223:110-118

1306. Meares, R.
    Behavior therapy and spasmodic torticollis
    Archives of General Psychiatry, 1973, 28:104-107

1307. Medina, J.L., Diamond, S. & Franklin, M.A.
    Biofeedback therapy for migraine
    Headache, 1976, 16:115-118

1308. Meichenbaum, D.
    Cognitive factors in biofeedback therapy
    Biofeedback and Self-Regulation, 1976, 1:201-216
        (Abst.)

1309. Meichenbaum, D.
    Toward a cognitive theory of self-control
    In G. E. Schwartz & D. Shapiro (Eds.), Consciousness
        and Self-Regulation
    New York: Plenum Press, 1976

1310. Meichenbaum, D.
      Cognitive Behavior Modification: An Integrative
         Approach
      New York: Plenum Press, 1976

1311. Mehearg, L.E. & Eschette, N.
      EMG measures and subjective reports of tension in
         feedback and no-feedback groups
      Proceedings of the Biofeedback Research Society
         Sixth Annual Meeting
      Monterey, 1975, 3 (Abst.)

1312. Melzack, R. & Perry, C.
      Self-regulation of pain: The use of alpha feedback
         and hypnotic training for the control of pain
      Experimental Neurology, 1975, 46:452-469

1313. Menzies, R.
      Conditioned vasomotor responses in human subjects
      Journal of Psychology, 1937, 4:75-120

1314. Menzies, R.
      Further studies of conditioned vasomotor responses
         in human subjects
      Journal of Experimental Psychology, 1941, 29:457-482

1315. Mercadel, D. & Murphy, P.
      The contributions of biofeedback training and cir-
         cadian rhythms in learning to relax
      Biofeedback and Self-Regulation, 1977, 2:315 (Abst.)

1316. Meyer-Osterkamp, S., Grusche, A. & Cohen, R.
      An investigation on operant control of heart rate
      Zeitschrift fur Klinische Psychologie, 1972, 3:213-231

1317. Michaels, R.R., Huber, M.H. & McCann, D.S.
      Evaluation of transcendental meditation as a
         method of reducing stress
      Science, 1976, 192:1242-1244

1318. Middaugh, S.J.
      Single motor unit control with EMG feedback, non-
         feedback performance, and discrimination of motor
         unit level events
      Psychophysiology, 1977, 14:102 (Abst.)

1319. Middaugh, P., Eissenberg, E. & Brener, J.
       The effect of artificial ventilation on cardio-
          vascular status and on heart rate conditioning in
          the curarized rat
       Psychophysiology, 1975, 12:520-526

1320. Millard, W.J.
       A retrospective consideration of neuromuscular
          blockade as a control procedure in autonomic
          response modification: Methodological ramifications
       Proceedings of the Biofeedback Research Society
          Sixth Annual Meeting
       Monterey, 1975, 10 (Abst.)

1321. Miller, M.P., Miller, T.P., Murphy, P.J., et al.
       The effects of EMG feedback and progressive re-
          laxation training on stress reactions in dental
          patients
       Biofeedback and Self-Regulation, 1976, 1:329-330
          (Abst.)

1322. Miller, N.E.
       Integration of neurophysiological and behavioral
          research
       Annals of the New York Academy of Sciences, 1961,
          92:830-839

1323. Miller, N.E.
       Visceral learning and other additional facts poten-
          tially applicable to psychotherapy
       International Psychiatry Clinics, 1968, 6:294-312

1324. Miller, N.E.
       Psychosomatic effects of specific types of training
       Annals of the New York Academy of Sciences, 1969,
          159:1025-1040

1325. Miller, N.
       Learning of visceral and glandular responses
       Science, 1969, 163:434-445

1326. Miller, N.E.
       Interactions between learned and physical factors in
          mental illness
       Seminars in Psychiatry, 1972, 4:239-254

1327. Miller, N.E.
       Learning of glandular and visceral responses:
          Postscript
       In D. Singh & C.T. Morgan (Eds.), Current Status of
          Physiological Psychology Readings
       Monterey: Brooks-Cole, 1972

1328. Miller, N.E.
       Synopsis of subsequent work on visceral learning
       In D. Singh & C. T. Morgan (Eds.), Current Status of
          Physiological Psychology
       Monterey: Brooks-Cole, 1972

1329. Miller, N.E.
       Biofeedback: Evaluation of a new technique
       New England Journal of Medicine, 1974, 290:684-685

1330. Miller, N.E.
       Application of learning and biofeedback to psychiatry
          and medicine
       In A. M. Freedman, H.K. Kaplan & B. J. Sadock (Eds.),
          Comprehensive Textbook of Psychiatry
       Baltimore: Williams & Wilkins, 1975

1331. Miller, N.E.
       Clinical applications of biofeedback: Voluntary
          control of heart rate, rhythm, and blood pressure
       In H. I. Russek (Ed.), New Horizons in Cardiovascular
          Practice
       Baltimore: University Park Press, 1975

1332. Miller, N.E. & Banuazizi, A.
       Instrumental learning by curarized rats of a
          specific visceral response, intestinal or cardiac
       Journal of Comparative and Physiological Psychology,
          1968, 65:17

1333. Miller, N.E., Barber, T.X., DiCara, L.V., Kamiya,
          J., Shapiro, D. & Stoyva, J. (Eds.)
       Biofeedback and Self-Control 1973: An Aldine Annual
          on the Regulation of Bodily Processes and Conscious-
          ness
       Chicago: Aldine Publishing Co., 1974

1334. Miller, N.E. & Carmona, A.
      Modification of a visceral response, salivation in
         thirsty dogs, by instrumental training with water
         reward
      Journal of Comparative and Physiological Psychology,
         1967, 63:1-6.

1335. Miller, N.E. & DiCara, L.
      Instrumental learning of heart rate changes in
         curarized rats: Shaping and specificity to
         discriminative stimulus
      Journal of Comparative and Physiological Psychology,
         1967, 63:12-19

1336. Miller, N.E. & DiCara, L.V.
      Instrumental learning of urine formation by rats;
         changes in renal blood flow
      American Journal of Physiology, 1968, 215:677-683

1337. Miller, N.E. & DiCara, L.V.
      New possibilities for glandular and visceral re-
         education
      Psychophysiology, 1969, 5:562 (Abst.)

1338. Miller, N.E., DiCara, L. & Banuazizi, A.
      Instrumental learning of glandular and visceral
         responses
      Conditional Reflex, 1968, 3:129

1339. Miller, N.E., DiCara, L.V., Solomon, H., et al.
      Learned modifications of autonomic functions: A review
         and some new data
      Circulation Research Supplement I, 1970, 27:3-11

1340. Miller, N.E. & Dworkin, B.R.
      Visceral learning: Recent difficulties with curarized
         rats and significant problems for human research
      In P. Obrist et al (Eds), Cardiovascular Psychophysiology
      Chicago: Aldine 1Publishing Co.,   1974

1341. Miller, N. & Dworkin, B.
      Effects of learning on visceral functions - biofeedback
      New England Journal of Medicine, 1977, 296:1274-1278

1342. Miller, N.E. & Dworkin, B.
       Critical issues in therapeutic applications of
         biofeedback
       In G. E. Schwartz & J. Beatty (Eds.), Biofeedback:
         Theory and Research
       New York: Academic Press, 1977

1343. Miller, R.M., Coger, R.W. & Dymond, A.M.
       Biofeedback skin conductance conditioning in dyshi-
         drotic eczema
       Archives of Dermatology, 1974, 109:737-738

1344. Mills, G.K. & Solyom, L.
       Biofeedback of EEG alpha in the treatment of ob-
         sessive ruminations: An exploration
       Journal of Behavior Therapy and Experimental
         Psychiatry, 1974, 5:37-41

1345. Misovich, S.G.
       Some effects of arousal, false GSR feedback and
         three types of drug reaction expectations on
         affective judgments
       Dissertation Abstracts, 1970, 30A:3095

1346. Misovich, S.
       Some effects of arousal and false GSR feedback on
         affective judgments
       Psychological Reports, 1974, 34:351-358

1347. Mitch, P.S., McGrady, A. & Iannone, A.
       Autogenic feedback training in treatment of migraine:
         A clinical report
       Proceedings of the Biofeedback Research Society
         Sixth Annual Meeting
       Monterey, 1975, 56 (Abst.)

1348. Mitch, P.S., McGrady, A. & Iannone, A.
       Autogenic feedback training in migraine: A treatment
         report
       Headache, 1976, 15:267-270

1349. Mittelmann, B. & Wolff, H.G.
       Affective states and skin temperature: Experimental
         study of subjects with "cold hands" and Raynaud's
         syndrome
       Psychosomatic Medicine, 1939, 1:271-292

1350. Moeller, T.A., Love, W.A. & Montgomery, D.D.
Correlates of personality in a hypertensive sample
Proceedings of the Biofeedback Research Society
Fifth Annual Meeting
Colorado Springs, 1974, 36 (Abst.)

1351. Montgomery, D.D. & Besner, H.F.
Effects of electromyographic relaxation training on
self reported sleep patterns in insomniacs
Proceedings of the Biofeedback Research Society
Fifth Annual Meeting
Colorado Springs, 1974, 102 (Abst.)

1352. Montgomery, D.D. & Besner, H.
Reduction of chronic onset insomnia through electro-
myographic relaxation training
Proceedings of the Biofeedback Research Society
Sixth Annual Meeting
Monterey, 1975, 21 (Abst.)

1353. Montgomery, D.D., Besner, H.F. & Weston, A.A.
Effects of the nature and modality of feedback
during a single session of electromyographic
relaxation training
Proceedings of the Biofeedback Research Society
Fifth Annual Meeting
Colorado Springs, 1974, 48 (Abst.)

1354. Montgomery, D.D., Love, W.A. & Moeller, T.A.
Effects of electromyographic feedback and relaxation
training on blood pressure in essential hypertension
Proceedings of the Biofeedback Research Society
Fifth Annual Meeting
Colorado Springs, 1974, 35 (Abst.)

1355. Montgomery, P.
Physiological response patterns obtained during
relaxation as a basis for individualizing biofeedback
Biofeedback and Self-Regulation, 1976, 1:359 (Abst.)

1356. Montgomery, P.S. & Ehrisman, W.J.
Biofeedback alleviated headaches, a follow-up
Headache, 1976, 16:64-65

1357. Moore, J.G. & Schenkenberg, T.
Psychic control of gastric acid: Response to antic-
ipated feeding and biofeedback training in a man
Gastroenterology, 1974, 66:954-959

1358. Moore, N.
Behavior therapy in bronchial asthma: A controlled
study
Journal of Psychosomatic Research, 1965, 9:257-276

1359. Moore, R.T.
Alpha training, instructional set, and hypnotic
susceptibility
Proceedings of the Biofeedback Research Society
Sixth Annual Meeting
Monterey, 1975, 64 (Abst.)

1360. Mordkoff, A.M.
The relationship between psychological and physiologi-
cal response to stress
Psychosomatic Medicine, 1964, 26:135-150

1361. Morgenson, D.F. & Martin, I.
Personality, awareness and autonomic conditioning
Psychophysiology, 1969, 5:536-547

1362. Morley, A.
Periodic diseases, physiological rhythms and feed-
back control: A hypothesis
Australas Annals of Medicine, 1970, 19:244-249

1363. Morley, S.
Migraine: A generalized vasomotor dysfunction? A
critical review of evidence
Headache, 1977, 17:71-74

1364. Moroz, I.
Use of the principles of adaptive bioregulation with
external feedback in the rehabilitation of children
with musculoskeletal diseases
Vopr Kurortol Fizioter Lech Fiz Kult., 1977, 1:33-36
(Russian)

1365. Morton, R.W., Dale, A., Klions, H., et al.
       Discrete muscle tension and relaxation responses in
         the forearm as a function of biofeedback and
         contralateral tension of relaxation
       Biofeedback and Self-Regulation, 1977, 2:309 (Abst.)

1366. Mosman, B.E.
       Conditioning of the single motor unit
       Dissertation Abstracts, 1973, 33B:3354

1367. Mulholland, T.
       The electroencephalogram as an experimental tool in
         the study of internal attention gradients
       Transactions of the New York Academy of Sciences,
         1962, 24:664-669

1368. Muholland, T.
       Variations in the response duration curve of successive
         cortical activation by a feedback stimulus
       Electroencephalography and Clinical Neurophysiology,
         1964, 16:394-395

1369. Mulholland, T.
       Occurrence of electroencephalographic alpha rhythm
         with eyes open
       Nature, 1965, 206:746

1370. Mulholland, T.
       Feedback electroencephalography
       Activitas Nervosa Superior, 1968, 10:410-438

1371. Mulholland, T.
       Feedback method: A new look at functional EEG
       Electroencephalography and Clinical Neurophysiology,
         1969, 27:688 (Abst.)

1372. Mulholland, T.
       The concept of attention and the electroencephalo-
         graphic alpha rhythm
       In C. R. Evans & T. Mulholland (Eds.), Attention in
         Neurophysiology
       London: Butterworths, 1969

1373. Mulholland, T.
Automatic control of visual displays by the attention
of the human viewer
In C. M. Williams & J. L. Debes, Proceedings of the
First National Conference on Visual Literacy, New
York: Pittman, 1970

1374. Mulholland, T.B.
Feedback electroencephalography II
Activitas Nervosa Superior, 1971, 4:266-276

1375. Mulholland, T.
Can you really turn on with alpha?
The R.M.Bucke Memorial Society Newsletter Review,
1972, 5:32-40

1376. Mulholland, T.B.
Occipital alpha revisited
Psychological Bulletin, 1972, 78:176-182

1377. Mulholland, T.
Objective EEG methods for studying covert shifts of
visual attention
In J. F. McGuigan & R. A. Schoonover (Ed), The
Psychophysiology of Thinking
New York: Academic Press, 1973, 109-151

1378. Mulholland, T.
Double stimulus feedback
Proceedings of the Biofeedback Research Society
Fifth Annual Meeting
Colorado Springs, 1974, 80 (Abst.)

1379. Mulholland, T.B.
Bilateral difference in the stability of the EEG
during feedback stimulation
Proceedings of the Biofeedback Research Society
Sixth Annual Meeting
Monterey, 1975, 69 (Abst.)

1380. Mulholland, T.B.
Biofeedback as scientific method
In G. Schwartz & J. Beatty (Eds.), Biofeedback:
Theory and Research.
New York: Academic Press, 1977

1381. Mulholland, T.B.
Biofeedback method for locating the most controlled
responses of EEG alpha to visual stimulation
In J. Beatty & H. Legewie (Eds.), Biofeedback and
Behavior
New York: Plenum Press, 1977

1382. Mulholland, T. & Benson, F.
Detection of EEG abnormalities with feedback stimu-
lation
Biofeedback and Self-Regulation, 1976, 1:47-61

1383. Mulholland, T. & Eberlin, P.
Effect of feedback contingencies on the control of
occipital alpha
Biofeedback and Self-Regulation, 1977, 2:43-57

1384. Mulholland, T., Eberlin, P., Goodman, D. et al.
Feedback methods for testing the mediation of an
EEG response to visual stimuli: I
Biofeedback and Self-Regulation, 1977, 2:287-288 (Abst.)

1385. Mulholland, T. & Evans, C.R.
An unexpected artefact in the human electroencephalo-
gram concerning the alpha rhythm and the orientation of the eyes
Nature, 1965, 207:36-37

1386. Mulholland, T. & Evans, C.R.
Oculomotor function and the alpha activation cycle
Nature, 1966, 211:1278-1279

1387. Mulholland, T., McLaughlin, T. & Benson, F.
Feedback control and quantification of the response
of EEG alpha to visual stimulation
Biofeedback and Self-Regulation, 1976, 1:411-422

1388. Mulholland, T. & Peper, E.
Occipital alpha and accommodative vergence, pursuit
tracking, and fast eye movements
Psychophysiology 1971, 8:556-575

1389. Mulholland, T. & Runnals, S.
A stimulus-brain feedback system for evaluation of
alertness
Journal of Psychology, 1962, 54:69-83

1390. Mulholland, T. & Runnals, S
       Increased occurrence of EEG alpha during increased
          attention
       Journal of Psychology, 1962, 54:317-330

1391. Mulholland, T. & Runnals, S.
       Evaluation of attention and alertness with a
          stimulus-brain feedback loop
       Electroencephalography and Clinical Neurophysiology,
          1962, 14:847-852

1392. Murphy, G.
       Experiments in overcoming self-deception
       Psychophysiology, 1970, 6:790-799

1393. Murphy, P.J., Darwin, J. & Murphy, D.A.
       EEG feedback training for cerebral dysfunction: A
          research program with learning disabled adolescents
       Biofeedback and Self-Regulation, 1977, 2:288 (Abst.)

1394. Murphy, P., Maurek, P. & Lakey, W.
       Effects of simultaneous divergent EEG feedback from
          both cerebral hemispheres on changes in verbal and
          spatial tasks
       Biofeedback and Self-Regulation, 1976, 1:337-338
          (Abst.)

1395. Murphy, P.J. & Smith, B.D.
       A comparison of different forms of mediation in the
          cardiac feedback procedure
       Proceedings of the Biofeedback Research Society
          Fifth Annual Meeting
       Colorado Springs, 1974, 92 (Abst.)

1396. Murphy, P.J. & Smith, B.D.
       Cognitive and respiratory mediation and tonic heart
          level in operant cardiac conditioning
       Proceedings of the Biofeedback Research Society
          Fifth Annual Meeting
       Colorado Springs, 1974, 93 (Abst.)

1397. Murphy, W.D., Fredericksen, L.W., Appel, M.A., et al.
       Effects of response specific instructions and ex-
          trinsic reinforcement on the operant deceleration
          of human heart rate
       Psychophysiology, 1976, 13:187 (Abst.)

1398. Murray, E.N. & Katkin, E.S.
      Comment on two recent reports of operant heart rate
        conditioning
      Psychophysiology, 1968, 5:192-195

1399. Myers, T.I. & Ramsay, D.A.
      A controlled, experimental study of meditation
      Proceedings of the Biofeedback Research Society
        Sixth Annual meeting
      Monterey, 1975, 78 (Abst.)

1400. McCanne, T.R. & Sandman, C.A.
      Instrumental heart rate responses and visual per-
        ception. A preliminary study
      Psychophysiology, 1974, 11:283-287

1401. McCanne, T.R. & Sandman, C.A.
      Determinants of human operant heart rate conditioning:
        A systematic investigation of several methodological
        issues
      Journal of Comparative and Physiological Psychology,
        1975, 88:609-618

1402. McCanne, T.R. & Sandman, C.A.
      The impact of two different reinforcers on conditional
        operant heart rate acceleration and deceleration
      Biological Psychology, 1975, 3:131-142

1403. McCanne, T.R. & Sandman, C.A.
      Human operant heart rate conditioning: The importance
        of individual differences
      Psychological Bulletin, 1976, 83:587-601

1404. McCanne, T.R. & Sandman, C.A.
      Proprioceptive awareness, information about response
        reinforcement contingencies and operant heart rate
        control
      Physiological Psychology, 1976, 4:369-375

1405. McFarland, R.A.
      Heart rate perception and heart rate control
      Psychophysiology, 1975, 12:402-405

1406. McFarland, R.A. & Bissell, H.S.
      Precise operant heart rate control employing three
         different amounts of information feedback
      Psychophysiology, 1971, 8:264 (Abst.)

1407. McFarland, R.A. & Campbell, C.
      Precise heart rate control and heart rate perception
      Perceptual and Motor Skills, 1975, 41:730

1408. McFarland, R.A. & Coombs, R.
      Anxiety and feedback as factors in operant heart
         rate control
      Psychophysiology, 1974, 11:53-57

1409. McFarland, R.A. & Herrmann, J.A.
      Precise voluntary control in humans
      Psychological Reports, 1974, 35:925-926

1410. McFarland, W.J.
      Biofeedback: A contemporary overview
      Journal of the Connecticut State Medical Society,
         1976, 40:689-704

1411. McGeorge, C.M.
      Biofeedback and the headache
      The New Zealand Psychologist, 1976, 5:16-25

1412. McGowan, E.J.
      The role of the systems engineer in biofeedback
      Proceedings of the Biofeedback Research Society
         Fifth Annual Meeting
      Colorado Springs, 1974, 108 (Abst.)

1413. McGrady, A., Mitch, P. & Iannone, A.
      Effect of direct feedback of systolic pressure in
         essential hypertension
      Biofeedback and Self-Regulation, 1977, 2:306 (Abst.)

1414. McGrady, A., Mitch, P.S., Iannone, A., et al.
      Effect of direct biofeedback of systolic blood
         pressure on systolic and diastolic blood pressure
         of essential hypertensives
      Proceedings of the Biofeedback Research Society
         Sixth Annual Meeting
      Monterey, 1975, 12 (Abst.)

1415. McGuigan, F.
Feedback of speech muscle activity during silent
reading: Two comments
Science, 1967, 157:579-581

1416. McKenzie, R.E., Ehrisman, W.J., Montgomery, P.S.,
et al.
The treatment of headaches by means of electroencephalographic biofeedback
Headache, 1974, 13:164-172

1417. McLaughlin, T.J. & Lewis, C.N.
Feedback EEG reactivity and the social responsivity
of psychiatric patients
Journal of Nervous and Mental Disease, 1975, 161:336-
342

1418. McLaughlin, T.J., Solomon, L. & Harrison, R.
The use of feedback encephalography to assess levels
of attention and motivated interests in paranoid
and nonparanoid schizophrenics
Journal of Nervous and Mental Disease, 1974, 159:422-
432

1419. McLean, P.D. & Milne, L.G.
Effect of exteroceptive feedback in controlling
electrodermal activity in preconditioned fears
Perceptual and Motor Skills, 1975, 40:487-493

1420. McLean, S., Toomim, H. & Taylor, L.
Biofeedback in Neuromuscular Reeducation: History,
Uses and Procedures
Los Angeles: Biofeedback Research Institute, 1975

1421. McMahon, C.E.
Voluntary control of "involuntary" functions:
The approach of the stoics
Psychophysiology, 1974, 11:710-714

1422. Nafliotis, H.
      Electromyographic feedback to improve ankle dorsi-
      flexion, wrist extension and hand grasp
      Physical Therapy, 1976, 56:821-825

1423. Nall, A.
      Alpha training and the hyperkinetic child: Is it
      effective?
      Academic Therapy, 1973, 9:5-19

1424. Naranjo, C. & Ornstein, R.
      On the Psychology of Meditation
      New York: Viking Press, 1971

1425. Netsell, R. & Cleeland, C.S.
      Modification of lip hypertonia in dysarthria using
      EMG feedback
      Journal of Speech and Hearing Disorders, 1973,
      58:131-140

1426. Neumann, E. & Blanton, R.
      The early history of electrodermal research
      Psychophysiology, 1970, 6:453-475

1427. Newman, R.W.
      Temperature regulation training in a cooling en-
      vironment
      American Industrial Hygiene Association Journal,
      1975, 36:610-617

1428. Newton, F.A., Bird, B.L., Ford, M., et al.
      Long-term control of 40 Hz EEG activity
      Psychophysiology, 1977, 14:84 (Abst.)

1429. Newton, F.A., Bird, B.L. & Sheer, D.L.
      Conditioning and suppression for 40 Hz EEG activity
      in humans: Analysis of volunary control and
      subjective states
      Proceedings of the Biofeedback Research Society
      Sixth Annual Meeting
      Monterey, 1975, 18 (Abst.)

1430. Newton, F.A., Bird, B.L., Sheer, D., et al.
        Biofeedback training of 40 Hz EEG activity in
          humans: Hardware, procedures and data
        Biofeedback and Self-Regulation, 1976, 1:338 (Abst.)

1431. Newton, G., Paul, J. & Bovard, E.W.
        Effect of emotional stress on finger temperature
        Psychological Reports, 1957, 3:341-343

1432. Neyer, M.A.
        Heart rate control with somatic and emotional
          instructions: Effects on sensorimotor and occi-
          pital alpha
        Psychophysiology, 1976, 13:176 (Abst.)

1433. Nicassio, P. & Bootzin, R.
        A comparison of progressive relaxation and autogenic
          training as treatments for insomnia
        Journal of Abnormal Psychology, 1974, 83:253-260

1434. Nideffer, R.M.
        Alpha and the development of human potential
        In D. Shapiro et al (Eds.), Biofeedback and Self-
          Control: 1972
        Chicago: Aldine Publishing Co., 1973

1435. Nideffer, R.M. & Deckner, C.W.
        A case study of improved athletic performance
          following use of relaxation procedures
        Perceptual and Motor Skills, 1970, 30:821-822

1436. Norton, G.R.
        Biofeedback treatment of long-standing eye closure
          reactions
        Journal of Behavior Therapy and Experimental
          Psychiatry, 1976, 7:277-278

1437. Norman, K.L.
        Dynamic processes in stimulus integration theory:
          Effects of feedback on averaging of motor movements
        Journal of Experimental Psychology, 1974, 102:399-
          408

1438. Nowlis, D.P. & Kamiya, J.
        The control of electroencephalographic alpha rhythms
          through auditory feedback and the associated
          mental activity
        Psychophysiology, 1970, 6:476-484

1439. Nowlis, D. & Rhead, J.
      Relation of eyes-closed resting EEG alpha activity
         to hypnotic susceptibility
      Perceptual and Motor Skills, 1968, 27:1047-1500

1440. Nowlis, D.P. & Wortz, E.C.
      Control of the ratio of midline parietal to midline
         frontal EEG alpha rhythms through auditory feed-
         back
      Perceptual and Motor Skills, 1973, 37:815-824

1441. Nunes, J.W. & Marks, I.M.
      Feedback of true heart rate during exposure in vivo
      Archives of General Psychiatry, 1975, 32:933-936

1442. Nunes, J.S. & Marks, I.M.
      Feedback of true heart rate during exposure in vivo
      Archives of General Psychiatry, 1976, 33:1346-1352

1443. O'Brien, J.S., Raynes, A.E. & Patch, V.D.
Treatment of heroin addiction with aversion therapy,
relaxation training and systematic desensitization
Behavior Research and Therapy, 1972, 10:77-80

1444. Obrist, P.A.
The cardiovascular-behavioral interaction: As it
appears today
Psychophysiology, 1976, 13:95-107

1445. Obrist, P., Black, A.H., Brener, J. & DiCara, L.
(Eds.),
Cardiovascular Psychophysiology
Chicago: Aldine Publishing Co., 1974

1446. Obrist, P.A., Galosy, R.A., Lawler, J.E., et al.
Operant conditioning of heart rate: Somatic correlates
Psychophysiology, 1975, 12:445-455

1447. Obrist, P.A., Howard, J.L., Lawler, J.E., et al.
The cardiac-somatic interaction
In P. A. Obrist, et al. (Eds.), Cardiovascular
Psychophysiology
Chicago: Aldine Publishing Co., 1974

1448. Obrist, P.A., Lawler, J.E., Howard, J.L., et al.
Sympathetic influences on cardiac rate and con-
tractibility during acute stress in humans
Psychophysiology, 1974, 11:405-427

1449. Obrist, P., LeGuyader, D., Howard, J. et al
Operant conditioning of heart rate: Somatic
correlates
Psychophysiology, 1972, 9:270 (Abst.)

1450. Obrist, P.A., Webb, R.A. & Sutterer, J.R.
Heart rate and somatic changes during aversive
conditioning and a simple reaction time task
Psychophysiology, 1969, 5:696-723

1451. Obrist, P.A., Webb, R.A., Sutterer, J.R. & Howard,
J.L.
The cardiac-somatic relationship: Some reformulations
Psychophysiology, 1970, 6:569-587

1452. Obrist, P.A., Webb, R.A., Sutterer, J.R., et al
       Cardiac deceleration and reaction time: An evaluation
         of two hypotheses
       Psychophysiology, 1970, 6:695-706

1453. Ogden, E. & Shock, N.W.
       Voluntary hypercirculation
       American Journal of the Medical Sciences, 1939,
         198:329-342

1454. O'Hanlon, J.F., Royal, J.W. & Beatty, J
       Theta regulation and radar vigilance performance
       In J. Beatty & H. Legewie (Eds.), Biofeedback and
         Behavior
       New York: Plenum Press, 1977

1455. Ohno, Y., Tanoka, Y., Takeya, T., et al.
       Modification of skin temperature by biofeedback
         procedures
       Journal of Behavior Therapy and Experimental
         Psychiatry, 1977, 8:31-34

1456. Olds, J.
       Operant conditioning of single unit responses
       Tokyo: Exerpta Medica Foundation International
         Congress Series, 1965, 87:372-80

1457. Orenstein, H.B. & McWilliams, B.
       Variations in electroencephalographic alpha activity
         under conditions of differential lighting and
         auditory feedback
       Biofeedback and Self-Regulation, 1976, 1:423-432

1458. Orme-Johnson, D.W.
       Autonomic stability and transcendental meditation
       Psychosomatic Medicine, 1973, 35:341-349

1459. Orne, M.T.
       The nature of hypnosis: Artifact and essence
       Journal of Abnormal and Social Psychology, 1959,
         58:277-299

1460. Orne, M.T.
       Hypnosis, motivation, and compliance
       American Journal of Psychiatry, 1966, 122:721-726

1461. Orne, M.T. & Paskewitz, D.A.
      Aversive situational effects on alpha feedback
         training
      Science, 1974, 186:458-460

1462. Orne, M. & Wilson, S.
      Alpha, biofeedback and arousal/activation
      In J. Beatty & H. Legewie (Eds.), Biofeedback and
         Behavior
      New York: Plenum Press, 1977

1463. Ornstein, R.E.
      The esoteric and modern psychologies of awareness
      In C. Naranjo & R. E. Ornstein, On the Psychology of
         Meditation Chapter 2
      The Viking Press, Inc., 1971

1464. Ortof, E.
      Cognitive and interpersonal considerations in
         biofeedback
      Contemporary Psychoanalysis, 1976, 12:446-454

1465. Osbourne, S.R.
      Autoregulation of phase relations between left
         and right occipital brain potentials through the
         use of immediate biological feedback
      Dissertation Abstracts, 1972, 32B:4901

1466. Osis, K. & Bokert, E.
      ESP and changed states of consciousness induced by
         meditation
      Journal of the American Society for Psychical
         Research, 1971, 65:17

1467. Otis, L.S. Turner, A.
      EMG training and headache reduction: Some methodo-
         logical issues
      Proceedings of the Biofeedback Research Society
         Sixth Annual Meeting
      Monterey, 1975, 100 (Abst.)

1468. Otis, L.S. & Low, D.W.
      The use of timers to reduce tension headache fre-
         quency: Failure to replicate
      Biofeedback and Self-Regulation, 1976, 1:349 (Abst.)

1469. Otis, L.S., McCormick, N.L. & Lukas, J.S.
       Voluntary control of tension headaches
       Proceedings of the Biofeedback Research Society
         Fifth Annual Meeting
       Colorado Springs, 1974, 23 (Abst.)

1470. Owen, S.
       An experiment in muscle re-education
       National Paraplegia Foundation Journal, 1974, July,
         10-12

1471. Owen, S.
       Biofeedback in rehabilitation
       Rehabilitation Gazette, 1974, 17:46-49

1472. Owen, S., Toomim, H. & Taylor, L.
       Biofeedback in Neuromuscular Rehabilitation
       Los Angeles: Biofeedback Research Institute, 1975

1473. Packer, L.E. & Selekman, W.L.
      Within-subjects controls in EMG and thermal biofeedback
        training: The baseline effect
      Biofeedback and Self-Regulation, 1977, 2:293-294
        (Abst.)

1474. Pagano, R.R. & Frumkin, L.R.
      The effect of transcendental meditation in right
        hemispheric functioning
      Biofeedback and Self-Regulation, 1977, 2:407-415

1475. Pagano, R.R., Rose, R.M., Stivers, R.M., et al.
      Occurrence of sleep in transcendental meditation
      Proceedings of the Biofeedback Research Society
        Sixth Annual Meeting
      Monterey, 1975, 76 (Abst.)

1476. Pagano, R.R., Rose, R.M., Stivers, R.M., et al.
      Sleep during transcendental meditation
      Science, 1976, 191:308-310

1477. Palmer, R.D. & Siegel, M.
      Electromyographic feedback in the treatment of
        primary open-angle glaucoma
      Biofeedback and Self-Regulation, 1977, 2:315-316
        (Abst.)

1478. Palmer, R.D. & Siegel, M.
      Electromyographic feedback in the treatment of
        strabismus
      Biofeedback and Self-Regulation, 1977, 2:316 (Abst.)

1479. Pappas, B.A., DiCara, L.V. & Miller, N.E.
      Learning of blood pressure response in the non-
        curarized rat: Transfer to the curarized state
      Physiology and Behavior, 1970, 5:1029-1032

1480. Parliament, V. & Reeves, J.L.
      The effects of alpha enhancement and cognitive and
        physiological relaxation
      Psychophysiology, 1977, 14:112 (Abst.)

1481. Parsky, L. & Papsdorf, J.D.
      EMG biofeedback suppression of vocalization in
        reading disabled Grade VI students
      Biofeedback and Self-Regulation, 1976, 1:330 (Abst.)

1482. Paskewitz, D.A.
A hybrid circuit to indicate the presence of alpha
activity
Psychophysiology, 1971, 8:107-112

1483. Paskewitz, D.A.
Biofeedback instrumentation: Soldering closed the
loop
American Psychologist, 1975, 30:371-378

1484. Paskewitz, D.A., Lynch, J.J., Orne, M.T. & Costello,
J.
The feedback control of alpha activity: Condition-
ing or disinhibition
Psychophysiology, 1970, 6:637-638 (Abst.)

1485. Paskewitz, D.A. & Orne, M.T.
The effect of cognitive tasks on the feedback
control of alpha activity
Psychophysiology, 1971, 8:263

1486. Paskewitz, D. & Orne, M.
Visual effects during alpha feedback training
Psychophysiology, 1972, 9:269 (Abst.)

1487. Paskewitz, D.A. & Orne, M.T.
Visual effects in alpha feedback training
Science, 1973, 181:360-363

1488. Paskewitz, D.A. & Orne, M.T.
On the reliability of baseline EEG alpha activity
Psychophysiology, 1973, 10:202-203

1489. Pasquali, E.
A relay controlled by alpha rhythm
Psychophysiology, 1969, 6:207-208

1490. Passini, F.T., Letsch, B.A. & Westlake, S.H.
Blood alcohol content and spontaneous alpha changes
in humans
Biofeedback and Self-Regulation, 1977, 2:283 (Abst.)

1491. Passini, F., Watson, C.G., Dehnel, L., et al.
Alpha wave biofeedback training therapy in alcoholics
Journal of Clinical Psychology, 1977, 33:292-299

1492. Patel, C.H.
Yoga and biofeedback in the management of hypertension
Lancet, 1973, 2:1053-1055

1493. Patel, C.
Yoga and biofeedback in the management of stress in
    hypertensive patients
Proceedings of the Biofeedback Research Society
    Sixth Annual Meeting
Monterey, 1975, 14 (Abst.)

1494. Patel, C.
12-month follow-up of yoga and biofeedback in the
    management of hypertension
Lancet, 1975, 1:62-65

1495. Patel, C.H.
Yoga and biofeedback in the management of "stress"
    in hypertensive patients
Clinical Science and Molecular Medicine, 1975, 48
    (Supp 2), 171-174

1496. Patel, C.
Yoga and biofeedback in the management of hypertension
Journal of Psychosomatic Research, 1975, 19:355-360

1497. Patel, C.
Reduction of serum cholesterol and blood pressure in
    hypertensive patients by behavior modification
Journal of the Royal College of General Practitioners
British Journal of General Practice, 1976, 26:211-
    215

1498. Patel, C.
Biofeedback as therapy with particular emphasis on
    hypertension
Biofeedback and Self-Regulation, 1976, 1:310-311
    (Abst.)

1499. Patel, C.
Biofeedback-aided relaxation and meditation in the
    management of hypertension
Biofeedback and Self-Regulation, 1977, 2:1-41

1500. Patel, C. & Carruthers, M.
       Coronary risk factor reduction through biofeedback-
          aided relaxation and meditation
       Journal of the Royal College of General Practitioners
          British Journal of General Practice, 1977 (In
          Press)

1501. Patel, C. & Datey, K.K.
       Relaxation and biofeedback technique in the manage-
          ment of hypertension
       Proceedings of the Biofeedback Research Society
          Fifth Annual Meeting
       Colorado Springs, 1974, 39 (Abst.)

1502. Patel, C.H. & Datey, K.K.
       Management of hypertension using biofeedback techniqu
          in relaxation and meditation
       Chest, 1974, 65:596 (Abst.)

1503. Patel, C. & Datey, K.K.
       Relaxation and biofeedback techniques in the manage-
          ment of hypertension
       Angiology, 1976, 27:106-113

1504. Patel, C.H. & North, W.R.
       Randomized control trial of yoga and biofeedback in
          management of hypertension
       Lancet, 1975, 2:93-95

1505. Patterson, D.M.
       Differential biofeedback training, pre-post cognitive
          style changes, and the role of the "preferred"
          hemisphere in spatial-intuitive vs. verbal-
          analytic subjects
       Biofeedback and Self-Regulation, 1977, 2:288-289
          (Abst.)

1506. Patton, G.W.R.
       Combined autonomic effects of concurrently applied
          stressors
       Psychophysiology, 1970, 6:707

1507.   Paul, G.L.
         Extraversion, emotionality and physiological re-
             sponse to relaxation training and hypnotic
             suggestion
         International Journal of Clinical and Experimental
             Hypnosis, 1969, 17:89-98

1508.   Paul, G.L.
         Inhibition of physiological response to stressful
             imagery by relaxation training and hypnotically
             suggested relaxation
         Behavior Research and Therapy, 1969, 7:249-256

1509.   Paul, G.L.
         Physiological effects of relaxation training and
             hypnotic suggestion
         Journal of Abnormal Psychology, 1969, 74:425-437

1510.   Paul, G.L. & Trimble, R.W.
         Recorded vs. "live" relaxation training and hypnotic
             suggestion: Comparative effectiveness for re-
             ducing physiological arousal and inhibiting stress
             response
         Behavior Therapy, 1970, 1:285-302

1511.   Pearne, D.H., Zigelbaum, S.D. & Peyser, W.P.
         Biofeedback assisted EMG relaxation for urinary
             retention and incontinence: A case report
         Biofeedback and Self-Regulation, 1977, 2:213-218

1512.   Pearse, B.A., Sargent, J.D., Walters, E.D., et al
         Exploratory observations of the use of an intensive
             autogenic biofeedback training (IAFT) procedure in
             a follow-up study of out-of-town patients having
             migraine and/or tension headaches
         Proceedings of the Biofeedback Research Society
             Sixth Annual Meeting
         Monterey, 1975, 53 (Abst.)

1513.   Pease, E.A.
         Voluntary control of the heart
         Boston Medical and Surgical Journal, 1889, 120:525-
             529

1514. Peck, C.L. & Kraft, G.H.
Electromyographic biofeedback for pain related to
muscle tension-study of tension headache, back and
jaw pain
Archives of Surgery, 1977, 112:889-895

1515. Peck, D.F.
Operant conditioning and physical rehabilitation
European Journal of Behavioral Analysis and Modi-
fication, 1976, 1:158-164

1516. Peck, D.F.
The use of EMG feedback in the treatment of a severe
case of blepharospasm
Biofeedback and Self-Regulation, 1977, 2:273-278

1517. Peek, C.J.
A critical look at the theory of placebo
Biofeedback and Self-Regulation, 1977, 2:327-335

1518. Pelletier, K.R.
Neurological, psychophysiological, and clinical
parameters of alpha, theta, and the voluntary
control of bleeding and pain
Proceedings of the Biofeedback Research Society
Fifth Annual Meeting
Colorado Springs, 1974, 112 (Abst.)

1519. Pelletier, K.R.
Neurological, psychophysiological, and clinical
differentiation of the alpha and theta altered
states of consciousness
Dissertation Abstracts International, 1974, 35/1:74-
14, 806

1520. Pelletier, K.
Influence of transcendental meditation upon auto-
kinetic perception
Perceptual and Motor Skills, 1974, 39:1031-1034

1521. Pelletier, K.R.
Diagnosis, procedures, and phenomenology of clinical
biofeedback
Proceedings of the Biofeedback Research Society
Sixth Annual Meeting
Monterey, 1975, 30 (Abst.)

1522.   Pelletier, K.R.
        Neurological substrates of consciousness: Impli-
           cations for psychosomatic medicine
        Journal of Altered States of Consciousness, 1975,
           2:75-85

1523.   Pelletier, K.R.
        Theory and applications of clinical biofeedback
        Journal of Contemporary Psychotherapy, 1975, 7:29-34

1524.   Pelletier, K.R.
        Adjunctive biofeedback with cancer patients: A case
           presentation
        Biofeedback and Self-Regulation, 1977, 2:317 (Abst.)

1525.   Pelletier, K.R.
        Mind as Healer, Mind as Slayer
        New York: Delacorte, 1977

1526.   Pelletier, K.R. & Garfield, C.
        Consciousness East and West
        New York: Harper & Row, 1976

1527.   Pelletier, K.R. & Peper, E.
        The chutzpah factor in psychophysiological parameters
           of altered states of consciousness
        Proceedings of the Biofeedback Research Society
           Fifth Annual Meeting
        Colorado Springs, 1974, 113 (Abst.)

1528.   Pelletier, K.R. & Peper, E.
        The chutzpah factor in altered states of conscious-
           ness
        Journal of Humanistic Psychology, 1977, 17:63-74

1529.   Pelletier, K.R. & Peper, E.
        Developing a biofeedback model: Alpha EEG feedback
           as a means for pain control
        The International Journal of Clinical and Experi-
           mental Hypnosis, 1977, 25:361-371

1530.   Pendleton, L.R. & Tasto, D.L.
        Effects of metronome-conditioned relaxation, metronome-
           induced relaxation, and progressive muscle re-
           laxation on insomnia
        Behavior Research and Therapy, 1976, 14:165-166

1531. Peper, E.
       Feedback regulation of the alpha electroencephalogram
       activity through control of the internal and
       external parameters
       Kybernetik, 1970, 7:107-112

1532. Peper, E.
       Comment on feedback training of parietal-occipital
       alpha asymmetry in normal human subjects
       Kybernetik, 1971, 9:156-158

1533. Peper, E.
       Reduction of efferent motor commands during alpha
       feedback as a facilitator of EEG alpha and a
       precondition for changes in consciousness
       Kybernetik, 1971, 9:226-231

1534. Peper, E.
       Localized EEG alpha feedback training: A possible
       technique for mapping subjective, conscious and
       behavioral experiences
       Kybernetik, 1972, 11:166-169

1535. Peper, E.
       Frontiers of clinical biofeedback
       In L. Birk (Ed.), Seminars in Psychiatry,
       New York: Grune & Stratton, 1973

1536. Peper, E.
       Holistic application of biofeedback to reduce
       symptoms of stress and as a technique for re-
       education: Backache as a case example
       Proceedings of the Biofeedback Research Society
          Fifth Annual Meeting
       Colorado Springs, 1974, 53 (Abst.)

1537. Peper, E.
       Problems in heart rate and alpha electroencephalograph
       feedback--is the control over the feedback stimulus
       meaningful?
       Kybernetik, 1974, 14:217-221

1538. Peper, E.
       Problems in biofeedback training: An experimental
       analogy--urination
       Perspectives in Biology and Medicine, 1976, 19:404-
          412

1539. Peper, E.
       Passive attention: The gateway to consciousness
          and autonomic control
       In P. G. Zimbardo & F. L. Ruch, (Eds.), Psychology
          and Life
       Chicago: Scott, Foresman & Co., 1976

1540. Peper, E.
       Mind/Body Integration: A Handbook for Biofeedback
       New York/Berkeley: Random House/Bookworks (In Press)

1541. Peper, E. & Ancoli, S.
       The two endpoints of an EEG continuum of meditation--
          alpha/theta and fast beta
       Biofeedback and Self-Regulation, 1977, 2:289-290
          (Abst.)

1542. Peper, E. & Grossman, E.R.
       Preliminary observation of thermal biofeedback
          training in children with migraine
       Proceedings of the Biofeedback Research Society
          Fifth Annual Meeting
       Colorado Springs, 1974, 63 (Abst.)

1543. Peper, E. & Mulholland, T.
       Methodological and theoretical problems in the
          voluntary control of electroencephalographic
          occipital alpha by the subject
       Kybernetik, 1970, 7, Bd., Heft 3 10-13

1544. Peper, E. & Robertson, J.A.
       Biofeedback use of common objects: The bathroom
          scale in physical therapy
       Biofeedback and Self-Regulation, 1976, 1:237-240

1545. Pettingill, J.A. & Simkins, L.D.
       Sensory mode of feedback and incentive effects of
          muscle relaxation
       Biofeedback and Self-Regulation, 1976, 1:335-336
          (Abst.)

1546. Phares, E.J.
       Locus of Control in Personality
       Morristown, New Jersey: Silver-Burdett, 1976

1547. Phillips, C.
       The modification of tension headache pain using EMG
          biofeedback
       Behavior Research and Therapy, 1977, 15:119-129

1548. Pickering, T.
       Yoga and biofeedback in hypertension
       Lancet, 1973, 2:1440-1441

1549. Pickering, T.G., Brucker, B., Frankel, H.L., et al.
       Mechanisms of learned voluntary control of blood
          pressure in patients with generalized bodily
          paralysis
       In J. Beatty & H. Legewie (Eds.), Biofeedback and
          Behavior
       New York: Plenum Press, 1977

1550. Pickering, T. & Gorham, G.
       Learned heart rate control by a patient with a
          ventricular parasystolic rhythm
       The Lancet, 1975, 1:252-253

1551. Pickering, T.G. & Miller, N.E.
       Learned voluntary control of heart rate and rhythm
          in two subjects with premature ventricular con-
          tractions
       British Heart Journal 1977, 39:152-159

1552. Pierce, D.S. & Wagman, I.H.
       A method of recording from single muscle fibres of
          motor units in human skeletal muscle
       Journal of Applied Physiology, 1964,19:366-370

1553. Plotkin, W.B.
       The eyes as a gateway to the mind: Effects of
          feedback, instructions, and the presence of light
          on subjective state and the degree of acquired
          control of occipital alpha
       Proceedings of the Biofeedback Research Society
          Fifth Annual Meeting
       Colorado Springs, 1974, 81 (Abst.)

1554. Plotkin, W.
       Occipital alpha and the "alpha experience"
       Proceedings of the Biofeedback Research Society
          Sixth Annual Meeting
       Monterey, 1975, 39 (Abst.)

1555.   Plotkin, W.B.
        On the self-regulation of the occipital alpha
        rhythm: Control strategies, states of conscious-
        ness, and the role of physiological feedback
        Journal of Experimental Psychology: General, 1976,
        105:66-99

1556.   Plotkin, W.B.
        Appraising the ephemeral "alpha phenomenon" a reply
        to Hardt & Kamiya
        Journal of Experimental Psychology: General, 1976,
        105:109-121

1557.   Plotkin, W.B.
        On the social psychology of experimental states
        associated with EEG alpha biofeedback training
        In J. Beatty & H. Legewie (Eds.), Biofeedback and
        Behavior
        New York: Plenum Press, 1977

1558.   Plotkin, W.B. & Cohen, R.
        Occipital alpha and the attributes of the "alpha
        experience"
        Psychophysiology, 1976, 13:16-21

1559.   Plotkin, W.B., Mazer, C. & Loewy, D.
        Alpha enhancement and the likelihood of an alpha
        experience
        Psychophysiology, 1976, 13:466-471

1560.   Plumlee, L.A.
        Operant conditioning of increases in blood pressure
        Psychophysiology, 1969, 6:283-290

1561.   Podlesny, J.A. & Raskin, D.C.
        Biofeedback: A failure to enhance alpha EEG
        Psychophysiology, 1974, 11:277 (Abst.)

1562.   Poirier, F.
        Biological feedback and medicine
        Union Med Canada, 1973, 102:1486-1490

1563.   Poirier, F.
        Treatment of epilepsy with biofeedback
        Proceedings of the Biofeedback Research Society
           Sixth Annual Meeting
        Monterey, 1975, 47 (Fr. Abs.)

1564.   Pollack, M.H.
        Biofeedback of blood pressure changes: A treatment
        for essential hypertension
        Biological Psychology Bulletin, 1973, 3:49-56

1565.   Pollack, M.H., & Zeiner, A.R.
        Physiological correlates of Bensonian relaxation
        training with controls for relaxation and setting
        Psychophysiology, 1976, 13:185 (Abst.)

1566.   Pollini, S. & Peper, E.
        18 Hz Beta activity: Recording limitation, problems
        and subjective reports
        Biofeedback and Self-Regulation, 1976, 1:338-339
        (Abst.)

1567.   Poon, L., Williams, R. & Burdette, L.
        Operant control of forearm blood flow (FBF)
        Psychophysiology, 1974, 11:231 (Abst.)

1568.   Pope, A.T. & Gersten, C.D.
        A semi-automated system for biofeedback-assisted
        relaxation therapy
        Proceedings of the Biofeedback Research Society
        Sixth Annual Meeting
        Monterey, 1975, 93 (Abst.)

1569.   Pope, A.T. & Gersten, C.D.
        A semi-automated system for biofeedback-assisted
        relaxation therapy
        Behavior Research Methods in Instrumentation, 1975,
        7:459-463

1570.   Pope, A.T. & Gersten, C.D.
        Computer automation of relaxation therapy employing
        EMG biofeedback
        Biofeedback and Self-Regulation, 1976, 1:363 (Abst.)

1571.   Pope, A.T. & Gersten, C.D.
        Computer automation of biofeedback training
        Behavior Research Methods and Instrumentation, 1977,
        9:164-168

1572.   Powell, D.A. & Joseph, J.A.
        Autonomic-somatic interaction and hippocampal theta
          activity
        Journal of Comparative and Physiological Psychology,
          1974, 87:978-986

1573.   Powers, W.T.
        Feedback: Beyond behaviorism
        Science, 1973, 179:351-356

1574.   Pratap, V.
        Svara yoga: A modality in biofeedback
        Proceedings of the Biofeedback Research Society
          Fifth Annual Meeting
        Colorado Springs, 1974, 111 (Abst.)

1575.   Premack, D.
        Mechanisms of self-control
        In W. Hunt (Ed.), Learning and Mechanisms of Self-
          Control in Smoking
        Chicago: Aldine Publishing Co., 1970

1576.   Premack, D. & Anglin, B.
        On the possibilities of self-control in man and
          animals
        Journal of Abnormal Psychology, 1973, 81:137-151

1577.   Prentke, E.M. & Beard, J.E.
        A surface electrode design for myolectric control
        Orthotics Prosthetics, 1969, 23:63-67

1578.   Pressner, J.A. & Savitsky, J.C.
        Effect of contingent and noncontingent feedback and
          subject expectancies on electroencephalogram
          biofeedback training
        Journal of Consulting and Clinical Psychology, 1977,
          45:713-714

1579.   Prewitt, M.J. & Adams, H.E.
        Alpha activity suppression and enhancement as a
          function of feedback and instructions
        Psychophysiology, 1976, 13:307-310

1580. Pribram, K.
Self-consciousness and intentionality
In G. E. Schwartz & D. Shapiro (Eds.), Consciousness
and Self-Regulation
New York: Plenum Press, 1976

1581. Price, K.P. & Tursky, B.
Vascular reactivity of migraines and nonmigraineurs
Headache, 1976, 16:210-216

1582. Prigitano, G.P.
Spider phobia: Autonomic reactions and biofeedback
control of heart rate variability
Dissertation Abstracts, 1973, 33B:3320

1583. Prigitano, G.P. & Johnson, H.J.
Biofeedback control of heart rate variability to phob
stimuli: A new approach to treating spider phobia
Proceedings of the Annual Convention, APA
Washington, D.C., American Psychological Association,
1972, pp. 403-404

1584. Provine, R.R. & Enoch, J.M.
On voluntary ocular accommodation
Perception and Psychophysis, 1975, 17:209-212

1585. Pryzbylik, A.T. & Howe, R.C.
A system for biofeedback conditioning of electro-
encephalographic activity
Medical and Biological Engineering, 1975, 13:577-582

1586. Quinn, I., Harbison, J. & McAllister, A.
An attempt to shape human penile responses
Behavior Research and Therapy, 1970, 8:213-216

1587.   Rachman, S.
        Studies in desensitization   I.   The separate effects
        of relaxation and desensitization
        Behavior Research and Therapy, 1965, 3:245-251

1588.   Rachman, S.
        The role of muscular relaxation in desensitization
        therapy
        Behavior Research and Therapy, 1968, 6:159-166

1589.   Radl, G.W.
        (Use of hybrid-analog laboratory computer with small
        capacity for the control of feedback signals by
        EMG amplitude)
        Biomed Tech (Stuttg), 1972, 17:96-102 (Ger.)

1590.   Ramamurthi, B., et al.
        Nonvolitional biofeedback in the management of
        mental illness
        In W. H. Sweet et al (Eds.), Neurosurgical Treatment
        in Psychiatry, Pain and Epilepsy
        Baltimore: University Park Press, 1977

1591.   Randle, R.J.
        Volitional control of visual accommodation
        Conference Proceedings No. 82, Adaptation and
        Acclimatization in Aerospace Medicine, 1971

1592.   Rao, S.
        Yoga and autohypnotism
        British Journal of Medical Hypnotism, 1965, 17:38-
        40

1593.   Rappaport, A.F., et al.
        EMG feedback for the treatment of bruxism: A
        stress control program
        In D. H. Morgan (Ed.), Diseases of the temporo-
        mandibular apparatus: A multidiscipline approach
        New York: C. V. Mosby (In Press)

1594. Rappaport, H. & Katkin, E.S.
Relationships among manifest anxiety, response to
stress and the perception of autonomic activity
Journal of Consulting and Clinical Psychology, 1972,
38:219-224

1595. Raskin, M., Johnson, G. & Rondestvedt, J.W.
Chronic anxiety treated by feedback-induced muscle
relaxation
Archives of General Psychiatry, 1973, 28:263-267

1596. Rasmussen, W.A.
Instrumental control of systolic blood pressure in
hypertensive subjects
Dissertation Abstracts, 1972, 33B:2819-2820

1597. Ray, W.J., Jr.
The relationship of locus of control, self report
measures, and feedback to the voluntary control of
heart rate
Dissertation Abstracts, 1972, 32B:4226

1598. Ray, W.J.
The relationship of locus of control, self-report
measures and feedback to the voluntary control
of heart rate
Psychophysiology, 1974, 11:527-534

1599. Ray, W.J., Frediani, A.W. & Harman, D.
Self-regulation of hemispheric asymmetry
Biofeedback and Self-Regulation, 1977, 2:195-200

1600. Ray, W.J. & Katahn, M.
Relation of anxiety to locus of control
Psychological Reports, 1968, 23:1196

1601. Ray, W.J. & Lamb, S.B.
Locus of control and voluntary control of heart rate
Psychosomatic Medicine, 1974, 36:180-182

1602. Ray, W. & Strupp, H.
Locus of control and the voluntary control of
heart rate
Psychophysiology, 1972, 9:270 (Abst.)

1603.   Rayter, B. & Sandler, L.
        The effect of cardiac variability and cardiac
          awareness upon heart rate conditionability
        Proceedings of the Biofeedback Research Society
          Sixth Annual Meeting
        Monterey, 1975, 45 (Abst.)

1604.   Reading, C. & Mohr, P.D.
        Biofeedback control of migraine: A pilot study
        British Journal of Social and Clinical Psychology,
          1976, 15:429-434

1605.   Reavley, W.
        The use of biofeedback in the treatment of writers
          cramp
        Journal of Behavior Therapy and Experiental Psychiatry,
          1975, 6:335-338

1606.   Reckless, J.B.
        A behavioral treatment of bronchial asthma in
          modified group therapy
        Psychosomatics, 1971, 12:168-173

1607.   Redmond, D.P., Gayler, M.S., McDonald, R.H., et al.
        Blood pressure and heart-rate response to verbal
          instructions and relaxation in hypertension
        Psychosomatic Medicine, 1974, 36:285-297

1608.   Reed, J.P.
        Determinants of EEG alpha wave control
        Dissertation Abstracts, 1973, 33B:5549

1609.   Reeves, J.L.
        EMG-biofeedback reduction of tension headache: A
          cognitive skills training approach
        Proceedings of the Biofeedback Research Society
          Sixth Annual Meeting
        Monterey, 1975, 98 (Abst.)

1610.   Reeves, J.L.
        EMG-biofeedback reduction of tension headache: A
          cognitive skills - training approach
        Biofeedback and Self-Regulation, 1976, 1:217-225

1611.   Reeves, J. & Mealiea, W.
        Biofeedback-assisted cue-controlled relaxation for
           the treatment of flight phobias
        Journal of Behavior Therapy and Experimental
           Psychiatry, 1975, 6:105-110

1612.   Regestein, Q.R., Buckland, G.H. & Pegram, G.V.
        Effect of daytime alpha rhythm maintenance on
           subsequent sleep
        Psychosomatic Medicine, 1973, 35:415-418

1613.   Regestein, Q.R., Pegram, G.V., Cooke, B., et al.
        Alpha rhythm percentage maintained during 4- and 12-
           hour feedback periods
        Psychosomatic Medicine, 1973, 35:215-222

1614.   Reinking, R.H.
        The influence of internal-external control and
           trait anxiety on acquisition of EMG control
        Biofeedback and Self-Regulation, 1976, 1:359 (Abst.)

1615.   Reinking, R.
        Follow-up and extension of "tension headache - what
           method is the most effective?"
        Biofeedback and Self-Regulation, 1976, 1:350 (Abst.)

1616.   Reinking, R. & Kohl, M.L.
        Effects of various forms of relaxation training on
           physiological and self-report measures of re-
           laxation
        Journal of Consulting and Clinical Psychology, 1975,
           43:595-600

1617.   Reinking, R., Tamayo, F. & Morgret, M.
        Comparative effectiveness of various forms of
           relaxation training
        Proceedings of the Biofeedback Research Society
           Sixth Annual Meeting
        Monterey, 1975, 85 (Abst.)

1618.   Reisman, S., Insko, C.A. & Valins, S.
        Triadic consistency and false heart rate feedback
        Journal of Personality, 1970, 38:629-640

1619.   Revland, P. & Hirschman, R.
        Imagery training and visual biofeedback: Relative
           effects on the self-regulation of heart rate
        Psychophysiology, 1976, 13:186-187 (Abst.)

1620.   Reyes, R.B.
        Operant conditioning of GSR amplitude under feed-
           back and non-feedback situations
        Phillipine Journal of Psychology, 1971, 4:79-87

1621.   Rhead, J.
        Relation of eyes closed resting EEG alpha activity
           to hypnotic susceptibility
        Perceptual and Motor Skills, 1968, 27:1047-1050

1622.   Rice, D.G.
        Operant GSR conditioning and associated electro-
           myogram responses
        Journal of Experimental Psychology, 1966, 71:908-912

1623.   Richter-Heinrich, E., et al.
        Blood pressure control through biofeedback in
           arterial and essential hypertension
        Z. Psychol., 1976, 184:538-550 (Ger.)

1624.   Rickles, W.H.
        Some theoretical aspects of the psychodynamics of
           successful biofeedback treatment
        Biofeedback and Self-Regulation, 1976, 1:360 (Abst.)

1625.   Riddick, C. & Meyer, R.G.
        The efficacy of automated relaxation training with
           response contingent feedback
        Behavior Therapy, 1973, 4:331-337

1626.   Roberts, A.H.
        Biofeedback techniques. The potential for the
           control of pain
        Minnesota Medicine, 1974, 57:167-171

1627.   Roberts, A.H., Kewman, D.G. & Macdonald, H.
        Voluntary control of skin temperature: Unilateral
           changes using hypnosis and auditory feedback
        Proceedings of the Biofeedback Research Society
           Fourth Annual Meeting
        Boston, 1972, 26 (Abst.)

1628. Roberts, A.H., Kewman, D.G. & MacDonald, H.
       Voluntary control of skin temperature: Unilateral
       changes using hypnosis and feedback
       Journal of Abnormal Psychology, 1973, 82:163-168

1629. Roberts, A.H., Schuler, J., Bacon, J., et al.
       Individual differences and autonomic control:
       Absorption, hypnotic susceptibility and the
       unilateral control of skin temperature
       Proceedings of the Biofeedback Research Society
       Fifth Annual Meeting
       Colorado Springs, 1974, 67 (Abst.)

1630. Roberts, A.H., Schuler, J., Bacon, J.R., et al.
       Individual differences and autonomic control:
       Absorption, hypnotic susceptibility and the
       unilateral control of skin temperature
       Journal of Abnormal Psychology, 1975, 84:272-279

1631. Roberts, L.E.
       Comparative psychophysiology of the electrodermal
       and cardiac control systems
       In P. A. Obrist et al (Eds.), Cardiovascular Psycho-
       physiology
       Chicago: Aldine, 1974

1632. Roberts, L.E.
       The role of exteroceptive feedback in learned
       electrodermal and cardiac control: Some attraction
       of and problems with discrimination theory
       In J. Beatty & H. Legewie (Eds.), Biofeedback and
       Behavior
       New York: Plenum Press, 1977

1633. Robinson, B.F., Epstein, S.E., Beiser, G.D. &
       Braunwald, E.
       Control of heart rate by the autonomic nervous
       system: Studies in man in the interrelationship
       between baroreceptor mechanisms and exercise
       Circulation Research, 1966, 19:400-411

1634. Rohland, T.A.
       Sensory feedback for powered limb prostheses
       Medical and Biological Engineering, 1975, 13:300-301

1635.   Rohm, C.E.T., Gibb, J.D. & Sorenson, R.
        Biofeedback hand temperature training and speaking
           behavior
        Biofeedback and Self-Regulation, 1976, 1:350-351
           (Abst.)

1636.   Rond, P.C.
        Biofeedback: When medication is not enough
        Journal of the Florida Medical Association, 1975,
           62:34-35

1637.   Rose, G., Norman, R. & Collins, J.
        Plasticity of visual evoked potentials in kittens
           demonstrated by operant conditioning
        Proceedings of the Biofeedback Research Society
           Fifth Annual Meeting
        Colorado Springs, 1974, 31 (Abst.)

1638.   Rosen, R.C.
        Suppression of penile tumescence by instrumental
           conditioning
        Psychosomatic Medicine, 1973, 35:509-514

1639.   Rosen, R.C.
        Implications of biofeedback for sexual dysfunction
        Proceedings of the Biofeedback Research Society
           Fifth Annual Meeting
        Colorado Springs, 1974, 12 (Abst.)

1640.   Rosen, R.C.
        Genital blood flow measurement: Feedback applications
           in sexual therapy
        The Journal of Sex and Mental Therapy, 1976, 2:184-
           196

1641.   Rosen, R.C.
        Operant control of sexual responses in man
        In G. E. Schwartz & J. Beatty (Eds.), Biofeedback:
           Theory and Practice
        New York: Academic Press, 1977

1642.   Rosen, R.C. & Kopel, S.
        Penile plethysmography and biofeedback in the treat-
           ment of a transvestite - exhibitionist
        Journal of Consulting and Clinical Psychology, 1977,
           45:908-916

1643.   Rosen, R.C., Shapiro, D. & Schwartz, G.E.
         Voluntary control of penile tumescence
         Psychosomatic Medicine, 1975, 37:479-483

1644.   Rosenboom, D. (Ed.)
         Biofeedback and the Arts: Results of early Experiment
         Vancouver: Aesthetic Research Center, 1976

1645.   Rosenfeld, J.P.
         The meaning of operantly conditioned changes in
            evoked responses
         In G. E. Schwartz & J. Beatty (Eds.), Biofeedback:
            Theory and Research
         New York: Academic Press, 1977

1646.   Rosenfeld, J.P. & Fox, S.S.
         Operant control of a brain potential evoked by a
            behavior
         Physiology and Behavior, 1971, 7:489-493

1647.   Rosenfeld, J.P. & Fox, S.S.
         Sequential representation of voluntary movement in
            cortical macropotentials: Direct control of
            behavior by operant conditioning of wave amplitude
         Journal of Neurophysiology, 1972, 35:879-891

1648.   Rosenfeld, J.P. & Hetzler, B.E.
         Operant-controlled evoked responses: Discrimination
            of conditioned and normally occurring components
         Science, 1973, 181:797-769

1649.   Rosenfeld, J.P., Hetzler, B.E. & Kosnik, W.
         Operant photic evoked potential control, unmediated
            by selective orientation
         Physiology and Behavior, 1974, 13:479-482

1650.   Rosenfeld, J.P. & Owen, R.L.
         Instrumental conditioning of photic evoked potentials:
            Mechanisms and properties of late component modi-
            fication
         Physiology and Behavior, 1972, 9:851-858

1651.   Rosenfeld, J.P., Rudell, A.P. & Fox, S.S.
         Operant control of neural events in humans
         Science, 1969, 165:821-823

1652.   Roth, S.R., Sterman, M.B. & Clemente, C.D.
         Comparison of EEG correlates of reinforcement,
             interval inhibition, and sleep
         Electroencephalography and Clinical Neurophysiology.
             1967, 23:509-520

1653.   Rotter, J.B.
         Generalized expectancies for internal versus ex-
             ternal control of reinforcement
         Psychological Monographs, 1966, 80:1-28

1654.   Rouse, L.O.
         LSD-25 in the treatment of epilepsy
         Proceedings of the Biofeedback Research Society
             Fourth Annual Meeting
         Boston, 1972, 40 (Abst.)

1655.   Rouse, L.O.
         Some new instrumentation and methodology for EEG
             biofeedback
         Proceedings of the Biofeedback Research Society
             Fifth Annual Meeting
         Colorado Springs, 1974, 109 (Abst.)

1656.   Rouse, L.O.
         Strobe trigger, compound alpha filter, and phase
             coherence detector for EEG biofeedback
         Behavior Research Methods and Instrumentation, 1974,
             6:335-337

1657.   Rouse, L.O.
         Orgasm, epilepsy, drugs and biofeedback
         Proceedings of the Biofeedback Research Society
             Sixth Annual Meeting
         Monterey, 1975, 50 (Abst.)

1658.   Rouse, L.O.
         EEG alpha spectral interactions as a function of
             arousal, affective and feedback bandpass variables
         Biofeedback and Self-Regulation, 1977, 2:283-284
             (Abst.)

1659.   Rouse, L., Peterson, J. & Shapiro, G.
        EEG alpha entrainment reaction to the biofeedback
           setting and some possible effects on epilepsy
        Proceedings of the Biofeedback Research Society
           Fifth Annual Meeting
        Colorado Springs, 1974, 18 (Abst.)

1660.   Rouse, L., Peterson, J. & Shapiro, G.
        EEG alpha entrainment reaction within the biofeed-
           back setting and some possible effects on epilepsy
        Physiological Psychology, 1975, 3:113-122

1661.   Rouse, L.O. & Solomon, G.F.
        Baseline procedures for application of EEG alpha
           biofeedback to rehabilitation of criminal offenders
        Corrective and Social Psychiatry and Journal of
           Applied Behavior Therapy, 1977, 23:56-60

1662.   Rubow, R. & Smith, K.
        Feedback parameters of electromyographic learning
        American Journal of Physical Medicine, 1971, 50:115-
           131

1663.   Rugh, J.D.
        A behavioral approach to the diagnosis and treatment
           of functional oral disorders: Biofeedback and
           self control techniques
        In J. D. Rugh, D. Perlis, & R. Disraeli (Eds.),
           Biofeedback in Dentistry: Research and Clinical
           Applications
        Phoenix: Semantodontics, 1976

1664.   Rugh, J.D.
        Learning differential control of balanced orofacial
           muscles
        Biofeedback and Self-Regulation, 1977, 2:209-310
           (Abst.)

1665.   Rugh, J.D., Perlis, D.B. & Disraeli, R.I. (Eds.)
        Biofeedback in Dentistry: Research and Clinical
           Applications
        Phoenix: Semantodontics, 1976

1666.   Rugh, J.D. & Schwitzgebel, R.I.
        Comparative evaluation of commercial EEG and EMG
          feedback devices
        Proceedings of the Biofeedback Research Society
          Sixth Annual Meeting
        Monterey, 1975, 89 (Abst.)

1667.   Rugh, J.D. & Schwitzgebel, R.L.
        Biofeedback apparatus: Supplier list
        Behavior Therapy, 1975, 6:238-240

1668.   Rugh, J.D. & Schwitzgebel, R.L.
        Instrumentation for behavioral assessment
        In A. R. Ciminero, K.S. Calhoun & H. E. Adams
          (Eds.), Handbook for Behavioral Assessment
        New York: Wiley & Sons, 1976

1669.   Rugh, J.D. & Schwitzgebel, R.L.
        Variability in commercial electromyographic biofeed-
          back devices
        Behavior Research Methods and Instrumentation, 1977,
          9:281-285

1670.   Rugh, J.D. & Solberg, W.K.
        The identification of stressful stimuli in natural
          environments using a portable biofeedback unit
        Proceedings of the Biofeedback Research Society
          Fifth Annual Meeting
        Colorado Springs, 1974, 54 (Abst.)

1671.   Rugh, J.D. & Solberg, W.K.
        Electromyographic studies of bruxist behavior before
          and during treatment
        Journal of California Dental Association, 1975,
          3:56-59

1672.   Rugh, J.D. & Solberg, W.K.
        Psychological implications in temporomandibular pain
          and dysfunction
        Oral Sciences Review, 1976, 7:3-30

1673.   Rugh, J.D. & Solberg, W.K.
        The identification of stressful stimuli in natural
            environments using a portable biofeedback unit
        In J. Rugh & W. Solberg (Eds.), Biofeedback in
            Dentistry
        Phoenix: Semantodontics, 1977

1674.   Runnals, S. & Mulholland, T.
        A method for the study of bilateral asymmetry of
            cortical activation
        American Journal of EEG Technology, 1964, 4:15-18

1675.   Runnals, S. & Mulholland, T.
        Selected demonstrations of voluntary regulation of
            cortical activation
        Bedford Research, 1965, 11:26

1676.   Russ, K.L.
        Effect of two different feedback paradigms on
            blood pressure levels of patients with essential
            hypertension
        Proceedings of the Biofeedback Research Society
            Fifth Annual Meeting
        Colorado Springs, 1974, 38 (Abst.)

1677.   Russ, K.L.
        EMG biofeedback of spasmodic torticollis: A case
            presentation
        Proceedings of the Biofeedback Research Society
            Sixth Annual Meeting
        Monterey, 1975, 28 (Abst.)

1678.   Russ, K.L.
        Informational, incentive, and electromyographic
            feedback techniques as applied to hypertensive
            patients: Contrasts and comparisons
        Biofeedback and Self-Regulation, 1977, 2:306-307
            (Abst.)

1679.   Russ, K.L., Hammer, R.L. & Adderton, M.
        Clinical Follow-up: Treatment and outcome of
            functional headache patients treated with bio-
            feedback
        Biofeedback and Self-Regulation, 1977, 2:298 (Abst.)

1680.   Russell, H.L.
        Fingertip temperature changes during relaxation and
            psychotherapy
        Psychophysiology, 1972, 9:279 (Abst.)

1681.   Russell, H.L., Hunter, S.H. & Russell, E.D.
        The ability of elementary school children to learn
            autoregulation of fingertip skin temperature:
            Preliminary results
        Proceedings of the Biofeedback Research Society
            Fifth Annual Meeting
        Colorado Springs, 1974, 64 (Abst.)

1682.   Russell, G. & Woolridge, C.P.
        Correction of an habitual head tilt using biofeed-
            back techniques: A case study
        Physiotherapy Canada, 1975, 27:181-187

1683.   Ryan, B.P. & Van Kirk, B.
        The establishment, transfer, and maintenance of
            fluent speech in 50 stutterers using delayed
            auditory feedback and operant procedures
        Journal of Speech and Hearing Disorders, 1974, 39:3-
            10

1684.   Sacks, B., Fenwick, P.B.C., Marks, I., et al.
        An investigation of the phenomenon of autocontrol of
           the alpha rhythm and possible associated feeling
           states using visual feedback
        Electroencephalography and Clinical Neurophysiology,
           1972, 32:461-463

1685.   Santee, J.L., Riggin, C.S., Kleinman, K.M., et al.
        Use of EMG feedback to increase foot dorsiflexion in
           stroke patients
        Psychophysiology, 1977, 14:88-89

1686.   Sargent, J.D.
        Biofeedback and biocybernetics
        In J.I. Martin (Ed.), Proceedings of the San Diego
           Biomedical Symposium 1976 - Vol 15
        New York: Academic Press, 1976

1687.   Sargent, J.D., Green, E.E. & Walters, E.D.
        The use of autogenic feedback training in a pilot
           study of migraine and tension headaches
        Headache, 1972, 12:120-124

1688.   Sargent, J.D., Green, E.E. & Walters, E.D.
        Preliminary report on the use of autogenic feedback
           techniques in the treatment of migraine and
           tension headache
        Psychosomatic Medicine, 1973, 35:129-135

1689.   Sargent, J.D., Walters, E.D. & Green, E.E.
        Psychosomatic self-regulation of migraine headaches
        Seminars in Psychiatry, 1973, 5:415-427

1690.   Sasmor, R.M.
        Operant conditioning of a small-scale muscle response
        Journal of the Experimental Analysis of Behavior,
           1966, 9:69-85

1691.   Savill, G.E. & Koppman, J.W.
        Voluntary temporal artery regulation compared with
           finger blood volume and temperature
        Proceedings of the Biofeedback Research Society
           Sixth Annual Meeting
        Monterey, 1975, 55 (Abst.)

1692.   Schaefer, S. & Engel, R.
        Operant control of autonomic functions: Biofeedback
           bibliography
        Perceptual and Motor Skills, 1973, 36:863-875

1693.   Schandler, S.L. & Grings, W.W.
        A system for providing tactile EMG biofeedback
        Behavior Research Methods and Instrumentation, 1974,
           6:541-542

1694.   Schandler, S.L. & Grings, W.W.
        An examination of methods for producing relaxation
           during short term laboratory sessions
        Behavior Research and Therapy, 1976, 14:419-426

1695.   Scherr, M.S.,Crawford, P.L., Sergent, C.B., et al.
        Effects of biofeedback techniques on chronic asthma
           in a summer camp environent
        Annals of Allergy, 1975, 35:289-295

1696.   Schmeidler, G. & Lewis, L.
        Mood changes after alpha feedback training
        Perceptual and Motor Skills, 1971, 32:709-710

1697.   Schneider, J.A.
        Finger temperature feedback procedures: Sympathetic
           inhibition training or placebo effect
        Psychotherapy: Theory, Research and Practice, 1976,
           13:141-147

1698.   Schneider, R.D., Sobol, M.P. & Herrmann, T.F., et
           al.
        A reexamination of the relationship between locus
           of control and voluntary heart rate change
        Biofeedback and Self-Regulation, 1977, 2:302 (Abst.)

1699.   Schneiderman, N.
        The relationship between learned and unlearned
           cardiovascular response
        In P. A. Obrist, et al (Eds.), Cardiovascular Psycho-
           physiology
        Chicago: Aldine Publishing Co., 1974

1700.   Schultz, J. & Luthe, W.
        Autogenic Training. A Psychophysiologic Approach in
            Psychotherapy
        New York: Grune & Stratton, 1959

1701.   Schultz, J.H. & Luthe, W.
        Autogenic Therapy: Autogenic Methods
        New York: Grune & Stratton, 1969

1702.   Schuster, M.M.
        Operant conditioning in gastrointestinal dysfunctions
        Hospital Practice, 1974, 135-143

1703.   Schuster, M.M.
        Biofeedback treatment of gastrointestinal disorders
        Medical Clinics of North America, 1977, 61:907-912

1704.   Schuster, M.M.
        Gastrointestinal tract dysfunctions respond to
            biofeedback
        Geriatrics, 1977, 32:32

1705.   Schwartz, G.E.
        Cardiac responses to self-induced thoughts
        Psychophysiology, 1971, 8:462-467

1706.   Schwartz, G.E.
        Learned control of cardiovascular integration in man
            through operant conditioning
        Psychosomatic Medicine, 1971, 33:57-62

1707.   Schwartz, G.E.
        Voluntary control of human cardiovascular integration
            and differentiation through feedback and reward
        Science, 1972, 175:90-93

1708.   Schwartz, G.E.
        Biofeedback as therapy: Some theoretical and
            practical issues
        American Psychologist, 1973, 28:666-673

1709.   Schwartz, G.E.
        Toward a theory of voluntary control of response
            patterns in the cardiovascular system
        In P. Obrist et al (Eds.), Cardiovascular Psycho-
            physiology
        Chicago: Aldine Publishing Co., 1974

1710.   Schwartz, G.E.
        Biofeedback, self-regulation and the patterning of
            physiological responses
        American Scientist, 1975, 63:314-324

1711.   Schwartz, G. E.
        Self-regulation of response patterning
        Biofeedback and Self-Regulation, 1976, 1:7-30

1712.   Schwartz, G.E.
        Biofeedback and cardiovascular self-regulation:
            Neurophysiological mechanisms
        In W. deJong, et al.(Eds.), Hypertension and Brain
            Mechanisms
        Progress in Brain Research, 43, Netherlands:
            Elsevier, 1977

1713.   Schwartz, G.E.
        Psychosomatic disorders and biofeedback: A psycho-
            biological model of disregulation
        In J. D. Maser & M. Seligman (Eds.), Psychopathology:
            Experimental Models
        San Francisco: W. H. Freeman and Co., 1977

1714.   Schwartz, G.E.
        Biofeedback and patterning of autonomic and central
            processes: CNS-Cardiovascular interactions
        In G. E. Schwartz & J. Beatty (Eds.), Biofeedback:
            Theory and Research
        New York: Academic Press, 1977

1715.   Schwartz, G.E.
        Biofeedback and physiological patterning in human
            emotion and consciousness
        In J. Beatty & H. Legewie (Eds.), Biofeedback and
            Behavior
        New York: Plenum Press, 1977

1716.   Schwartz, G.E. & Beatty, J. (Eds.)
        Biofeedback: Theory and Research
        New York: Academic Press, 1977

1717.   Schwartz, G.E., Davidson, R. & Maer, F.
        Right hemisphere lateralization for emotion in the
            human brain: Interactions with cognition
        Science, 1975, 190:286-288

1718.   Schwartz, G.E., Davidson, R.J. & Pugash, E.
        Voluntary control of patterns of EEG parietal
            asymmetry: Cognitive concomitants
        Psychophysiology, 1976, 13:498-504

1719.   Schwartz, G.E., Davidson, R.J. & Pugash, E.
        Voluntary control of patterns of EEG parietal
            symmetry: Cognitive concomitants
        Psychophysiology, 1976, 13:166 (Abst.)

1720.   Schwartz, G.E., Fair, P., Greenberg, P., et al.
        Facial expression and depression: An electromyo-
            graphic study
        Psychosomatic Medicine, 1974, 36:458 (Abst.)

1721.   Schwartz, G.E., Fair, P.L., Salt, P., et al.
        Facial muscle patterning to affective imagery in
            depressed and nondepressed subjects
        Science, 1976, 192:489-491

1722.   Schwartz, G.E., Fair, P.L., Salt, P., et al.
        Facial expression and imagery in depression: An
            electromyographic study
        Psychosomatic Medicine, 1976, 38:337-347

1723.   Schwartz , G.E. & Johnson, H.J.
        Affective visual stimuli as operant reinforcers of
            the GSR
        Journal of Experimental Psychology, 1969, 80:28-32

1724.   Schwartz, G.E. & Shapiro, D.
        Biofeedback and essential hypertension: Current
            findings and theoretical concerns
        Seminars in Psychiatry, 1973, 5:493-503

1725.   Schwartz, G.E. & Shapiro, D.
        Consciousness and Self-Regulation
        New York: Plenum Press, 1976

1726.   Schwartz, G.E., Shapiro, D. & Tursky, B.
        Learned control of cardiovascular interaction in man
            through operant conditioning
        Psychosomatic Medicine, 1971, 33:57-62

1727. Schwartz, G.E., Vogler, J. & Young, L.
Heart rate self-regulation as skill learning:
   Strength-endurance vs. cardiac reaction time
Psychophysiology, 1975, 12:234 (Abst.)

1728. Schwartz, G., Shapiro, D. & Tursky, B.
Self-control of patterns of human diastolic blood
   pressure and heart rate through feedback and
   reward
Psychophysiology, 1972, 9:270 (Abst.)

1729. Schwartz, G.E., Shaw, G. & Shapiro, D.
Specificity of alpha and heart rate control through
   feedback
Psychophysiology, 1972, 9:269 (Abst.)

1730. Schwartz, G.E., Young, L.D. & Volger, J.
Heart rate regulation as skill learning: Strength-
   endurance versus cardiac reaction time
Psychophysiology, 1976, 13:472

1731. Schwitzgebel, R.L.
Survey of electromechanical devices for behavior
   modification
Psychological Bulletin, 1968, 70:444-459

1732. Schwitzgebel, R.L. & Rugh, J.D.
"Of bread, circuses, and alpha machines."
American Psychologist, 1975, 30:363-370

1733. Scopp, A.L.
Relaxation training: Cognitive and affective
   components
Proceedings of the Biofeedback Research Society
   Sixth Annual Meeting
Monterey, 1975, 71 (Abst.)

1734. Scott, C.H.
An electromyographic investigation of bilaterally
   recorded action potentials from the orbicularis
   oris muscle in stutterers and nonstutterers
Archives of Physical Medicine, 1972, 53:589 (Abst.)

1735.   Scott, J. & Timmons, B.
        On the relationship between frontalis EMG activity
          and skin temperature: A preliminary model with
          very little data
        Proceedings of the Biofeedback Research Society
          Fifth Annual Meeting
        Colorado Springs, 1974, 65 (Abst.)

1736.   Scott, R.W., Blanchard, E.B., Edmundson, E.D., et
          al.
        A shaping procedure for heart-rate control in
          chronic tachycardia
        Perceptual and Motor Skills, 1973, 37:327-338

1737.   Scott, R.W., Peters, R.D., Gillespie, W.J., et al.
        The use of shaping and reinforcement in the operant
          acceleration and deceleration of heart rate
        Behavior Research and Therapy, 1973, 11:179-185

1738.   Scripture, E.W., Smith, T.L. & Brown, E.M.
        On the education of muscular control and power
        Studies of the Yale Psychology Laboratory, 1894,
          2:114

1739.   Scully, H.E. & Basmajian, J.V.
        Motor-unit training and influence of manual skill
        Psychophysiology, 1969, 5:625-632

1740.   Scully, H.E. & Basmajian, J.V.
        Effect of nerve stimulation on trained motor unit
          control
        Archives of Physical Medicine and Rehabilitation,
          1969, 50:32-33

1741.   Scully, T.
        A 128 point amplitude-frequency histogram algorithm
          and hardware for real-time EEG analysis
        Biofeedback and Self-Regulation, 1977, 2:325 (Abst.)

1742.   Sedlacek, K.
        EMG, GSR and thermal biofeedback in the treatment of
          hypertension
        Biofeedback and Self-Regulation, 1976, 1:311-312
          (Abst.)

1743.   Sedlacek, K.
        EMG and thermal feedback as a treatment for Raynaud's
            Disease
        Biofeedback and Self-Regulation, 1976, 1:318 (Abst.)

1744.   Sedlacek, K. & Heczey, M.
        A specific biofeedback treatment for dysmenorrhea
        Biofeedback and Self-Regulation, 1977, 2:294 (Abst.)

1745.   Segal, J.
        Biofeedback as a medical treatment
        Journal of the American Medical Association, 1975,
            232:179-180

1746.   Seifert, A.R. & Lubar, J.F.
        Reduction of epileptic seizures through EMG biofeedback
            training
        Biological Psychology, 1975, 3:157-184

1747.   Selye, H.
        The evolution of the stress concept
        American Scientist, 1973, 61:692-699

1748.   Selye, H.
        Confusion and controversy in the stress field
        Journal of Human Stress, 1975, 1:37-44

1749.   Selye, H.
        The Stress of Life
        New York: McGraw-Hill, 1974

1750.   Selye, H.
        Stress Without Distress
        New York: McGraw-Hill, 1974

1751.   Selzer, F.A. & Fehmi, L.G.
        Auto-regulation of EEG alpha wave production as a
            function of the direction of conjugate lateral eye
            movements
        Proceedings of the Biofeedback Research Society
            Fifth Annual Meeting
        Colorado Springs, 1974, 82 (Abst.)

1752. Selzer, F. & Fehmi, L.G.
       Effects of rhythmical auditory signals on the electro-
       encephalogram (EEG)
       Proceedings of the Biofeedback Research Society
       Sixth Annual Meeting
       Monterey, 1975, 66 (Abst.)

1753. Shagass, C.
       Conditioning the human occipital alpha rhythm to a
       voluntary stimulus. A quantitative study
       Journal of Experimental Psychology, 1942, 31:367-379

1754. Shambes, G.M. & Waterland, J.C.
       Control of motor units in skill and postural muscles
       in normal man. An electromyographic study
       American Journal of Physiology and Medicine, 1973,
       52:114-123

1755. Shanks, E.M. & Brener, J.M.
       Instructional control of diastolic blood pressure in
       human subjects
       Psychophysiology, 1974, 11:240 (Abst.)

1756. Shapiro, A.P., et al.
       Relationships of perception, cognition, suggestion
       and operant conditioning in essential hypertension
       Progress in Brain Research, 1975, 42:299-312

1757. Shapiro, A.K.
       Contribution to a history of the placebo effect
       Behavioral Science, 1960, 5:109-135

1758. Shapiro, D.
       Recommendations of ethics committee regarding bio-
       feedback techniques and instrumentation: Issues
       of public and professional concern
       Psychophysiology, 1973, 10:533-535

1759.   Shapiro, D.
        Role of feedback and instructions in the voluntary
           control of human blood pressure
        Japanese Journal of Biofeedback Research, 1973, 1:2-
           9 (Japanese)

1760.   Shapiro, D.
        Operant-feedback control of human blood pressure:
           Some clinical issues
        In P. A. Obrist et al (Eds.), Cardiovascular
           Psychophysiology
        Chicago: Aldine Publishing Co., 1974

1761.   Shapiro, D.
        Biofeedback
        In R. O. Pasnau, (Ed.), Consultation-Liaison
           Psychiatry
        New York: Grune & Stratton, 1975

1762.   Shapiro, D.
        Biofeedback and the regulation of complex psycho-
           logical processes
        In J. Beatty & H. Legewie (Eds.), Biofeedback and
           Behavior
        New York: Plenum Press, 1977

1763.   Shapiro, D.
        A monologue on biofeedback and psychophysiology
        Psychophysiology, 1977, 14:213-227

1764.   Shapiro, D., Barber, T.X., DiCara, L.V., Kamiya, J.,
           Miller, N.E. & Stoyva, J.(Eds.),
        Biofeedback and Self-Control, 1972: An Aldine
           Annual on The Regulation of Bodily Processes and
           Consciousness
        Chicago: Aldine Publishing Co., 1973

1765.   Shapiro, D. & Crider, A.B.
        Operant electrodermal conditioning under multiple
           schedules of reinforcement
        Psychophysiology, 1967, 4:168-175

1766.   Shapiro, D., Crider, A.B. & Tursky, B.
        Differentiation of an autonomic response through
           operant reinforcements
        Psychonomic Science, 1964,, 1:147-148

1767.   Shapiro, D., Mainardi, J.A. & Surwit, R.S.
         Biofeedback and self-regulation in essential hyper-
            tension
         In G. E. Schwartz & J. Beatty (Eds), Biofeedback:
            Theory and Research
         New York: Academic Press, 1977

1768.   Shapiro, D. & Schwartz, G.E.
         Biofeedback and visceral learning: Clinical appli-
            cations
         Seminars in Psychiatry, 1972, 4:171-184

1769.   Shapiro, D. & Schwartz, G.E.
         Control of diastolic blood pressure in man by
            feedback and reinforcement
         Psychophysiology, 1972, 9:296-304

1770.   Shapiro, D. & Schwartz, G.E.
         Comparison of varied instructions and feedback in
            the voluntary control of human blood pressure
         Psychophysiology, 1974, 11:231 (Abst.)

1771.   Shapiro, D., Schwartz, G.E. & Benson, H.
         Biofeedback: A behavioral approach to cardiovascular
            control
         In R. S. Eliot (Ed.), Stress and the Heart
         New York: Futura, 1974

1772.   Shapiro, D., Schwartz, G.E., Shnidman, S., et al.
         Operant control of fear-related electrodermal res-
            ponses in snakephobic subjects
         Psychophysiology, 1972, 9:271 (Abst.)

1773.   Shapiro, D., Schwartz, G.E. & Tursky, B.
         Control of diastolic blood pressure in man by
            feedback and reinforcement
         Psychophysiology, 1972, 9:296-304

1774.   Shapiro, D. & Surwit, R.S.
         Operant conditioning: A new theoretical approach in
            psychosomatic medicine
         International Journal of Psychiatry in Medicine,
            1974, 5:377-387

1775. Shapiro, D., Tursky, B., Gershon, E. & Stern, M.
       Effects of feedback and reinforcement on the control
       of human systolic blood pressure
       Science, 1969, 163:588-589

1776. Shapiro, D., Tursky, B. & Schwartz, G.E.
       Control of blood pressure in man by operant con-
       ditioning
       Supplements in Circulation Research, 1970, 26:I-27
       to I-32

1777. Shapiro, D., Tursky, B. & Schwartz, G.E.
       Differentiation of heart rate and systolic blood
       pressure in man by operant conditioning
       Psychosomatic Medicine, 1970, 32:417-423

1778. Shapiro, D., Tursky, B. & Schwartz, G.E.
       Decreased systolic blood pressure through operant
       conditioning techniques in patients with essential
       hypertension
       Science, 1971, 173:740-742

1779. Shapiro, D. & Watanabe, T.
       Timing characteristics of operant electrodermal
       modification: Fixed-interval effects
       Japanese Psychological Research, 1971, 13:123-130

1780. Shapiro, D. & Watanabe, T.
       Reinforcement of spontaneous electrodermal activity:
       A cross-cultural study in Japan
       Psychophysiology, 1972, 9:340-344

1781. Shapiro, D.H. & Zifferblatt, S.M.
       Zen meditation and behavioral self-control: Simi-
       larities, differences, and clinical applications
       American Psychologist, 1976, 31:519-532

1782. Shapiro, D., Barber, T.X., DiCara, L.V., Kamiya, J.,
       Miller, N.E. & Stoyva, J. (Eds.)
       Biofeedback and Self-Control 1972: An Aldine Annual
       on the Regulation of Bodily Processes and Conscious-
       ness
       Chicago: Aldine Publishing Co., 1973

1783. Shatus, E.L.
       Electromyographic biofeedback training in mild
          hemiparesis
       Newsletter for Research in Mental Health and Be-
          havioral Sciences, 1976, 18:5-7

1784. Shealy, C.N.
       Biogenic technique in management of pain
       Biofeedback and Self-Regulation, 1976, 1:252 (Abst.)

1785. Shean, G.D.
       Instrumental modification of the galvanic skin
          response: Conditioning or control
       Journal of Psychosomatic Research, 1970, 14:155-160

1786. Shean, G.D. & Stange, P.W.
       The effects of varied respiratory rate and volume
          upon finger pulse volume
       Psychophysiology, 1971, 8:401-405

1787. Shearn, D.
       Does the heart learn?
       Psychological Bulletin, 1961, 58:452-458

1788. Shearn, D.W.
       Operant conditioning of heart rate
       Science, 1962, 137:530-531

1789. Shedivy, D.I. & Kleinman, K.M.
       Lack of correlation between frontalis EMG and either
          neck EMG or verbal ratings of tension
       Psychophysiology, 1977, 14:182-186

1790. Sheer, D.E.
       Demonstration of a miniature portable unit for
          recording 40 Hz EEG in humans
       Proceedings of the Biofeedback Research Society
          Sixth Annual Meeting
       Monterey, 1975, 19 (Abst.)

1791. Sheer, D.E.
       Biofeedback training of 40 Hz EEG and behavior
       In N. Burch & H. L. Altshuler (Eds.), Behavior and
          Brain Electrical Activity
       New York: Plenum Press, 1975

1792. Sheridan, C.L., Boehm, M.B., Ward, L.B., et al.
Autogenic biofeedback, autogenic phrases and bio-
feedback compared
Biofeedback and Self-Regulation, 1976, 1:315-316
(Abst.)

1793. Sheridan, C.L., Vaughan, K.S., Wallerstedt, M.J.,
et al.
Electromyographic biofeedback and proressive relaxation compared: Interactions with gender and
type of dependent measure
Biofeedback and Self-Regulation, 1977, 2:320-431
(Abst.)

1794. Sherman, R.A.
Case reports of treatment of phantom limb pain with
a combination of electromyographic biofeedback and
verbal relaxation techniques
Biofeedback and Self-Regulation, 1976, 1:353 (Abst.)

1795. Sherman, R.A. & Mayfield, D.W.
Effects of the biofeedback environment on frontal
EMG and blood pressure
Biofeedback and Self-Regulation, 1977, 2:310 (Abst.)

1796. Shinkman, P.G., Bruce, C.J. & Pfingst, B.E.
Operant conditioning of single unit response
patterns in visual cortex
Science, 1974, 184:1194-1196

1797. Shipman, W.G., Oken, D., Goldstein, I.B., et al.
A study in the psychophysiology of muscle tension.
II. Personality factors
Archives of General Psychiatry, 1964, 11:330-345

1798. Shipman, W., Oken, D. & Heath, H.
Muscle tension and effort at self-control during
anxiety
Archives of General Psychiatry, 1970, 23:359-368

1799. Shnidman, S.R.
Instrumental conditioning of orienting responses
using positive reinforcement
Journal of Experimental Psychology, 1970, 83:491-494

1800. Shnidman, S.R. & Shapiro, D.
       Instrumental modification of elicited autonomic
          responses
       Psychophysiology, 1970, 7:395-401

1801. Shoemaker, J.E. & Tasto, D.L.
       The effects of muscle relaxation on blood pressure
          of essential hypertensives
       Behavior Research and Therapy, 1975, 13:29-43

1802. Shouse, M.N. & Lubar, J.F.
       Management of the hyperkinetic syndrome in children
          concurrent with sensorimotor rhythm biofeedback
          training
       Biofeedback and Self-Regulation, 1976, 1:339 (Abst.)

1803. Shouse, M.N. & Lubar, J.F.
       Management of the hyperkinetic syndrome with methyl-
          phenidate and SMR biofeedback training
       Biofeedback and Self-Regulation, 1977, 2:290 (Abst.)

1804. Sidorov, I. & Efimov, V.N.
       Simple schemes for carrying out a directed experiment
          with bioregulated feedback
       Fiziol Zh SSSR, 1974, 60:459-461

1805. Siegel, M.E.
       Biofeedback as an educational technology
       Educational Technology, 1977, 17:37

1806. Silverman, A.J. & McGough, W.E.
       Personality, stress and venous flow rates
       Journal of Psychosomatic Research, 1971,
          15:315

1807. Silverman, S. & Sherwood, M.
       Operant conditioning of the amplitude component of
          the EEG
       Psychophysiology, 1972, 9:269 (Abst.)

1808. Sim, M.K.
       Treatment of disease without the use of drugs I.
          Research on biofeedback training
       Singapore Medical Journal, 1976, 17:167-173

1809.   Simard, T.G.
        Fine sensorimotor control in healthy children: An
           electromyographic study
        Pediatrics, 1969, 43:1035-1041

1810.   Simard, T.G. & Basmajian, J.V.
        Methods in training the conscious control of motor
           units
        Archives of Physical Medicine, 1967, 48:12-19

1811.   Simard, T.G. & Basmajian, J.V.
        Effects of ischemia on trained motor units
        American Journal of Physical Medicine, 1968, 47:64-
           71

1812.   Simard, T.G. & Ladd, H.W.
        Pre-orthotic training--an electromyographic study
           in normal adults
        American Journal of Physical Medicine, 1969, 48:301-
           312

1813.   Simard, T.G. & Ladd, H.W.
        Conscious control of motor units with thalidomide
           children: An electromyographic study
        Developmental Medicine and Child Neurology, 1969,
           11:743-748

1814.   Simard, T. & Ladd, H.
        Differential control of muscle segments by quadriplegic
           patients: Electromyographical procedural in-
           vestigation
        Archives of Physical Medicine and Rehabilitation,
           1971, 52:447-454

1815.   Simard, T.G. & Ladd, H.W.
        Hand orthotic device influence on fine neuromuscular
           control
        Archives of Physical Medicine and Rehabilitation,
           1976, 57:258-263

1816.   Sime, W.E. & DeGood, D.E.
        Stress testing recovery EMG for evaluation of
           biofeedback and progressive muscle relaxation
           training effects
        Biofeedback and Self-Regulation, 1977, 2:317-318
        (Abst.)

1817.   Sime, W. & DeGood, D.
        Effect of EMG biofeedback and progressive muscle
        relaxation training on awareness of frontalis
        muscle tension
        Psychophysiology, 1977, 14:522-530

1818.   Sime, W.E., DeGood, D.E. & Noble, B.J.
        "Awareness" of frontalis muscle tension before and
        after EMG biofeedback relaxation training
        Psychophysiology, 1976, 13:164 (Abst.)

1819.   Simon, J.
        Creativity and altered states of consciousness
        The American Journal of Psychoanalysis, 1977, 37:3-
        12

1820.   Simonton, O.C. & Simonton, S.
        Belief systems and management of the emotional
        aspects of malignancy
        Journal of Transpersonal Psychology, 1975, 7:29-47

1821.   Simpson, D.D.
        Relaxation and biofeedback training using finger
        pulse volume
        JSAS Catalog of Selected Documents in Psychology,
        1973, 3:41(MS #341)

1822.   Simpson, D.D. & Nelson, A.E.
        Specificity of finger pulse volume feedback during
        relaxation
        Biofeedback and Self-Regulation, 1976, 1:433-443

1823.   Simpson, D.E.
        Heart rate feedback, anxiety, and psychophysiological
        reactions under neural and stress conditions
        Dissertation Abstracts, 1969, 30B:2408-2409

1824.   Simpson, H.M. & Climan, M.H.
        Pupillary and electromyographic changes during an
        imagery task
        Psychophysiology, 1971, 8:483-490

1825.   Simpson, H.M. & Paivio, A.
        Changes in pupil size during an imaginary task
        without motor response involvement
        Psychonomic Science, 1966, 5:405-406

1826.   Simpson, H., Paivio, A. & Rogers, T.
        Occipital alpha activity of high and low visual
           imagers during problem solving
        Psychonomic Science, 1967, 8:49-50

1827.   Singer, J.
        A Jungian view of biofeedback training
        Journal of Transpersonal Psychology, 1976, 8:112-
           118

1828.   Sirota, A.D. & Mahoney, M.J.
        Relaxing on cue: The self regulation of asthma
        Journal of Behavior Therapy and Experimental
           Psychiatry 1974, 5:65-66

1829.   Sirota, A., Schwartz, G.E. & Shapiro, D.
        Effects of feedback control of heart rate on judg-
           ments of electric shock intensity
        Proceedings of the Biofeedback Research Society
           Fourth Annual Meeting
        Boston, 1972, 36 (Abst.)

1830.   Sirota, A.D., Schwartz, G.E. & Shapiro, D.
        Effects of feedback control of heart rate on
           judgments of electric shock intensity
        Psychophysiology, 1973, 10:212-213 (Abst.)

1831.   Sirota, A.D., Schwartz, G.E. & Shapiro, D.
        Voluntary control of human heart rate: Effects on
           reactions to aversive stimuli
        Journal of Abnormal Psychology, 1974, 83:261-267

1832.   Sirota, A.D., Schwartz, G.E. & Shapiro, D.
        Voluntary control of human heart rate: Effect on
           reaction to aversive stimulation. A replication
           and extension
        Journal of Abnormal Psychology, 1976, 85:473-477

1833.   Sirota, A.D., Shapiro, D. Schwartz, G.E.
        Self-regulation of heart rate and perception of a
           noxious stimulus
        Proceedings of the Biofeedback Research Society
           Sixth Annual Meeting
        Monterey, 1975, 41 (Abst.)

1834.   Sirota, A.D., Shapiro, D. & Schwartz, G.E.
         Heart rate feedback and instructional effects on
            subjective reaction to aversive stimuli
         Psychophysiology, 1977, 14:82 (Abst.)

1835.   Sisson, D.E.
         A case of voluntary control of accommodation
         Journal of General Psychology, 1937, 17:170-174

1836.   Sisson, D.E..
         Voluntary control of accommodation
         Journal of General Psychology, 1938, 18:195-198

1837.   Sittenfeld, P.
         The control of the EEG theta rhythm
         Proceedings of the Biofeedback Research Society
            Fourth Annual Meeting
         Boston, 1972, 32 (Abst.)

1838.   Sittenfeld, P.
         The control of the EEG theta rhythm
         In D. Shapiro et al (Eds.), Biofeedback and Self-
            Control: 1972
         Chicago: Aldine Publishing Co., 1973

1839.   Sittenfeld, P., Budzynski, T. & Stoyva, J.
         Differential shaping of EEG theta rhythms
         Biofeedback and Self-Regulation, 1976, 1:31-46

1840.   Slattery, P. & Taub, E.
         Specificity of temperature self-regulation to
            feedback loci
         Biofeedback and Self-Regulation, 1976, 1:316 (Abst.)

1841.   Slaughter, J., Hahn, W. & Renaldi, P.
         Instrumental conditioning of heart rate in the
            curarized rat with varied amounts of pretraining
         Journal of Comparative and Physiological Psychology,
            1970, 72:356-360

1842.   Small, M.M. & Hull, E.I.
         Clinical applications of biofeedback technology: A
            review of the literature and five case histories
         Journal Supplement Abstract Service, APA, 1975, MS
            #1117, 1-44

1843. Smith, H.M., Jr., Basmajian, J.V. & Vanderstoep, S.F.
Inhibition of neighboring motoneurons in conscious
control of single spinal motoneurons
Science, 1974, 183:975-976

1844. Smith, J.C.
Meditation as psychotherapy: A review of the
literature
Psychological Bulletin, 1975, 82:558-564

1845. Smith, K.U. & Ansell, S.
Closed loop digital computer system for study of
sensory feedback effects on brain rhythms
American Journal of Physical Medicine, 1965, 44:125-
137

1846. Smith, K.U. & Henry, J.P.
Cybernetic foundations for rehabilitation
American Journal of Physical Medicine, 1967, 46:379-
467

1847. Smith, R.
Frontalis muscle tension and personality
Psychophysiology, 1973, 10:311-312

1848. Smith, O.C.
Action potentials from single motor units in vol-
untary contraction
American Journal of Physiology, 1934, 108:629

1849. Snape, W.J., Jr., Carlson, G.M., Matarazzo, S.A.,
et al.
Evidence that abnormal myoelectrical activity
produced colonic motor dysfunction in the irritable
bowel syndrome
Gastroenterology, 1977, 72:383-387

1850. Snyder, C. & Noble, M.
Operant conditioning of vasoconstriction
Journal of Experimental Psychology, 1968, 77:263-268

1851. Sobell, L.C. & Sobell, M.B.
A self-feedback technique to monitor drinking be-
havior in alcoholics
Behavior Research and Therapy, 1973, 11:237-238

1852. Sokolow, M., et al.
       Preliminary studies relating portably recorded blood
          pressures to daily life events in patients with
          essential hypertension
       In: Koster, M. (Ed.), Psychosomatics in Essential
          Hypertension
       Basil: S. Karger, 1970

1853. Solbach, P. & Sargent, J.D.
       A follow-up evaluation of the Menninger pilot
          migraine study using thermal training
       Biofeedback and Self-Regulation, 1977, 2:298-299
          (Abst.)

1854. Solberg, W.K. & Rugh, J.D.
       The use of biofeedback devices in the treatment of
          bruxism
       Southern California Dental Association Journal,
          1972, 40:852-853

1855. Solberg, W.K. & Rugh, J.D.
       Biofeedback-induced muscle relaxation used in the
          treatment of bruxism
       Journal of Dental Research, 1973, 52:73 (Abst.)

1856. Sovak, M., Fronek, A., Helland, D.R., et al.
       Effects of vasomotor changes in the upper extremities
          on the hemodynamics of the carotid arterial beds:
          A possible mechanism of biofeedback therapy of
          migraine
       In J. I. Martin (Ed.), Proceedings of the San Diego
          Biomedical Symposium 1976 - Vol 15
       New York: Academic Press, 1976

1857. Spanos, N.P.
       Barber's reconceptualization of hypnosis: An evalua-
          tion of criticisms
       Journal of Experimental Research in Personality,
          1970, 4:241-258

1858. Spanos, N.P.
       A reply to Tellegen's "Comments on 'Barber's Re-
          conceptualization of Hypnosis'"
       Personality, 1970, 4:268-269

1859.   Spanos, N.P.   & Barber, T.X.
        "Hypnotic" experiences as inferred from subjective
           reports: Auditory and visual hallucinations
        Journal of Experimental Research in Personality,
           1968, 3:136-150

1860.   Spanos, N.P.   & Barber, T.X.
        Toward a convergence in hypnosis research
        American Psychologist, 1974, 29:500-511

1861.   Spanos, N.P., Barber, T.X.   & Lang, G.
        Cognition and self-control: Cognitive control of
           painful sensory input
        In H. London & R. E. Nisbett (Eds.), Thoughts and Feeling:
           Feeling: Cognitive Alteration of Feeling States
        Chicago: Aldine Publishing Co., 1974

1862.   Spanos, N.P.   & Chaves, J.F.
        Hypnosis research: A methodological critique of
           experiments generated by two alternative paradigms
        American Journal of Clinical Hypnosis, 1970, 13:108-
           127

1863.   Spearing, D.L.   & Poppen, R.
        The use of feedback in the reduction of foot dragging
           in a cerebral palsied client
        Journal of Nervous and Mental Disease, 1974, 159:148-
           151

1864.   Spencer, K., Dale, A., Blankstein, K., et al.
        Are biofeedback effects epiphenomenal?   Voluntary
           heart rate changes directly mediated by muscle
           tension, respiration, and cognitive strategies
        Biofeedback and Self-Regulation, 1976, 1:321 (Abst.)

1865.   Spilker, B., Kamiya, J., Callaway, E.   & Yeager, C.L.
        Visual evoked responses in subjects trained to
           control alpha rhythms
        Psychophysiology, 1969, 5:683-695

1866.   Sroufe, L.A.
        Learned stabilization of cardiac rate with respira-
           tion experimentally controlled
        Journal of Experimental Psychology, 1969, 81:391-393

1867.   Sroufe, L.A.
        Effects of depth and rate of breathing on heart rate
           and heart rate variability
        Psychophysiology, 1971, 8:648-655

1868.   Stambaugh, E.E. & House, A.E.
        Multimodality treatment of migraine headache: A
           case study utilizing biofeedback, relaxation,
           autogenic and hypnotic treatments
        American Journal of Clinical Hypnosis, 1977, 19:235-
           240

1869.   Stanford, R.G. & Lovin, C.
        EEG alpha activity and ESP performance
        Journal of the American Society for Psychical
           Research, 1970, 64:375

1870.   Stanford, R.G.
        EEG alpha activity and ESP performance: A repli-
           cative study
        Journal of the American Society for Psychical
           Research, 1971, 65:144-154

1871.   Staples, R. & Coursey, R.F.
        A comparison of EMG feedback with two other re-
           laxation techniques
        Proceedings of the Biofeedback Research Society
           Sixth Annual Meeting
        Monterey, 1975, 86 (Abst.)

1872.   Staudenmayer, H.
        Awareness: Of signal or process?
        Proceedings of the Biofeedback Research Society
           Sixth Annual Meeting
        Monterey, 1975, 2 (Abst.)

1873.   Staudenmayer, H. & Kinsman, R.A.
        Trial by trial method of training frontalis muscle
           relaxation: Awareness and modes of feedback
           (Report #17).
        Denver, Colorado: Psychophysiology Research Labora-
           tories, National Jewish Hospital and Research
           Center, August, 1974

1874.   Staudenmayer, H. & Kinsman, R.A.
        Awareness during electromyographic biofeedback: Of
           signal or process
        Biofeedback and Self-Regulation, 1976, 1:191-199

1875.   Staudenmayer, H., Kinsman, R.A. & Yaroush, R.
        Posttraining transfer of awareness in EMG bio-
           feedback training
        Biofeedback and Self-Regulation, 1976, 1:334-335

1876.   Steffen, J.J.
        Electromyographically induced relaxation in the
           treatment of chronic alcohol abuse
        Journal of Consulting and Clinical Psychology,
           1975, 43:275

1877.   Stein, A. & Lewis, D.H.
        Motor unit myoelectric control
        IEEE Transactions on Human Factors in Electronics,
           1967, 8:253-254

1878.   Steinberg, E.P. & Schwartz, G.E.
        Biofeedback and electrodermal self-regulation in
           psychopathy
        Journal of Abnormal Psychology, 1976, 85:408-415

1879.   Steiner, T.E., Butler, R., Reynolds, A., et al
        Covariation in heart rate, blood pressure, skin
           temperature, and photoelectric plethysmogram
           during biofeedback for peripheral vasomotor
           control
        Biofeedback and Self-Regulation, 1977, 2:295-296
           (Abst.)

1880.   Stenn, P.G., Brown, R. & Laidley, L.
        Assessment and retraining of functioning: Bio-
           feedback and the problem of excessive muscular
           tension
        Psychophysiology, 1976, 13:164-165 (Abst.)

1881.   Stephens, J.A. & Taylor, A.
        The effect of visual feedback on physiological
           muscle tremor
        Electroencephalography and Clinical Neurophysiology,
           1974, 36:457-464

1882.   Stephens, J.H., Harris, A.H. & Brady, J.V.
        Large magnitude heart rate changes in subjects
           instructed to change their heart rates and given
           exteroceptive feedback
        Psychophysiology, 1972, 9:283-285

1883.   Stephens, J.H., Harris, A.H., Brady, J.V., et al.
        Psychological and physiological variables associated
           with large magnitude voluntary heart rate changes
        Psychophysiology, 1975, 12:381-387

1884.   Stephens, W.J. & Fenz, W.D.
        The effect of motivation on cardiac activity in a
           reaction time task under conditions of augmented
           feedback
        Psychophysiology, 1971, 8:264 (Abst.)

1885.   Stephensen, N.L.
        Two cases of successful treatment of Raynaud's
           Disease with relaxation and biofeedback training
           and supportive therapy
        Biofeedback and Self Regulation, 1976, 1:318-319
           (Abst.)

1886.   Stephenson, N.L.
        Successful treatment of blepharospasm with relaxation
           training and biofeedback
        Biofeedback and Self-Regulation, 1976, 1:331 (Abst.)

1887.   Steptoe, A.
        Blood pressure control: A comparison of feedback
           and instructions using pulse wave velocity measure-
           ments
        Psychophysiology, 1976, 13:528-535

1888.   Steptoe, A.
        Voluntary blood pressure reduction measured with
           pulse transit time: Training conditions and
           reactions to mental work
        Psychophysiology, 1977, 14:492-498

1889.   Steptoe, A.
        Blood pressure control with pulse wave velocity
           feedback: Methods of analysis and training
        In J. Beatty & H. Legewie (Eds.), Biofeedback and
           Behavior
        New York: Plenum Press, 1977

REFERENCES

1890. Steptoe, A. & Johnston, D.
       The instructional control of blood pressure: A
         comparison with biofeedback
       Psychophysiology, 1976, 13:177. (Abst.)

1891. Steptoe, A. & Johnston, D.
       The control of blood pressure using pulse-wave
         velocity feedback
       Journal of Psychosomatic Research, 1976, 20:417-424

1892. Steptoe, A. & Johnston, D.
       The control of blood pressure with instructions and
         pulse wave velocity feedback
       European Journal of Behavioral Analysis and Modi-
         fication, 1976, 1:147-154

1893. Steptoe, A., Mathews, A. & Johnston, D.
       The learned control of differential temperature in
         the human earlobes: Preliminary study
       Biological Psychology, 1974, 1:237-242

1894. Sterman, L.T.
       Clinical biofeedback
       American Journal of Nursing, 1975, 75:2006-1009

1895. Sterman, M.B.
       Studies of EEG biofeedback training in man and cat
       Highlights of 17th Annual Conference VA Cooperative
         Studies in Mental Health and Behavioral Sciences,
         1972, 55-60

1896. Sterman, M.B.
       Neurophysiologic and clinical studies of sensori-
         motor EEG biofeedback training: Some effects on
         epilepsy
       Seminars in Psychiatry, 1973, 5:507-524

1897. Sterman, M.B.
       Somatic and cognitive correlates of the sensorimotor
         rhythm in man
       Proceedings of the Biofeedback Research Society
         Fifth Annual Meeting
       Colorado Springs, 1974, 19 (Abst.)

1898. Sterman, M.B.
       Clinical implications of EEG biofeedback training:
       A critical appraisal
       In G. E. Schwartz & J. Beatty (Eds.), Biofeedback:
       Theory and Research
       New York: Academic Press, 1977

1899. Sterman, M.B.
       Effects of brain surgery and EEG operant condition-
       ing on seizure latency following monomethyl
       hydrazine intoxication in the cat
       Biofeedback and Self-Regulation, 1976, 1:340 (Abst.)

1900. Sterman, M.B.
       Sensorimotor EEG operant conditioning: Experimental
       and clinical effects
       Pavlovian Journal of Biological Science, 1977,
       12:63-92

1901. Sterman, M.B.
       Effects of sensorimotor EEG feedback training on
       sleep and clinical manifestations of epilepsy
       In J. Beatty & H. Legewie (Eds.), Biofeedback and
       Behavior
       New York: Plenum Press, 1977

1902. Sterman, M.B., Ayres, M.E. & Goodman, S.J.
       Case study: Effects of SMR suppression on EEG and
       motor patterns in a quadriplegic patient
       Biofeedback and Self-Regulation, 1976, 1:340-341
       (Abst.)

1903. Sterman, M.B., Feinstein, B. & Macdonald, L.R.
       Quantitative analysis of baseline and biofeedback
       training effects with central and occipital
       cortical frequencies in man
       Proceedings of the Biofeedback Research Society
       Sixth Annual Meeting
       Monterey, 1975, 67 (Abst.)

1904. Sterman, M.B. & Friar, L.
       Suppression of seizures in an epileptic following
       EEG feedback training
       Electroencephalography and Clinical Neurophysiology,
       1972, 33:89-95

1905. Sterman, M.B., Howe, R.C. & MacDonald, L.R
Facilitation of spindle-burst sleep by conditioning
of electroencephalographic activity while awake
Science, 1970, 167:1146-1148

1906. Sterman, M.B., Lubar. J.L. & Harper, R.M.
Effects of central cortical EEG feedback training on
power-spectral characteristics and seizure: In-
cidence in uncontrolled epileptics
Biofeedback and Self-Regulation, 1977, 2:291 (Abst.)

1907. Sterman, M.B., Lucas, E.A. & Macdonald, L.R.
Periodicity within sleep and operant performance in
the cat
Brain Research, 1972, 38:327-341

1908. Sterman, M.B., Macdonald, L.R., Lucia, M., et al.
Effects of operant conditioning of central cortical
EEG patterns in epilepsy
Biofeedback and Self-Regulation, 1976, 1:347 (Abst.)

1909. Sterman, M.B., Macdonald, L.R. & Stone, R.K.
Biofeedback training of the sensorimotor EEG rhythm
in man: Effects on epilepsy
Epilepsia, 1974, 15:395-416

1910. Stern, G.S. & Berrenberg, J.L.
Biofeedback training in frontalis muscle relaxation
and enhancement of belief in personal control
Biofeedback and Self-Regulation, 1977, 2:173-182

1911. Stern, R.M.
Operant conditioning of spontaneous GSR's: Negative
results
Journal of Experimental Psychology, 1967, 75:128-130

1912. Stern, R.M.
Behavioral and physiological effects of false heart
rate feedback: A replication and extension
Psychophysiology, 1972, 9:21-29

1913. Stern, R.M.
Detection of one's own spontaneous GSR's
Psychonomic Science, 1972, 29:354-356

1914. Stern, R.M. & Kaplan, B.E.
       Galvanic skin response: Voluntary control and ex-
           ternalization
       Journal of Psychosomatic Research, 1967, 10:349-353

1915. Stern, R.M. & Lewis, N.L.
       Ability of actors to control their GSR's and express
           emotions
       Psychophysiology, 1968, 4:294-299

1916. Stern, R.M. & Pavloski, R.P.
       Operant conditioning vascoconstriction: A veri-
           fication
       Journal of Experimental Psychology, 1974, 102:330-
           332

1917. Stern, R.M. & Ray, W.J.
       Biofeedback and the Control of Internal Bodily
           Activity
       Richard D. Irwin Co., Homewood, Il, 1975

1918. Stern, R.M. & Tyler, R.W.
       Augmented heart rate feedback: Differential effects
           during rest and stress
       Psychophysiology, 1969, 5:583-584 (Abst.)

1919. Stewart, R.A.C.
       Self-realization as the bases of psychotherapy: A
           look at two eastern based practices, Transcendental
           Meditation and alpha brain wave biofeedback
       Social Behavior and Personality, 1974, 2:191-200

1920. Stoffer, G.S., Jensen, J.S. & Nesset B.
       Cold stress tolerance as a function of biofeedback
           temperature training and internal-external locus
           of control
       Biofeedback and Self-Regulation, 1977, 2:295 (Abst.)

1921. Stone, R.A. & DeLeo, J.
       Psychotherapeutic control of hypertension
       The New England Journal of Medicine, 1976, 294:80-
           84

1922. Stoudenmire, J.
Effects of muscle relaxation training on state and
trait anxiety in introverts and extroverts
Journal of Personality and Social Psychology, 1972,
24:273-275

1923. Stoudenmire, J.
The effect of length of sessions and spacing of
sessions on muscle relaxation training
Journal of Community Psychology, 1973, 1:235-236

1924. Stoudenmire, J.
A comparison of muscle relaxation training and
music in the reduction of state and trait anxiety
Journal of Clinical Psychology, 1975, 31:490-492

1925. Stoyva, J.M.
Finger electromyographic activity during sleep: Its
relation to dreaming in deaf and normal subjects
Journal of Abnormal Psychology, 1965, 70:343-349

1926. Stoyva, J.M.
The public (scientific) study of private events
In E. H. Hartman (Ed.), Sleep and Dreaming
Boston: Little, Brown & Co., 1970

1927. Stoyva, J.
Biofeedback techniques and the conditions for
hallucinatory activity
In F. J. McGuigan & R. Schoonover (Eds.), The
Psychophysiology of Thinking
New York: Academic Press, 1973

1928. Stoyva, J.
Self-Regulation: A context for biofeedback
Biofeedback and Self-Regulation, 1976, 1:1-5

1929. Stoyva, J.M.
Self-regulation and stress related disorders--a
perspective on biofeedback
In D. Mostovsky (Ed.), Behavior Control and Modi-
fication of Physiological Activity
New York: Prentice-Hall, 1976

1930. Stoyva, J.M.
A psychophysiological model of stress disorders as a
rationale for biofeedback training
In F. J. McGuigan (Ed.), Proceedings of the Second
Meeting of the American Association for the
Advancement of Tension Control
Blacksburg, Virginia: University Publications, 1976,
47-66

1931. Stoyva, J.
Why should muscular relaxation by clinically useful?
Some data and 2 1/2 models
In J. Beatty & H. Legewie (Eds.), Biofeedback and
Behavior
New York: Plenum Press, 1977

1932. Stoyva, J.M.
A rationale for biofeedback training in stress re-
lated disorders
In F. Antonelli (Eds.), Therapy in Psychosomatic
Medicine (Vol. I)
Rome: Edizioni Luigi Pozzi, 1977

1933. Stoyva, J.M.
Similarities of self-regulatory discharges occurring
during biofeedback training and autogenic standard
exercises
In W. Luthe & F. Antonelli (Eds.), Therapy in
Psychosomatic Medicine: Autogenic Therapy
Rome: Edizioni Luigi Pozzi, 1977

1934. Stoyva, J.M.
Guidelines in the training of general relaxation
In J. V. Basmajian (Ed.), Biofeedback: A Handbook
for Clinicians
Baltimore: Williams & Wilkins (In Press)

1935. Stoyva, J.M.
Behavioral techniques in muscle skeletal disorders
In O. Pomerleau & J. P. Brady, Behavioral Medicine:
Theory and Practice
Baltimore: Williams & Wilkins (In Press)

1936.   Stoyva, J., Barber, T.X., DiCara, L.V., Kamiya, J.,
        Miller, N.E. & Shapiro, D., (Eds.).
        Biofeedback and Self-Control 1971: An Aldine Annual
          on the Regulation of Bodily Processes and Conscious-
          ness
        Chicago: Aldine Publishing Co., 1972

1937.   Stoyva, J. & Budzynski, T.H.
        Cultivated low arousal - an anti-stress response?
        In L. V. DiCara (Ed.), Limbic and Autonomic Nervous
          Systems Research
        New York: Plenum Press, 1974

1938.   Stoyva, J., Budzynski, T., Sittenfeld, P., et al
        A two-step EMG-theta feedback training in sleep
          onset insomnia: Preliminary results
        Proceedings of the Biofeedback Research Society
          Fifth Annual Meeting
        Colorado Springs, 1974, 103 (Abst.)

1939.   Stoyva, J. & Budzynski, T.B.
        Applications of muscle and EEG feedback for anxiety,
          stress disorders and exploration of conscious
          states
        Mental Health Program Reports, 1975, 6:109-121

1940.   Stoyva, J.M., Forsyth, R.P. & Kamiya, J.
        Blood pressure during sleep in the rhesus monkey,
          before and after work on stressful operant
          schedules
        American Journal of Physiology, 1968, 214:1122-1125

1941.   Stoyva, J.M. & Kamiya, J.
        Electrophysiological studies of dreaming as the
          prototype of a new strategy in the study of
          consciousness
        Psychological Review, 1968, 75:192-205

1942.   Strauss, N.
        The placebo effects of biofeedback
        Biofeedback and Self-Regulation, 1976, 1:335 (Abst.)

1943. Strayer, I., Scott, W.B. & Bakan, P.
       A re-examination of alpha feedback training:
         Operant conditioning or perceptual differentiation
       Canadian Journal of Psychology, 1973, 27:247-253

1944. Stroebel, C.F. & Glueck, B.C.
       Biofeedback treatment in medicine and psychiatry:
         An ultimate placebo?
       Seminars in Psychiatry, 1973, 5:379-393

1945. Strupp, H.
       Specific vs non-specific factors in psychology and
         the problem of control
       Archives of General Psychology, 1970, 23:393-401

1946. Stunkard, A.
       New therapies for the eating disorders
       Archives of General Psychiatry, 1972, 26:391-398

1947. Stunkard, A.J. & Mahoney, M.J.
       Behavioral treatment of the eating disorders
       In H. Leitenberg (Ed.), Handbook of Behavior Modi-
         fication
       New York: Appleton-Century-Crofts, 1975

1948. Sue, D.
       The role of relaxation in systematic desensitization
       Behavior Research and Therapy, 1972, 10:153-158

1949. Surwit, R.S.
       Biofeedback: A possible treatment for Raynaud's
         Disease
       Seminars in Psychiatry, 1973, 5:483-490

1950. Surwit, R.S.
       Simple vs complex feedback displays in the training
         of digital temperature
       Journal of Consulting and Clinical Psychology, 1977,
         45:146-147

1951. Surwit, R.S., Hager, J.L. & Feldman, T.
       The role of feedback in voluntary control of blood
         pressure in instructed subjects
       Psychophysiology, 1977, 14:97 (Abst.)

1952.   Surwit, R.S. & Shapiro, D.
        Skin temperature feedback and concomitant cardio-
            vascular changes
        Proceedings of the Biofeedback Research Society
            Fifth Annual Meeting
        Colorado Springs, 1974, 69 (Abst.)

1953.   Surwit, R.S. & Shapiro, D.
        Digital temperature autoregulation and associated
            cardiovascular changes
        Psychophysiology, 1976, 13:165 (Abst.)

1954.   Surwit, R. & Shapiro, D.
        Cardiovascular biofeedback, muscle activity in
            biofeedback and meditation -- relaxation training
            in borderline essential hypertensives
        Biofeedback and Self-Regulation, 1976, 1:312 (Abst.)

1955.   Surwit, R.S. & Shapiro, D.
        Biofeedback and meditation in the treatment of
            borderline hypertension
        In J. Beatty & H. Legewie (Eds.), Biofeedback and
            Behavior
        New York: Plenum Press, 1977

1956.   Surwit, R.S., Shapiro, D. & Feld, J.L.
        Digital temperature autoregulation and associated
            cardiovascular changes
        Psychophysiology, 1976, 13:242-248

1957.   Suter, S.
        Independent biofeedback self-regulation of EEG
            alpha and skin resistance
        Biofeedback and Self-Regulation, 1977, 2:255-258

1958.   Suter, S., Beatty, J. & Strickler, J.
        Skin temperature over the external carotid arteries
            during spatial versus verbal tasks
        Biofeedback and Self-Regulation, 1977, 2:291-292
            (Abst.)

1959.   Suter, S. & Dillingham, C.
        Time perception during biofeedback enhanced and
            suppressed alpha
        Biofeedback and Self-Regulation, 1976, 1:360-361
            (Abst.)

1960.   Suter, S., Griffin, G., Smallhouse, P., et al.
        Lateral shifts in temporal alpha: Discrimination,
          conscious correlates, biofeedback control, and
          effects on hemisphere-specialized tasks
        Biofeedback and Self-Regulation, 1977, 2:284-285
          (Abst.)

1961.   Suter, S., Johnson, T., Franconi, L., et al
        Independent biofeedback control of EEG alpha and
          skin conductance
        Biofeedback and Self-Regulation, 1977, 2:285 (Abst.)

1962.   Suzuki, S., Watanabe, T. & Simizu, K.
        Effect of visual feedback on voluntary control of
          the skin potential response to detection of
          deception
        Japanese Journal of Psychology, 1969, 40:59-67
          (Japan)

1963.   Swaan, D., Van Wieringen, P.C.W. & Fokkema, S.D.
        Auditory electromyographic feedback therapy to
          inhibit undesired motor activity
        Archives of Physical Medicine and Rehabilitation,
          1974, 55:251-254

1964.   Tafts, J.C. & Blankstein, K.R.
        Volunteer effects on the feedback control of heart
          rate: Achieving tendency
        Proceedings of the Biofeedback Research Society
          Fifth Annual Meeting
        Colorado Springs, 1974, 90 (Abst.)

1965.   Takebe, K. & Basmajian, J.V.
        Gait analysis in stroke patients to assess treatments
          of foot-drop
        Archives of Physical Medicine and Rehabilitation,
          1976, 57:305-310

1966.   Takebe, K., Kukulka, C.G. & Narayan, M.G., et al.
        Biofeedback treatment of foot-drop after stroke
          compared with standard rehabilitation technique
          (Part 2): Effects on nerve conductor velocity and
          spasticity
        Archives of Physical Medicine and Rehabilitation,
          1976, 57:9-11

1967.   Takeya, T.
        A biofeedback study of postural sway
        Folia Psychiatrica Neurologie Japan, 1976, 30:494-
          504

1968.   Tanji, J. & Kato, M.
        Volitionally controlled single motor unit discharges
          and cortical motor potentials in human subjects
        Brain Research, 1971, 29:343-346

1969.   Tanji, J. & Kato, M.
        Recruitment of motor units in voluntary contraction
          of a finger muscle in man
        Experimental Neurology, 1973, 40:759-770

1970.   Tarchanoff, J.R.
        Voluntary acceleration of the heart beat in man
        In D. Shapiro et al (Eds.), Biofeedback and Self-
          Control
        Chicago: Aldine Publishing Co., 1973, 3-20

1971.   Tart, C.
        Altered States of Consciousness
        New York: Wiley, 1969

1972.   Tart, C.T.
        Scientific foundation for the study of altered
            states of consciousness
        Journal of Transpersonal Psychology, 1971, 3:93-
            124

1973.   Tart, C.T.
        States of Consciousness
        New York: Dutton, 1975

1974.   Tart, C.T.
        The basic nature of altered states of consciousness:
            A system approach
        The Journal of Transpersonal Psychology, 1977, 8:45-
            64

1975.   Tasto, D.L.
        Systematic desensitization, muscle relaxation and
            visual imagery in the counter-conditioning of
            four-year-old phobic child
        Behavior Research and Therapy, 1969, 7:409-411

1976.   Tasto, D.L. & Chesney, M.A.
        Muscle relaxation treatment for primary dysmenorrhea
        Behavior Therapy, 1974, 5:668-672

1977.   Tasto, D. & Hinkle, J.E.
        Muscle relaxation treatment for tension headaches
        Behavior Research and Therapy, 1973, 11:347-349

1978.   Tasto, D.L. & Huebner, L.A.
        The effects of muscle relaxation and stress on the
            blood pressure levels of normotensives
        Behavior Research and Therapy, 1976, 14:89-91

1979.   Taub, E.
        Self-regulation of human tissue temperature
        In G. E. Schwartz & J. Beatty (Eds.), Biofeedback:
            Theory and Research
        New York: Academic Press, 1977

1980.   Taub, E. & Emurian, C.
        Autoregulation of skin temperature using a variable
            intensity feedback light
        Proceedings of the Biofeedback Research Society
            Fourth Annual Meeting
        Boston, 1972, 25 (Abst.)

1981.   Taub, E. & Emurian, C.S.
        Self-regulation of skin temperature using a variable
            intensity light
        In J. Stoyva et al (Eds.), Biofeedback and Self-
            Control: 1972
        Chicago: Aldine Publishing Co., 1973

1982.   Taub, E. & Emurian, C.S.
        Feedback aided self-regulation of skin temperature
            with a single feedback locus: I. Acquisition and
            reversal training
        Biofeedback and Self-Regulation, 1976, 1:147-148

1983.   Taub, E., Emurian, C. & Howell, P.
        Further progress in training self-regulation of skin
            temperature
        Proceedings of the Biofeedback Research Society
            Fifth Annual Meeting
        Colorado Springs, 1974, 70 (Abst.)

1984.   Taylor, C.B., Farquhar, J.W., Nelson, E., et al.
        Relaxation therapy and high blood pressure
        Archives of General Psychiatry, 1977, 34:339-342

1985.   Taylor, L.P.
        Muscle reeducation of post CVA victim using the
            electromyometer with audio feedback
        Proceedings of the Biofeedback Research Society
            Sixth Annual Meeting
        Monterey, 1975, 27 (Abst.)

1986.   Taylor, L.P. & Bongar, B.M.
        Clinical applications in biofeedback
        Los Angeles: Psychology Press, 1976

1987.   Taylor, N.B. & Cameron, H.G.
        Voluntary acceleration of the heart
        American Journal of Physiology, 1922, 61:385-398

1988.   Tebecis, A.K., Ohno, Y., Takeya, T., et al.
        Fine body movement during autogenic training:
            Longitudinal and short term changes
        Biofeedback and Self-Regulation, 1977, 2:417-426

1989. Tellegen, A.
       Some comments on Barber's "reconceptualization" of
         hypnosis
       Personality, 1970, 4:259-267

1990. Teng, E.L., McNeal, D.R., Kralj, J., et al.
       Electrical stimulation and feedback training:
         Effects on the voluntary control of paretic
         muscles
       Archives of Physical Medicine and Rehabilitation,
         1976, 57:228-233

1991. Teplitz, T.A.
       Operant conditioning of blood pressure: A critical
         review and some psychosomatic considerations
       Communications in Behavioral Biology, Part A,
         1971, 6:197-202

1992. Thompson, D.L. & Russell, H.L.
       Learning voluntary control of fingertip skin temper-
         ature: Issues, questions and answers
       Biofeedback and Self-Regulation, 1976, 1:316-317
         (Abst.)

1993. Thornton, E.W. & Hagan, P.J.
       A failure to explain the effects of false heart-rate
         feedback on affect by induced changes in physio-
         logical response
       British Journal of Psychology, 1976, 32:838-843

1994. Thornton, E.W. & Van-Toller, C.
       Effect of immunosympathectomy on operant heart rate
         conditioning in the curarized rat
       Physiology and Behavior, 1973, 10:197-201

1995. Thornton, E.W. & Van-Toller, C.
       Operant conditioning of heart rate changes in the
         functionally decorticate curarized rat
       Physiology and Behavior, 1973, 10:983-989

1996. Throop, W.F. & MacDonald, A.P.
       Internal-external locus of control: A bibliography
       Psychological Reports, 1971, 1-28

1997. Thysell, R.V.
       Reaction time of single motor units
       Psychophysiology, 1969, 6:174-185

1998.   Tiep, B.L., Alaniz, J. & Cordell, J.
        Respiratory biofeedback. Two non-invasive approaches
          in the treatment of patients with chronic ob-
          structive disease
        In J. I. Martin (Ed.), Proceedings of the San Diego
          Biomedical Symposium, 1976 - Vol 15
        New York: Academic Press, 1976

1999.   Timken, K.R.
        Biofeedback - a brief review
        Dallas Medical Journal, 1974, (Sept), 432-436

2000.   Timken, K.R., Chambers, J., Hall, J.A., et al.
        Biofeedback: A demand for clinical expertise
        Texas Medicine, 1975, 71:44-47

2001.   Timmons, B.A.
        Expectancy as a factor in reaction to delayed
          auditory feedback
        Perceptual and Motor Skills, 1971, 33:1219-1222

2002.   Timmons, B.A.
        Delayed auditory feedback as a factor influencing
          retention
        Perceptual and Motor Skills, 1974, 38:399-402

2003.   Timmons, B.A. & Boudreau, J.P.
        Auditory feedback as a major factor in stuttering
        Journal of Speech and Hearing Disorders, 1972,
          37:476-484

2004.   Timmons, B.A. & Boudreau, J.P.
        Age, sex, and delay time as factors affecting
          reaction to delayed auditory feedback
        Perceptual and Motor Skills, 1976, 43:27-30

2005.   Timmons, B. & Kamiya, J.
        The psychology and physiology of meditation and
          related phenomena: A bibliography
        Journal of Transpersonal Psychology, 1970, 2:41-59

2006.   Timmons, B. & Kanellakos, D.
        The psychology and physiology of meditation and
          related phenomena: Bibliography II
        Journal of Transpersonal Psychology, 1974, 6:32-38

2007. Timmons, B., Zilberg, N. & Scott, J.
       Respiratory movements: Psychophysiology and potential
          clinical biofeedback applications
       Proceedings of the Biofeedback Research Society
          Sixth Annual Meeting
       Monterey, 1975, 74 (Abst.)

2008. Todd, F. & Kelly, R.J.
       The use of hypnosis to facilitate conditioned
          relaxation responses. A report of three cases
       Journal of Behavior Therapy and Experimental
          Psychiatry, 1970, 1:295-298

2009. Toomim, H. & Johnson, H.E.
       Electromyometer feedback in paraplegia: A case
          study in neuromuscular reeducation
       Proceedings of the Biofeedback Research Society
          Fifth Annual Meeting
       Colorado Springs, 1974, 27 (Abst.)

2010. Toomim, M.K.
       GSR biofeedback techniques in psychotherapy
       Proceedings of the Biofeedback Research Society
          Fifth Annual Meeting
       Colorado Springs, 1974, 73 (Abst.)

2011. Toomim, M.K.
       EMG and GSR feedback in psychotherapy
       Biofeedback and Self-Regulation, 1976, 1:361 (Abst.)

2012. Toomim, M. & Toomim, H.
       Biofeedback-fact and fantasy --does it hold impli-
          cations for gifted children?
       Gifted Child Quarterly, 1973, 17:48-55

2013. Toomim, M.K. & Toomim, H.
       Psychodynamic correlates of the paradoxically
          invariant GSR
       Proceedings of the Biofeedback Research Society
          Sixth Annual Meeting
       Monterey, 1975, 31 (Abst.)

2014. Tophoff, M.
       Massed practice, relaxation and assertion training
          in the treatment of Gilles de la Tourette's Syndrome
       Journal of Behavior Therapy and Experimental
          Psychiatry, 1973, 4:71-73

2015.   Townsend, R.E. & Addario, D.
        Treatment of chronic anxiety with feedback-mediated
           electromyographic relaxation: A comparison study
        Proceedings of the Biofeedback Research Society
           Sixth Annual Meeting
        Monterey, 1975, 84 (Abst.)

2016.   Townsend, R.E., House, J.F. & Addario, D.
        Comparison of biofeedback-mediated relaxation and
           group therapy in treatment of chronic anxiety
        American Journal of Psychiatry, 1975, 132:598-601

2017.   Traczyk, W.Z., Whitmoyer, D.I. & Sawyer, C.H.
        EEG feedback control of midbrain electrical stimu-
           lation inducing sleep or arousal in rabbits
        Acta Biologiae Experimentalis (Warszawa), 1969,
           29:135-152

2018.   Travis, T., Kondo, C. & Knott, J.
        A controlled study of alpha enhancement
        Psychophysiology, 1972, 9:268 (Abst.)

2019.   Travis, T.A., Kondo, C.Y. & Knott, J.
        Interaction effects of sex of subject and experimenter
           in biofeedback training
        Proceedings of the Biofeedback Research Society
           Fourth Annual Meeting
        Boston, 1972, 34 (Abst.)

2020.   Travis, T.A., Kondo, C.Y. & Knott, J.R.
        Interaction of hypnotic suggestion and alpha en-
           hancement
        American Journal of Psychiatry, 1973, 130:1389-1391

2021.   Travis, T.A., Kondo, C. & Knott, J.R.
        Subjective reports following feedback training of
           the occipital alpha rhythm
        Proceedings of the Biofeedback Research Society
           Fifth Annual Meeting
        Colorado Springs, 1974, 79 (Abst.)

2022.   Travis, T., Kondo, C.Y. & Knott, J.R.
        Alpha conditioning: A controlled study
        Journal of Nervous and Mental Disease, 1974,
           158:163-173

2023.   Travis, T., Kondo, C.Y. & Knott, J.R.
        Personality variables and alpha enhancement: A
            correlative study
        British Journal of Psychiatry, 1974, 124:542-544

2024.   Travis, T.A., Kondo, C.Y. & Knott, J.R.
        Parameters of eyes-closed alpha enhancement
        Psychophysiology, 1974, 11:674-681

2025.   Travis, T.A., Kondo, C.Y. & Knott, J.R.
        Subjective aspects of alpha enhancement
        The British Journal of Psychiatry, 1975, 127:122-126

2026.   Travis, T.A., Kondo, C.Y. & Knott, J.R.
        Alpha enhancement research: A review
        Biological Psychiatry, 1975, 10:69-89

2027.   Travis, T.A., Kondo, C.Y., Knott, J.R.
        Heart rate, muscle tension, and alpha production of
            transcendental meditators and controls
        Proceedings of the Biofeedback Research Society
            Sixth Annual Meeting
        Monterey, 1975, 77 (Abst.)

2028.   Travis, T.A., Kondo, C.Y. & Knott, J.R.
        Heart rate, muscle tension, and alpha production of
            transcendental meditators and relaxation controls
        Biofeedback and Self-Regulation, 1976, 1:387-394

2029.   Trombly, C.A.
        Myoelectric control of orthotic devices: For the
            severely paralyzed
        The American Journal of Occupational Therapy, 1968,
            22:385-389

2030.   Troyer, W.G., Twentyman, C.T., Gatchel, R.J., et al.
        Learned heart rate control in patients with ischemic
            heart disease
        Psychophysiology, 1973, 10:213 (Abst.)

2031.   Trowill, J.A.
        Instrumental conditioning of the heart rate in the
            curarized rat
        Journal of Comparative Physiology and Psychology,
            1967, 63:7-11

2032.   Tubbs, W. & Carnahan, C.
        Clinical biofeedback for primary dysmenorrhea: A
            pilot study
        Biofeedback and Self-Regulation, 1976, 1:323 (Abst.)

2033.   Tunner, W., Oelkers, C., Ferstl, R., et al.
        Systematic desensitization and self-control train-
            ing in the treatment of speech anxiety
        In J. C. Bregelmann (Eds.), Progress in Behavior
            Therapy
        Berlin: Springer, 1975

2034.   Turin, A.
        Biofeedback for migraines
        Proceedings of the Biofeedback Research Society
            Sixth Annual Meeting
        Monterey, 1975, 54 (Abst.)

2035.   Turin, A.
        Biofeedback and suggestion in finger temperature
            training: An effect for the controls but not the
            "treatments"
        Biofeedback and Self-Regulation, 1977, 2:296 (Abst.)

2036.   Turin A. & Johnson, W.G.
        Biofeedback therapy for migraine headaches
        Archives of General Psychiatry, 1976, 33:517-519

2037.   Turin, A. & Nideffer, R.M.
        Biofeedback training, migraine-like headaches and
            smoking: A serendipitous finding
        Proceedings of the Biofeedback Research Society
            Fifth Annual Meeting
        Colorado Springs, 1974, 24 (Abst.)

2038.   Tursky, B.
        Integrators as measuring devices of bioelectric output
        Clinical and Pharmacological Therapy, 1964, 5:887-892

2039.   Tursky, B.
        The indirect recording of human blood pressure
        In P. Obrist, A.H. Black, J. Brener et al (Eds.),
            Cardiovascular Psychophysiology
        Chicago: Aldine Publishing Co., 1974

2040.   Tursky, B. & Shapiro, D.
        Operant conditioning of systolic blood pressure
        Psychophysiology, 1969, 5:563 (Abst.)

2041.   Tursky, B., Shapiro, D. & Schwartz, G.E.
        Automated constant cuff pressure system to measure
            average systolic and diastolic blood pressure in
            man
        IEEE Transactions on Bio-Medical Engineering, 1972,
            19:271-276

2042.   Twemlow, S.W., Bowen, W.T. & Wilson, T.
        Personality and functional change in alcoholic
            following alpha-theta biofeedback
        Proceedings of the Biofeedback Research Society
            Sixth Annual Meeting
        Monterey, 1975, 62 (Abst.)

2043.   Twemlow, S., Bowen, W.T. & Williams, R.O.
        Subjective responses to brainwave biofeedback
            training in drug dependent veterans: A factor
            analytic study
        Biofeedback and Self-Regulation, 1976, 1:355-356
            (Abst.)

2044.   Twemlow, S.W., et al.
        Sociocultural predictors of self-actualization in
            EEG--Biofeedback-treated alcoholics
        Psychological Reports, 1977, 40:591-598

2045.   Twentyman, C.T. & Lang, P.J.
        The learned control of heart rate: Fixed time
            feedback
        Psychophysiology, 1977, 14:114 (Abst.)

2046.   Tyson, P.D. & Audette, R.
        The controversy over the relationship between alpha
            waves and experiences during feedback
        Biofeedback and Self-Regulation, 1977, 2:285-286
            (Abst.)

2047. Uchiyama, K., Lutterjohann, M. & Shah, M.T.
Biofeedback-assisted desensitization treatment of
writers cramp
Journal of Behavior Therapy and Experimental
Psychiatry, 1977, 8:169-172

2048. Upton, A.R. & Longmere, D.
The effects of feedback on focal epileptic discharges
in man. A preliminary report
Canadian Journal of Neurological Sciences, 1975,
2:153-167

2049.   Vachon, L. & Rich, E.S., Jr.
         Visceral learning in asthma
         Psychosomatic Medicine, 1976, 38:122-130

2050.   Vaitl, D.
         Heart rate control under false feedback conditions
         Proceedings of the Biofeedback Research Society
            Fourth Annual Meeting
         Boston, 1972, 20 (Abst.)

2051.   Vaitl, D., Pepping, G., Lichter, K., et al.
         Compensatory HR changes during an open loop feedback
            procedure
         Psychophysiology, 1977, 14:107 (Abst.)

2052.   Valins, S.
         Cognitive effects of false heart-rate feedback
         Journal of Personality and Social Psychology, 1966,
            4:400-408

2053.   Valle, R.S., Chisholm, R.C. & DeGood, D.E.
         The relationship of state and trait personality
            factors to alpha-controlling ability
         Proceedings of the Biofeedback Research Society
            Sixth Annual Meeting
         Monterey, 1975, 38 (Abst.)

2054.   Valle, R.S. & DeGood, D.E.
         Alpha control and self-reported drug use
         Biofeedback and Self-Regulation, 1976, 1:356 (Abst.)

2055.   Valle, R.S. & DeGood, D.E.
         Effects of state-trait anxiety on the ability to
            enhance and suppress EEG alpha
         Psychophysiology, 1977, 14:1-7

2056.   Valle, R.S. & Levine, J.M.
         Expectation effects in alpha wave control
         Psychophysiology, 1975, 12:306-309

2057.   Van Egeren, L.F., Feather, B.W. & Hein, P.L.
         Desensitization of phobias: Some psychophysiological
            propositions
         Psychophysiology, 1971, 8:213-228

2058. Van Twyver, H.B. & Kimmel, H.D.
        Operant conditioning of the GSR with concomitant
          measurement of two somatic variables
        Journal of Experimental Psychology, 1966, 72:841-846

2059. Vasilescu, C. & Dieckmann, G.
        Electromyographic investigation in torticollis
        Applied Neurophysiology, 1976, 38:153-160

2060. Victor, R., Shapiro, D. & Mainardi, J.A.
        Voluntary control of heart rate: Effects on heart
          rate and pain during the cold pressor test
        Biofeedback and Self-Regulation, 1976, 1:322 (Abst.)

2061. Vogt, A.T.
        Electromyograph responses and performance success
          estimates as a function of internal-external
          control
        Perceptual and Motor Skills, 1975, 41:977-978

2062. Volow, M. and Hein, P.
        Bidirectional operant conditioning of peripheral
          vasomotor responses with augmented feedback and
          prolonged training
        Psychophysiology, 1972, 9:271 (Abst.)

2063. Volow, M.R., Erwin, C.W., Cipolat, A., et al.
        Operant conditioning of skin potential level (SP2)
        Psychophysiology, 1974, 11:242 (Abst.)

2064. Volpe, R.
        Feedback facilitated relaxation training in school
          counseling
        Canadian Counselor, 1975, 9:202-215

2065. Volpe, R.
        Feedback facilitated relaxation training as primary
          prevention of drug abuse in early adolescence
        Journal of Drug Education, 1977, 7:179-194

2066. Wagman, I.H., Pierce, D.S. & Burger, R.E.
       Proprioceptive influence in volitional control of
          individual motor units
       Nature, 1965, 207:957-958

2067. Wagner, M.J.
       Effects of music and biofeedback on alpha brainwave
          rhythm and attentiveness of musicians and non-
          musicians
       Journal of Research in Music Education, 1975, 23:3-
          13

2068. Wagner, M.J.
       Brainwaves and biofeedback: A brief history-
          implication for music research
       Journal of Music Therapy, 1975, 12:46-58

2069. Wagner, C., Bourgeois, A., Levenson, H., et al.
       Multidimensional locus of control and voluntary
          control of GSR
       Perceptual and Motor Skills, 1974, 39:1142.

2070. Wallace, R.K.
       Physiological effects of Transcendental Meditation
       Science, 1970, 167:1751-1754

2071. Wallace, R.K. & Benson, H.
       The physiology of meditation
       Scientific American, 1972, 266:84-90

2072. Wallace, R.K., Benson, H. & Wilson, A.F.
       A wakeful, hypometabolic physiologic state
       American Journal of Physiology, 1971, 221:795-799

2073. Walls, R.T., Majumder, R.K., Gulkus, S.P., et al.
       Galvanic skin response arousal as a function of
          positive versus negative feedback in retarded adults
       Journal of Mental Deficiency Research, 1975, 19:57-
          61

2074. Walsh, D.H.
       Social, cognitive and electroencephalographic effects
          in alpha feedback training
       Dissertation Abstracts 1972, 33:1775

2075. Walsh, D.H.
       Effects of instructional set, reinforcement, and
       individual differences in EEG alpha feedback
       training
       Proceedings of the Biofeedback Research Society
       Fourth Annual Meeting
       Boston, 1972, 31 (Abst.)

2076. Walsh, D.H.
       Interactive effects of alpha feedback and instructional
       set on subjective state
       Psychophysiology 1974, 11:428-435

2077. Walsh, P., Dale, A. & Anderson, D.E.
       Comparison of biofeedback pulse wave velocity and
       progressive relaxation in essential hypertension
       Perceptual and Motor Skills, 1977, 44:839-843

2078. Walsh, P., Dale, A., Brethauer, L., et al.
       A comparison of pulse wave velocity feedback coupled
       with verbal sphygmomanometric feedback vs deep
       relaxation treatments in drug-controlled and non-
       drugged essential hypertensives
       Biofeedback and Self-Regulation, 1976, 1:313 (Abst.)

2079. Wargin, M. & Fahrion, S.L.
       A case study: Synchronized alpha training for the
       obsessive-compulsive headache patient
       Biofeedback and Self-Regulation, 1977, 2:299 (Abst.)

2080. Warren, C.G. & Lehmann, J.F.
       Training procedures and biofeedback methods to
       achieve controlled partial weight bearing: An
       assessment
       Archives of Physical Medicine and Rehabilitation,
       1975, 56:449-455

2081. Warrenburg, S., Pagano, R., Woods, M., et al.
       Oxygen consumption, HR, EMG & EEG during progressive
       muscle relaxation (PMR) and Transcendental Medi-
       tation (TM)
       Biofeedback and Self-Regulation, 1977, 2:321 (Abst.)

2082.   Watanabe, T. & Shapiro, D.
         Operant control of spontaneous skin potential
         responses in Japanese and American subjects: A
         comparative study
         Japanese Journal of Psychology, 1971, 42:79-86

2083.   Watanabe, T., Shapiro, D. & Schwartz, G.E.
         Meditation as an anorexic state: A critical review
         and theory
         Psychophysiology, 1972, 9:279 (Abst.)

2084.   Watson, S.J., Jr.
         Effect of delayed auditory feedback on process and
         reactive schizophrenic subjects
         Journal of Abnormal Psychology, 1974, 83:609-615

2085.   Webb, C.
         The use of myoelectric feedback in teaching facial
         expression to the blind
         Proceedings of the Biofeedback Research Society
         Fifth Annual Meeting
         Colorado Springs, 1974, 49 (Abst.)

2086.   Webb, C.
         The use of myoelectric feedback in teaching facial
         expression to the blind
         American Foundation for the Blind Research Bulletin,
         1974, 27:231-262

2087.   Webb, C.
         The use of myoelectric feedback in teaching facial
         expression to the blind
         Biofeedback and Self-Regulation, 1977, 2:147-160

2088.   Weber, E.S.P. & Fehmi, L.G.
         The therapeutic use of EEG biofeedback
         Proceedings of the Biofeedback Research Society
         Fifth Annual Meeting
         Colorado Springs, 1974, 13 (Abst.)

2089.   Webster, D.R. & Azrin, N.H.
         Required relaxation: A method of inhibiting
         agitative-disruptive behavior of retardates
         Behavior Research and Therapy, 1973, 11:67-78

2090. Weinstein, S.
       Biofeedback: A new, dramatic addition to the
         therapeutic armamentarium
       International Journal of Neuroscience, 1976, 6:263-
         264

2091. Weinstock, S.A.
       A tentative procedure for the control of pain:
         Migraine and tension headaches
       Proceedings of the Biofeedback Research Society
         Fourth Annual Meeting
       Boston, 1972, 37 (Abst.)

2092. Weinstock, S.A.
       Some physiological correlates of analgesia in
         various stages of hypnotic depth
       Proceedings of the Biofeedback Research Society
         Fourth Annual Meeting
       Boston, 1972, 44 (Abst.)

2093. Weinstock, S.A.
       A tentative procedure for the control of pain:
         Migraine and tension headaches
       In D. Shapiro, et al, (Eds.), Biofeedback and Self-
         Control
       Chicago: Aldine Publishing Co, 1972

2094. Weinstock, S.A.
       A suggested use for electromyography in physical
         rehabilitation
       Proceedings of the Biofeedback Research Society
         Fifth Annual Meeting
       Colorado Springs, 1974, 28 (Abst.)

2095. Weinstock, S.A.
       The relationship between hypnotic susceptibility and
         the production of alpha waves
       Proceedings of the Biofeedback Research Society
         Fifth Annual Meeting
       Colorado Springs, 1974, 83 (Abst.)

2096. Weinstock, S.A.
       A biofeedback approach to the problem of obesity
       Proceedings of the Biofeedback Research Society
         Sixth Annual Meeting
       Monterey, 1975, 26 (Abst.)

2097. Weinstock, S.A.
       The reestablishment of intestinal control of
           functional colitis
       Biofeedback and Self-Regulation, 1976, 1:324 (Abst.)

2098. Weiss, S., Dale, A., Anderson, P., et al.
       The roles of instruction and coronary proneness in
           biofeedback control of pulse wave velocity
       Biofeedback and Self-Regulation, 1977, 2:302-303
           (Abst.)

2099. Weiss, T.
       Biofeedback training for cardiovascular dysfunctions
       Medical clinics of North America, 1977, 61:913-928

2100. Weiss, T. & Engel, B.T.
       Voluntary control of premature ventricular con-
           tractions in patients
       American Journal of Cardiology, 1970, 26:666 (Abst.)

2101. Weiss, T. & Engel, B.T.
       Operant conditioning of heart rate in patients with
           premature ventricular contractions
       Psychosomatic Medicine, 1971, 33:301-321

2102. Weiss, T. & Engel, B.T.
       Operant conditioning of increased ventricular heart
           rate in patients with complete heart block
       Psychophysiology, 1977, 11:231 (Abst.)

2103. Weiss, T. & Engel, B.T.
       Evaluation of an intra-cardiac limit of learned
           heart rate control
       Psychophysiology, 1975, 12:310-312

2104. Welgan, P.R.
       Learned control of gastric acid secretions in
           ulcer patients
       Psychosomatic Medicine, 1974, 36:411-419

2105. Welgan, P.R.
       Biofeedback control of stomach acid secretions and
           gastrointestinal reactions
       In J. Beatty & H. Legewie (Eds.), Biofeedback and
           Behavior
       New York: Plenum Press, 1977

2106. Wells, D.T.
       Large magnitude voluntary heart rate changes under
          conditions of high motivation and extended
          practice
       Psychophysiology, 1970, 6:636

2107. Wells, D.T.
       Large magnitude voluntary heart rate changes
       Psychophysiology, 1973, 10:260-269

2108. Weltman, G., Groth, H. & Lyman, J.
       A myoelectric system for training functional
          dissociation of muscles
       Archives of Physical Medicine and Rehabilitation,
          1962, 43:534-537

2109. Wenger, M.A. & Bagchi, B.K.
       Studies of autonomic functions in practitioners of
          yoga in India
       Behavioral Science, 1961, 6:312-323

2110. Wenger, M.A., Bagchi, B.K. & Anand, B.K.
       Experiments in India on "voluntary" control of the
          heart and pulse
       Circulation, 1961, 24:1319-1325

2111. Wenger, M.A., Engel, B.T. & Clemens, T.L.
       Studies of autonomic response patterns: Rationale
          and methods
       Behavioral Science, 1957, 2:216-221

2112. Wentworth-Rohr, I.
       Biofeedback applications in psychotherapy
       In H. Grayson & C. Loew (Eds.), Changing Approaches
          to Psychotherapy
       New York: Spectrum Publications (In Press)

2113. Werbach, M.R
       EEG biofeedback and higher states of consciousness
       Proceedings of the Biofeedback Research Society
          Fifth Annual Meeting
       Colorado Springs, 1974, 84 (Abst.)

2114. Werbach, M.
       Psychiatric applications of biofeedback
       Psychiatry Digest, 1974, 35:23-27

2115. Werbach, M.
       Biofeedback and Psychotherapy
       American Journal of Psychotherapy, 1977, 31:376-382

2116. Werbach, M.
       EEG biofeedback and higher states of consciousness
       Journal of Biofeedback, 1977, 3:2-7

2117. West, L.J., Neill, K.C. & Hardy, J.D.
       Effects of hypnotic suggestion on pain perception
          and galvanic skin response
       American Archives of Neurology and Psychiatry, 1952,
          68:549-560

2118. West, H.F. & Savage, W.E.
       Voluntary acceleration of the heart beat
       Archives of Internal Medicine, 1918, 22:290-295

2119. Whatmore, G.B.
       Long-term results of neuromuscular feedback train-
          ing: A statistical evaluation
       Proceedings of the Biofeedback Research Society
          Fifth Annual Meeting
       Colorado Springs, 1974, 50 (Abst.)

2120. Whatmore, G.B.
       The concept of physiopathology in biofeedback
          training
       Proceedings of the Biofeedback Research Society
          Sixth Annual Meeting
       Monterey, 1975, 81 (Abst.)

2121. Whatmore, G.B.
       A neurophysiologic view of functional disorders
       Psychosomatics, 1962, 3:371-378

2122. Whatmore, G.B. & Ellis, R.M., Jr.
       Some neurophysiologic aspects of depressed states:
          An electromyographic study
       Archives of General Psychiatry, 1959, 1:70-80

2123. Whatmore, G.B. & Ellis, R.M., Jr.
       Further neurophysiologic aspects of depressed states
          An electromyographic study
       Archives of General Psychiatry, 1962, 6:243-253

2124.   Whatmore, G.B. & Ellis, R.M., Jr.
        Some neurophysiologic aspects of schizophrenia: An
           electromyographic study
        American Journal of Psychiatry, 1964, 120:1166-1169

2125.   Whatmore, G. & Kohli, D.
        Dysponesis: A neuropsychologic factor in functional
           disorders
        Behavioral Science, 1968, 13:102-124

2126.   Whatmore, G. & Kohli, D.
        The Physiopathology and Treatment of Functional
           Disorders
        New York: Grune & Stratton, 1974

2127.   Whisenant, W.F. & Murphy, P.J.
        Bilateral EEG biofeedback and creativity
        Biofeedback and Self-Regulation, 1977, 2:322 (Abst.)

2128.   White, P.D. & Alexander, A.B.
        The role of the contingent feedback stimulus in EMG
           biofeedback treatments of tension headache
        Psychophysiology, 1977, 14:86 (Abst.)

2129.   White, T.W., Holmes, D.S. & Bennett, D.H.
        Effects of instructions, biofeedback and cognitive
           activity on heart rate control
        Journal of Experimental Psychology-Human Learning
           and Memory, 1977, 3:477-484

2130.   Whitehead, W.E., Drescher, V.M. & Blackwell, B.
        Rate of learning to control heart rate differen-
           tially is negatively correlated with subjective
           awareness of heart beat
        Biofeedback and Self-Regulation, 1976, 1:322-323
           (Abst.)

2131.   Whitehead, W.E., Drescher, V.M., Heiman, P. &
           Blackwell, B
        Relation of heart rate control to heart beat per-
           ception
        Biofeedback and Self-Regulation, 1977, 2:371-392

2132.   Whitehead, W.E., Lurie, E. & Blackwell, B.
        Classical conditioning procedures facilitate
            biofeedback training to lower blood pressure in
            essential hypertension
        Psychophysiology, 1976, 13:176 (Abst.)

2133.   Whitehead, W.E., Renault, P.F. & Goldiamond, I.
        Modification of human acid secretion with operant
            conditioning procedures
        Journal of Applied Behavior Analysis, 1975, 8:147-
            156

2134.   Whittome, V.J & Lader, M.H.
        Operant GSR conditioning: An attempt to condition
            differentially the two sides of the body
        Journal of Psychosomatic Research, 1972, 16:421-424

2135.   Wickramasekera, I.
        Effects of EMG feedback training on susceptibility
            to hypnosis: Preliminary observations
        Proceedings, 79th Annual Convention American
            Psychological Association, 1971, 783-784

2136.   Wickramasekera, I.
        Effects of "hypnosis" and task motivational in-
            structions in attempting to influence the
            "voluntary" self deprivation of money
        Journal of Personality and Social Psychology, 1971,
            19:311-314

2137.   Wickramasekera, I.
        Instructions and EMG feedback in systematic de-
            sensitization: A case report
        Behavior Therapy, 1972, 3:460-465

2138.   Wickramasekera, I.
        Electromyographic feedback training and tension
            headache: Preliminary observations
        American Journal of Clinical Hypnosis, 1972, 15:83-
            85

2139.   Wickramasekera, I.
        Application of verbal instructions and EMG feedback
            training to the management of tension headache:
            Preliminary observations
        Headache, 1973, 13:74-76

2140.   Wickramasekera, I.
        Temperature feedback for the control of migraine
        Journal of Behavior Therapy and Experimental
            Psychiatry, 1973, 4:343-345

2141.   Wickramasekera, I.
        Effects of electromyographic feedback on hypnotic
            susceptibility: More preliminary data
        Journal of Abnormal Psychology, 1973, 82:74-77

2142.   Wickramasekera, I.
        Heart-rate feedback and the management of cardiac
            neurosis
        Journal of Abnormal Psychology, 1974, 83:578-580

2143.   Wickramasekera, I.
        Biofeedback, Behavior Therapy and Hypnosis
        Chicago: Nelsen-Hall, 1976

2144.   Wickramasekera, I. & Truong, X.T.
        Biofeedback
        Archives of Physical Medicine and Rehabilitation,
            1974, 55:483-484

2145.   Wildgruber, C., Lutzenberger, W., Elbert, T., et al
        Average pattern biofeedback: The method and a first
            step toward a clinical application
        Biofeedback and Self-Regulation, 1977, 2:326 (Abst.)

2146.   Willerman, L., Skeen, J. T. & Simpson, J.S.
        Retention of learned temperature change during
            problem solving
        Perceptual and Motor Skills, 1976, 43:995-1002

2147.   Williams, J.L. & Adkins, J.R.
        Voluntary control of heart rate during anxiety
            and oxygen deprivation
        Psychological Record, 1974, 24:3-16

2148.   Williams, P.
        EEG-alpha feedback: A comparison of two control
            groups
        Psychosomatic Medicine, 1977, 39:44-47

2149. Williams, R.
       Biofeedback: A technology for self- transaction
       Journal of Transpersonal Psychology, 1976, 8:119-
       127

2150. Williams, R.B.
       HR and forearm blood flow (FBF) feedback in the
          treatment of a case of severe essential hyper-
          tension
       Psychophysiology, 1973, 12:237 (Abst.)

2151. Williams, R.B.
       HR feedback in the treatment of torticollis
       Psychophysiology, 1975, 12:237 (Abst.)

2152. Williams, R.B., Poon, L. & Burdette, L.J.
       Locus of control and vasomotor response to sensory
          processing
       Psychosomatic Medicine, 1977, 39:127-133

2153. Wilson, A.F., Honsberger, R., Chico, J.T., et al.
       Transcendental meditation and asthma
       Respiration, 1975, 32:74-80

2154. Wilson, C., Hord, D., Townsend, R., et al.
       Lack of a specific theta suppression effect on
          performance during a visual sonar vigilance task
       Biofeedback and Self-Regulation, 1976, 1:341-342
          (Abst.)

2155. Winer, L.R.
       Biofeedback: A guide to the clinical literature
       American Journal of Orthopsychiatry, 1977, 47:626-
          638

2156. Wolf, S.L., Ledbetter, W.D. & Basmajian, J.F.
       Effects of a specific cutaneous cold stimulus on
          single motor unit activity of medical gastronemius
          muscle in man
       American Journal of Physical Medicine, 1976, 55:177-
          183

2157. Wolpert, R. & Wooldridge, C.P.
       The use of electromyography as biofeedback therapy
          in the management of cerebral palsy: A review and
          case study
       Physiotherapy Canada, 1975, 27:5-9

2158. Woodruff, D.S.
Biofeedback control of the EEG alpha rhythm and its
effect on reaction time in the young and old
Dissertation Abstracts, 1972, 33B:1833-1834

2159. Woodruff, D.S.
Relationships among EEG alpha frequency, reaction
time, and age: A biofeedback study
Psychophysiology, 1975, 12:673-681

2160. Woolfolk, R.L.
Psychophysiological correlates of meditation
Archives of General Psychiatry, 1975, 32:1326-1333

2161. Woolridge, C.P., et al.
Biofeedback - background and application to physical
rehabilitation
Bulletin of Prosthetic Research, 1976, Spring, 25-37

2162. Wulbert, M.
Operant control of physiological activity and its
relationship to emotionality
Dissertation Abstracts, 1972, 33B:456

2163. Wyler, A.R.
Operant conditioning of epileptic neurons in
monkeys and its theoretical application of EEG
operant conditioning in humans
Pavlovian Journal, 1977, 12:130-146

2164. Wyler, A.R. & Fetz, E.E.
Behavioral control of firing patterns of normal and
abnormal neurons in chronic epileptic cortex
Experimental Neurology, 1974, 42:448-464

2165. Wyler, A.R., Fetz, E.E. & Ward, A.A.
Firing patterns of epileptic and normal neurons in
the chronic alumena focus in undrugged monkeys
during different behavioral states
Brain Research, 1975, 98:1-20

2166. Wyricka, W. & Sterman, M.B.
Instrumental conditioning of sensorimotor cortex EEG
spindles in the waking cat
Physiology and Behavior, 1968, 3:703-707

2167.   Wyricka, W., Sterman, M.B.   & Clemente, C.D.
        Conditioning of induced electroencephalographic
          sleep patterns in the cat
        Science, 1962, 137:616-618

2168. Yamaguchi, Y., Niwa, K. & Nigi, T.
Feedback of midfrontal theta activity during mental
work and its voluntary control
Electroencephalography and Clinical Neurophysiology,
1973, 34:704-705

2169. Yates, A.J.
Delayed auditory feedback
Psychological Bulletin, 1963, 60:213-232

2170. Yemm, R.
Neurophysiologic studies of temperomandibular joint
dysfunction
Oral Sciences Reviews, 1976, 7:31-53

2171. Yock, T.J.
Relaxation and occipital alpha
Proceedings of the Biofeedback Research Society
Fifth Annual Meeting
Colorado Springs, 1974, 85 (Abst.)

2172. Young, L.D. & Blanchard, E.B.
Sex differences in the ability to control heart
rate
Psychophysiology, 1972, 9:667-668

2173. Young, L.D. & Blanchard, E.B.
Effects of auditory feedback of varying information
content on the self-control of heart rate
Journal of General Psychology, 1974, 91:61-68

2174. Young, L.D., Langford, H.G. & Blanchard, E.G.
Effect of operant conditioning of heart rate on
plasma renin activity
Psychosomatic Medicine, 1976, 38:278-281

2175. Young, L.R. & Stark, L.
Variable feedback experiments testing a sampled
data model for eye tracking movements
IEEE Transactions on Human Factors Electronics,
963, HFE-4, 38-51

2176.   Zappala, A.
        Influence of training and sex on the isolation and
            control of single motor units
        American Journal of Physical Medicine, 1970,
            49:348-361

2177.   Zeiner, A.R.   & Pollak, M.H.
        Bidirectional changes in digital skin temperature
            using biofeedback in a cold room
        Psychophysiology, 1977, 14:104-105 (Abst.)

2178.   Zirkel, K., Stewart, R.A.C. & Preston, C.
        Personality and attitudinal correlates of ability
            to increase alpha production in EEG biofeedback
            training
        Psychologia, 1977, 20:98-106

BIOFEEDBACK SOCIETY OF AMERICA NINTH ANNUAL MEETING
Albuquerque, New Mexico, March 3-7, 1978

Titles of papers from Proceedings. Proceedings may be
ordered from the Biofeedback Society of America, U.C.M.C.
C268, 4200 East 9th Avenue, Denver, Colorado 80262.

2179. Adler, S. & Lehrer, P.M.
Psychophysiological effects of autogenic training
and progressive relaxation

2180. Aleo, S. & Nicassio, P.
Auto-regulation of duodenal ulcer disease: A
preliminary report of four cases

2181. Bachers, A.
Atypical EMG biofeedback levels in a patient who
subsequently developed laryngeal cancer

2182. Baldwin, B.G., Benjamins, J.K., Meyers, R.M., &
Grant, C.W.
EMG biofeedback with hyperactive children: A time
series analysis

2183. Benjamins, J.K.
Alpha feedback relaxation procedures with high
and low mental image clarity: An analogue desensitization study

2184. Berger, J.E.
The roles of individual differences, biofeedback,
and awareness in the learning of heart rate de-
celeration and acceleration

2185. Besner, H.F.
Biofeedback - possible placebo in treating chronic
onset insomnia

2186. Birbaumer, N., Elbert, T., Lutzenberger, W., &
Rockstroh, B.
Biofeedback of slow cortical potentials

2187. Bird, B.L. and Cataldo, M.F.
       A behavioral neurology approach to movement dis-
       orders

2188. Blanchard, E.B.
       A case study of the use of temperature biofeedback
       in the treatment of chronic pain

2189. Blankstein, K.R., Cook, B. Manchester, P., &
       McVicar, R.
       Self-regulation of heart rate in young coronary-
       prone males

2190. Boller, J.D. & Flom, R.P.
       Treatment of the common migraine: Systematic
       application of biofeedback and autogenic training

2191. Bowles, C. & Smith, J.
       EMG biofeedback and progressive relaxation training:
       Clinical and home application in a comparative
       study of two groups of normal subjects

2192. Carlson, J.G. & Feld, J.L.
       Incentives and locus of control in frontal EMG
       training

2193. Cram, J.R.
       EMG biofeedback and the treatment of tension head-
       aches: A systematic analysis of treatment
       components

2194. Crosson, B., Andreychuk, T., Tiemann, K. &
       Phillips, C.
       Combined use of hypnosis and biofeedback in the
       treatment of migraines: A pilot study

2195. Cunningham, M.D. & Murphy, P.J.
       The effects of bilateral EEG biofeedback on verbal,
       visual-spatial, and creative skills in learning
       disabled male adolescents

2196. Dale, A., Anderson, D., Blankstein, K., Klions, H.,
       & Tane, K.
       With-in subject control designs and bidirectional
       control of frontalis muscle tension: Methodological
       comparison between pre-experiment and running
       baselines

2197. Diamond, S., Diamond-Falk, J. & DeVeno, T.
       The value of biofeedback in the treatment of
          chronic headache: Five-year retrospective study

2198. Dirks, M., Riordan, H. & Canfield, M.
       Blood histamine level as a factor in skin conductance
          and response

2199. Dunn, M., Davis, J. & Webster, T.
       Voluntary control of muscle spasticity with EMG bio-
          feedback in three spinal cord injured quadriplegics

2200. Datey, K.K.
       Biofeedback training and hypnosis in the management
          of hypertension

2201. Decker, W.A. & McCann, E.J.
       Electromyograph biofeedback for relief of tension
          headaches: Comparison of peripherally and cen-
          trally focused generalization of training
          strategies

2202. DeGood, D., Klaus, D., Tennenbaum, D. & Greenwald, D.
       "Length of training" as a factor in the biofeedback
          treatment of psychosomatic symptoms

2203. Ebert, B., Kuhmann, W. & Vaitl, D.
       Primary and secondary effects of experimentally
          manipulated biofeedback training for heart rate
          control in cardiophobic patients

2204. Engelhardt, L.
       Awareness and relaxation through biofeedback in
          public schools

2205. Farris, C.L.
       Biofeedback as an adjunct to family therapy in the
          initial interview -- a situational test pro-
          cedure

2206. Finley, W.W., Musicant, R.A., Billings, S.D. &
          Rosser, M.
       Biofeedback of auditory far-field potentials from
          the brainstem: Implications for sensory modifi-
          cation

2207.   Freedman, R., Hauri, P., Coursey, R. & Frankel, B.
        Behavioral treatment of insomnia: A collaborative
           study

2208.   Freedman, R., Lynn, S.J. & Ianni, P.
        Biofeedback treatment of Raynaud's phenomenon

2209.   Fridlund, A.J. & Fowler, S.C.
        An eight-channel, computer-controlled scanning
           electromyograph for measurement of multiple
           muscle groups

2210.   Gersten, C.D. & Pope, A.T.
        Continuous vs. intermittent EMG feedback effects on
           muscle tension reduction during Jacobsonian re-
           laxation training

2211.   Glaus, K.D. & Kotses, H.
        Generalization of conditioned frontalis tension:
           A closer look

2212.   Greene, W.A. & Gohl, M.
        Evaluation of nudes as a function of heart rate
           changes as influenced by instructions and true
           and false feedback

2213.   Hardt, J.V.
        A dedicated microcomputer for multi-channel,
           multi-subject biofeedback

2214.   Hardt, J.V.
        Personality change through voluntary control of EEG
           alpha activity

2215.   Hardt, J.V. & Kamiya, J.
        Treating high anxiety with alpha feedback

2216.   Harris, M.E., Ray, W.J. & Stern, R.M.
        Symptom related differences in biofeedback perfor-
           mances of gastric and migraine patients

2217.   Hartje, J.C. & Diver, C.E.
        Variation in hand temperature as a correlate to
           migraine severity

2218. Hatch, J.P. & Gatchel, R.J.
       The effects of biofeedback schedules on the operant
          modification of human heart rate

2219. Hauri, P.
       Biofeedback techniques in the treatment of serious
          chronic insomniacs

2220. Hawkins, R.C. & Wiedel, T.C.
       The effects of ingested calories and biofeedback
          training upon finger temperature changes in normal
          and overweight college students

2221. Hendler, N., Matthews, D., Avella, J., Long, D., &
          Gordon, J.
       The "effect of person" on EMG biofeedback responses

2222. Holliday, J.E. & Munz, D.C.
       EMG feedback training and changes in locus of
          control

2223. Hughes, R. & Collins, N.
       Group instruction in relaxation training with
          nursery school children

2224. Hurley, G.
       Motorically activating vs motorically inhibiting
          instructions in EMG feedback training

2225. Ingram, A. & Bourgeois, A.E.
       The enhancement of learned cardiac deceleration
          through reflexive techniques and biofeedback

2226. Jankel, W.R.
       EMG feedback in spasmodic torticollis

2227. Jeffrey, T.B.
       The effects of operant conditioning and electro-
          myographic biofeedback on the relaxed behavior
          of hyperkinetic children

2228. Jones, M. R. & Barnes, J.A.
       The effects of EEG analysis on computer-assisted
          instruction

2229.   Kay, M., Shively, M. & Kilkenny, J.
        Training of sensorimotor rhythm in developmental
        disabled children through EEG biofeedback

2230.   Keen, J. & Montgomery, D.D.
        Interoceptive reinforcement and laterality in
        thermal training facilitated by an elicited
        operant paradigm

2231.   Kotses, H. & Glaus, K.D.
        Facial muscle tension influences peak expiratory
        flow rate in normals and in asthmatic children

2232.   Kravitz, E., Glaros, A., Moore, M. & Stauffer, T.
        EMG feedback and differential relaxation training
        to promote pain relief in chronic low back pain
        patients

2233.   Kremsdorf, R.B. & Costell, S.
        Biofeedback and cognitive skills training: An
        evaluation of their relative efficacy

2234.   Lindley, B.S., Cunningham, D.M. & Abbott, D.W.
        An experimental stress situation for the evaluation
        of biofeedback assisted control of arousal

2235.   Maly, K. & Murphy, P.
        Concordance in measures of fear due to trait anxiety
        and EMG-feedback assisted desensitization

2236.   Marlatt, G.A., Pagano, R.R., Rose, R.R. & Marques,
        J.K.
        Effects of meditation and relaxation training on
        alcohol use in male social drinkers

2237.   Mathew, R.J., Largen, J.W., Claghorn, J. L., Dobbins,
        K. & Meyer, J.S.
        Relationship between volitional alteration in skin
        temperature and regional cerebral bloodflow in
        normal subjects

2238.   Matulich, W.J., Rugh, J.D. & Perlis, D.B.
        A comparison of group and individual EMG feedback
        for tension headaches

2239.   Morasky, R.L. & Trusk, T.C.
        Finger temperature control as a negative feedback
           system

2240.   Myers, H.K., Corson, J.A. & Klassen, G.A.
        Cardiovascular control during a painful stimulus:
           The use of skin resistance biofeedback

2241.   Naifeh, K. & Kamiya, J.
        Respiratory changes associated with sleep onset:
           Implications for biofeedback

2242.   Patmon, R. & Murphy, P.J.
        Differential treatment efficacy of EEG and EMG
           feedback for hyperactive adolescents

2243.   Reeves, J.L., Shapiro, D. & Cobb, L.F.
        Relative influences of heart rate biofeedback and
           cognitive/belief factors in the perception of
           cold pressor pain: A pilot study

2244.   Reinking, R.H.
        Biofeedback as an adjunct to alcoholism treatment

2245.   Rickles, W.H.
        Treatment of a case of hyperhidrosis with vapor
           pressure feedback

2246.   Rubow, R.
        Design and rationale for a parametric vibro-
           tactual feedback stimulator

2247.   Russ, K.L., Kass, M. & O'Connell, M.F.
        EMG biofeedback applied to patients with elevated
           intraocular pressure: A yoked-control study
           employing double-blind methodology

2248.   Schandler, S.L.
        Use of muscle biofeedback relaxation in the treatment
           of eczema

2249.   Schneider, J.A.
        Rapid absolute blood pressure feedback: Introducing
           a new method of providing blood pressure feedback

2250.   Sedlacek, K.W. & Cohen, J.
        Biofeedback treatment of essential hypertension

2251.   Shabsin, H.S., Bahler, W.W. & Lubar, J.F.
        A comparison of 12-15 Hz, Rolandic activity (SMR)
            during eyes open and eyes closed conditions and
            its concurrence with occipital alpha

2252.   Sheridan, C.L., Zimmer, J.G., Finch, W.S. & Eifler,
        M.F.
        Personality, peripheral temperature, and responsive-
            ness to induction of a relaxation response

2253.   Steiner, T.E., Butler, R., Reynolds, A., Bender, K.,
            Hawley, L. & Barenberg, F.
        Photoelectric plethysmograph feedback for the
            training of peripheral vasodilations with regard
            to thermal state of subject

2254.   Surwit, R.S., Pilon, R.N. & Fenton, C.H.
        Behavioral treatment of Raynaud's disease

2255.   Suter, S., Krone, A. & Matthews, S.
        Hemispheric, cognitive, and sex differences in
            biofeedback regulation of occipital alpha

2256.   Traynham, R.N.
        The effects of experimental meditation, feedback,
            and relaxation training on electromyograph and
            self-report measures of relaxation and altered
            states of consciousness

2257.   Wand, G., Slattery, P., Haskell, J. & Taub. E.
        Anatomical specificity of thermal self-regulatory
            effect: Feedback locus on the web dorsum

2258.   Warrenburg, S., Pagano, R., Woods, M. & Hlastala, M.
        Respiratory changes during progressive relaxation
            and Transcendental Meditation

2259.   Werbach, M.R. & Sandweiss, J.H.
        Finger temperature characteristics of migraineurs
            undergoing biofeedback - assisted relaxation
            training

2260.   Werder, D.S.
        An exploratory study of childhood migraine using
            thermal biofeedback as a treatment alternative

2261.   Wong, K., Hochhaus, L. & Murphy, P.
        Operant conditioning of alpha rhythm: The effects
            of biofeedback and instruction on alpha dis-
            crimination, enhancement, and subjective exper-
            ience

2262.   Wong, K. & Zeiner, A.
        The effects of high and low frequency EEG alpha
            enhancement on mood change

2263.   Yock, T.J.
        Electromyographic feedback as a relaxation procedure:
        A psychophysiological evaluation

2264.   Zigrang, P. & Murphy, P.J.
        The effects of individual differences in physio-
            logical reactivity on learning control of EMG
            and GSR responses through biofeedback training

Papers Read By Title Only

2265.   Amenhauser, C.G. & Shipley, R.
        Application of biofeedback treatment techniques
            within a rural drug and alcohol treatment center

2266.   Bagnall, L.M. & Burgar, C.G.
        A basic procedure for the selection of clinical
            biofeedback equipment

2267.   Benjamins, J.K. & Schofield, W.D.
        The treatment of sleep onset insomnia with finger
            temperature feedback and self monitoring: A
            case study

2268.   Carter, J.L. & Russell, H.L.
        Gains on academic learning tasks in learning
            disabled children receiving electromyographic
            feedback and relaxation training

2269. DeWitt, D.J.
       Neuropsychologic parameters of an EMG feedback pro-
       gram with learning disabled males

2270. Flick, G.L.
       EEG and electrodermal responses in normal and
       dyslexic children

2271. Friedman, H.
       EMG biofeedback of spasmodic torticollis: Case
       presentation of two brothers

2272. Froehner, C. & Suter, S.
       Biofeedback-induced frequency changes and time
       perception

2273. Gibb, J.D. & Rohm, C.E.T., Jr.
       EMG trained listener: Two heads are better than
       one

2274. Grove, R.N., Denver, D.R., Metivier, A. & Lavertue,
       P.
       The behavioral pharmacology of EMG biofeedback:
       Sensitivity of frontalis and sternomastoid activity
       distributions to oral ethanol – a preliminary
       report

2275. Jensen, J.S. & Stoffer, G.R.
       Treatment of essential blepharospasm with EMG
       biofeedback

2276. Klass, J., Lister, P. & Mount, J.
       A pilot study of EMG biofeedback applied to stuttering

2277. Long, A.
       Psychodiagnostic procedures as a preface to bio-
       feedback training

2278. Moore, R.T.
       The interaction of personality and intellectual
       variables with handwarming in alcoholics

2279. O'Connell, M.F. & Russ, K.L.
       A case report comparing two types of biofeedback
       in the treatment of irritable bowel syndrome

2280. Peiffer, A.L., Charlesworth, E.A. & Kotzen, F.
       Incorporation of biofeedback into a program for
          substance abusers: Initial evaluation

2281. Prager-Decker, I.J. & Decker, W.A.
       Arousal reactions to a media induced psychosocial
          stressor following muscle relaxation training

2282. Rouse, L.O.
       Clinical factors in the holistic treatment of
          hypertension

2283. Saunders, M., Larsen, L. & Hornstra, R.K.
       Outcome in a stress management project using multi-
          modal feedback

2284. Sedlacek, K.W. & Soroka, G.
       Biofeedback treatment of tinnitus

2285. Silverstein, L.
       Contraindications in biofeedback training for
          cardiac arrhythmia: A case study

2286. Stoffer, G.S. & Jensen, J.S.
       Task onset as a source of stress in biofeedback
          tasks: Clinical and nonclinical data

2287. Stramler, J.
       Computer analysis of EEG biofeedback epochs: A
          new approach in brain research

2288. Swabb, L.A. & Swabb, L.J.
       Management of essential blepharospasm through
          biofeedback

2289. Wentworth-Rohr, I.
       The reduction of anxiety related symptoms in
          schizophrenics through biofeedback-behavior
          therapy techniques

2290. Werder, D.S.
       The Personal Orientation Inventory as a predictor
          of success and change with biofeedback training

2291.   Wilkinson, M.
        A critical view of the use of frontalis EMG feedback
        as a general relaxation training technique

2292.   Zeiner, A.R., Pollak, M.H. & Schneider, R.A.
        Treatment of essential hypertension with biofeedback
        and relaxation training

PUBLICATIONS OF THE BIOFEEDBACK SOCIETY OF AMERICA

2293. Proceedings of the Sixth Annual Meeting
Monterey, California, 1975

2294. Proceedings of the Seventh Annual Meeting
Colorado Springs, Colorado, 1976

2295. Proceedings of the Eighth Annual Meeting
Orlando, Florida, 1977

2296. Proceedings of the Ninth Annual Meeting
Albuquerque, New Mexico, 1978

2297. A Survey of Biofeedback Training Opportunities at
Clinical Internship Facilities
Prepared by Jeffrey Cram and Stephen Warrenburg

2298. Introduction to the Methods of Autogenic Therapy
Prepared by W. Luthe, M.D.
The contents present practical information essential
for application and research in biofeedback,
autogenic therapy and autogenic feedback training

Information on ordering is available from the Biofeedback
Society of America, U.C.M.C. C268, 4200 East Ninth Avenue,
Denver, CO 80262

FILMS ON BIOFEEDBACK

2299. Biofeedback: The Yoga of the West
Hartley Productions, Inc.
Cat Rock Road, Cos Cob, Connecticut 06807

2300. Dialogue on Biofeedback
U. S. Department of Agriculture, Office of
Communication, Motion Picture Services, 14th and
Independence, S.W., Washington, D.C. 20250

THE BIOFEEDBACK SOCIETY OF AMERICA

The Biofeedback Society of America (BSA) is an open forum for the exchange of ideas, methods and results of biofeedback and related studies. Emphasis is primarily on scientific and clinical investigations of human behavior and human potential, both in experimental and applied settings.

The objectives of the Biofeedback Society are (1) to advance biofeedback as a means of human welfare by the encouragement of scientific research and the improvement of research methods, (2) to improve the clinical uses of biofeedback through high standards of professional ethics, conduct and education, (3) to increase the diffusion of knowledge about biofeedback through meetings, workshops and publications.

As stated by Thomas B. Mulholland, Ph.D., President of the Society, 1970-1971:

"From the historian's vantage, a new scientific topic is preceded by a series of innovations, discoveries and conceptualizations, which, in an inevitable way, have led to that new branch of science. For the contemporary observer scientific developments are accelerated and a topic may emerge within a decade seeming to spring suddenly on the scene. This is the case for biofeedback, which has the qualities of creative innovation, rapid emergence, unprecedented application and new direction.

"Biofeedback is applied to behavioral science whereby some recordable feature of a physiological process is connected by an external path to a stimulator or display which is seen, heard, or felt, forming a closed loop. It is differentiated from similar developments in physiology by the inclusion of psychological processes such as perception, cognition and voluntary control.

"As recently as a few years ago, only a small number of researchers in the United States and Europe had been working and publishing on the problems of feedback psycho-physiology. Now many scientists here and abroad are actively working in this new area of research. Biofeed-back includes the application of feedback methods to the study and control of the brain rhythms, cortical evoked potentials, galvanic skin response, skeletal muscle, motor units and motor neurons, blood pressure, skin temperature and other physiological processes. The Biofeedback Society of America is inherently interdisci-plinary."

The Biofeedback Society of America has been in existence since 1968. As the Society was formed it was called the Biofeedback Research Society. With the growth of the Society and the expansion of biofeedback into other areas, the membership approved a name change to the Biofeedback Society of America (in the summer of 1976). This change and the consequent revision of the bylaws allowed for the creation of two Society divisions, applied and experimental, and allowed a mechanism for the recognition of state societies as chapters of the national organization.

GUIDE TO THE KEYWORD INDEX

The following section presents a number of keywords which appear in the titles of the citations in this book. Below each keyword are the numbers of the citations which contain this keyword or include work on this topic. For example, if one is searching for the work on EMG, one might look at the topic "Electromyography". One might also check "EMG Feedback", which is a different topic.

It is suggested that before using this keyword section, the reader spend a few moments reviewing the topics to gain a familiarity with the terms.

KEYWORD INDEX

Buccinator Muscle
      102

Cancer
      605   1524   1820   2181

Cardiac Control (see also Heart Rate)
      118   142   187   191   192
      200   209   251   252   253
      257   261   265   336   362
      368   377   421   422   424
      445   469   474   518   519
      521   522   523   547   561
      566   568   580   581   582
      618   633   639   679   804
      810   830   834   882   972
      991   1007   1129   1395   1396
     1400   1404   1405   1406   1407
     1408   1432   1444   1445   1447
     1448   1451   1452   1513   1550
     1551   1631   1632   1699   1705
     1706   1707   1709   1712   1714
     1726   1727   1729   1730   1771
     1787   1866   1867   1884   1952
     1953   1954   1956   2030   2050
     2051   2099   2103   2110   2142
     2203   2225   2240

Cardiac-Somatic Relationship
     1444   1446   1447   1449   1450
     1451   1771

Case Study
      80   83   182   184   542
      583   584   585   586   593
      606   607   674   863   924
      965   982   1174   1187   1229
     1249   1435   1511   1524   1677
     1682   1794   1842   1868   1902
     2009   2079   2137   2157   2188

Central Nervous System
      115   169   172   292   312
     1098   1714

Conversion Reaction
    83   463

Cortical Activity
    107   179   474   490   570
    575   906   1022   1291   1292
   1368   1647   1675   1903   1906
   1908   1968   2164   2186

Counseling
    410   534   859   1186   2064

Counterconditioning
   1040   1041   1042   1975

Creativity
    725   726   732   1107   1291
   1292   1434   1819   2127   2195

Criminal Rehabilitation
    612   1661

Cross Cultural Studies
   1780   2082

Curare
     69   159   160   162   163
    164   173   174   177   257
    407   432   475   476   477
    479   480   481   482   484
    501   687   689   770   771
    900   905   1319   1332   1335
   1340   1479   1841   1994   1995
   2031

Demand Characteristics
     62

Dental Applications
    304   319   329   330   355
    356   489   493   556   672
    673   674   756   851   1011
   1066   1067   1068   1321   1593
   1663   1664   1665   1670   1671
   1672   1673   1854   1855   2170

Hand Temperature
145	392	393	408	497
625	626	864	1167	1168
1635	2217	2278		

Headache (also see specific type)
13	14	15	59	134
406	464	465	485	1180
1356	1411	1416	1467	1679
2079	2197			

Healing
726	732

Hearing Loss
2206

Heart Rate (see also Cardiac Control)
20	36	79	109	110
121	124	125	126	143
151	161	162	186	188
189	190	196	198	199
201	202	203	204	205
206	207	208	209	213
221	228	229	230	231
232	233	249	250	256
258	259	260	263	264
285	346	351	363	367
371	373	376	387	402
405	411	435	436	440
441	443	445	446	476
477	481	482	483	484
491	500	520	524	525
526	527	528	529	543
568	569	579	602	638
639	654	655	656	657
658	659	660	661	679
687	689	699	744	764
776	777	805	807	818
819	828	829	841	842
849	872	873	874	875
876	877	883	900	905
967	972	983	994	1035
1038	1063	1091	1125	1126
1140	1142	1143	1144	1145
1192	1193	1194	1195	1197

Hemiplegia
                42   974   1163

Hemispheric Laterality
          339   638   1379   1465   1505
          1599   1717   1960   2230   2255

Heroin
          1443

High Blood Pressure (see also Hypertension)
          18   433   1108   1984

Historical Aspects of Biofeedback
          16   53   54   58   333
          334   412   431   492   596
          599   622   623   706   714
          722   910   918   931   932
          933   934   935   936   937
          938   939   940   941   942
          943   944   945   946   947
          948   949   950   951   959
          963   964   1016   1063   1097
          1109   1119   1200   1210   1242
          1294   1313   1314   1349   1426
          1453   1738   1753   1835   1836
          1848   1987   2118

Huntington's Chorea
          1267

Hyperhidrosis (Sweating)
          2245

Hyperkinesis/Hyperactivity
          244   722   1235   1236   1423
          1802   1803   2182   2227   2242

Hypertension
          2   133   137   138   139
          140   181   214   239   268
          380   414   415   416   417
          509   513   613   630   643
          695   768   805   835   931
          948   1069   1070   1071   1072

Sensorimotor Rhythm (SMR) (Cont.)

1432	1802	1803	1896	1897
1900	1901	1902	1909	2166
2229	2251			

Serum Cholesterol

1497

Sex Differences (See also Individual Differences)

422	424	427	1057	1793
2004	2019	2172	2176	2255

Sexual Applications

80	182	228	553	624
627	749	860	887	1152
1153	1586	1638	1639	1640
1641	1642	1643		

Shaping Procedure

437	1335	1586	1736	1737
1839				

Single Case Design

81	82	154	1026

Single Motor Unit Activity

57	86	87	88	89
92	95	96	98	104
105	574	635	723	724
817	820	821	822	823
973	996	1022	1023	1024
1046	1047	1184	1217	1218
1318	1366	1456	1552	1739
1740	1754	1796	1810	1811
1813	1843	1848	1877	1968
1969	1997	2066	2156	2176

Skeletal Response

162	177	180	571	649
663	700	740	902	933
940	941	943	945	947
951	1130	1552	1935	

Skin Conductance

656	1025	1126	1343	1961
2198				

Sphincter Control
 1082

Spinal Cord Injury
 288   289   2199

Stimulus Control Procedure
 186

Strabismus
 1478

Stress
  48   129   234   240   268
 280   310   317   401   419
 446   500   567   568   676
 677   678   685   705   801
 815   880   904   991   1017
1021   1055   1070   1071   1121
1219   1273   1274   1294   1317
1321   1360   1431   1448   1493
1495   1510   1536   1593   1594
1670   1673   1747   1748   1749
1750   1806   1816   1823   1918
1929   1930   1932   1937   1938
1978   2234   2286

Stress Management
 557   736   2283

Stressor
 351   352   418   443   502
1506

Stroke
 101   103   597   761   1073
1074   1685   1965   1966

Stuttering (see also Speech Problems)
 287   348   765   782   921
 925   1146   1147   1174   1683
1734   2003   2276

Visual Acuity
719

Visual Effects
1486   1487

Visual Feedback

9	28	57	190	503
653	799	858	928	1290
1619	1684	1881	1962	

Visual Field
333   334

Visual Stimulation

342	709	799	1381	1384
1387	1723			

Voluntary Control

57	58	101	124	125
199	201	205	207	232
233	252	253	255	289
292	334	410	461	569
598	603	655	656	657
659	660	727	730	731
820	821	822	823	841
858	860	875	901	908
910	923	964	983	1025
1168	1192	1210	1271	1278
1279	1286	1287	1331	1421
1429	1469	1513	1518	1543
1549	1597	1598	1601	1602
1627	1628	1643	1691	1707
1709	1718	1759	1770	1831
1832	1835	1836	1848	1864
1914	1951	1962	**1990**	1992
2060	2069	2100	2110	2147
2168	2199	2214		

Wakefulness

891	906	907	978	1239

Weight Control

6	515	773	774	813
1102	1269	1946	1947	2096
2220				